Web Content Mining
With Java

Web Content Mining With Java

Techniques for exploiting the World Wide Web

Tony Loton

LOTONtech Limited, Middlewich, UK

JOHN WILEY & SONS, LTD

Library of Congress Cataloguing-in-Publication Data
(has been applied for)

British Library Cataloguing in Publication Data

A catalogue record for this book is available from the British Library

ISBN 0 470 84311 X

Typeset in 10.5/13pt Sabon by Vision Typesetting, Manchester
Printed and bound in Great Britain by Biddles Ltd., Guildford and King's Lynn
This book is printed on acid-free paper responsibly manufactured from sustainable forestry,
in which at least two trees are planted for each one used for paper production.

Contents

PREFACE   xi
ABOUT THE AUTHOR   xix
ACKNOWLEDGEMENTS   xxi

1. SURVEYING THE SCENE   1

    1.1 What's it all About?   1
        1.1.1 The world of web services   2
        1.1.2 The world of web technology   2
        1.1.3 What is web mining?   3
    1.2 The Master Plan   4
        1.2.1 The big picture   4
        1.2.2 The grand design   5
        1.2.3 UML notation   7
        1.2.4 Java code presentation   8
    1.3 Software Download   10
    1.4 Copyright Implications   11
    1.5 Chapter Review   12

2. LANGUAGE OF THE WEB   13

    2.1 Web Application Delivery Channels   14
        2.1.1 Applets as a delivery channel   14
        2.1.2 Servlets as a delivery channel   19
        2.1.3 Applets vs. servlets: the verdict   24
    2.2 HTTP Communication   24
        2.2.1 Compiling and running the HTTPApplet   26
        2.2.2 Beyond the proxy and through the firewall 27
    2.3 Performance Implications   29
    2.4 Chapter Review   30
        2.4.1 API classes and interfaces introduced in this chapter 31

3. HTML AND XML PARSING   33

    3.1 The Design   33

	3.1.1	SAX and DOM	33
3.2	Generic Parsing		35
	3.2.1	WebParserWrapper and WebParser	35
3.3	Parsing HTML		38
	3.3.1	HTMLParserWrapper	38
3.4	Parsing XML		52
	3.4.1	XMLParserWrapper	52
	3.4.2	DOMParserWrapper	57
3.5	Compiling and Running the Parsers		60
	3.5.1	Introducing XHTML	61
3.6	Chapter Review		63
	3.6.1	API classes and interfaces introduced in this chapter	64

4. DATA FILTERS AND STRUCTURED QUERIES — 67

4.1	The Design		67
4.2	Filtering		68
	4.2.1	Operator	68
	4.2.2	Filter	72
	4.2.3	FilterViewer	73
4.3	Structured Queries		85
	4.3.1	QueryEngine	87
	4.3.2	SqlGui	98
4.4	Chapter Review		105
	4.4.1	API classes and interfaces introduced in this chapter	106

5. BUILDING A PORTAL WITH JAVA — 109

5.1	The Design		109
5.2	Data Sources		109
	5.2.1	Yahoo!Finance data source	110
	5.2.2	ShareServlet data source	111
5.3	Servlet Portal		112
	5.3.1	Servlet portal in action	112
	5.3.2	Servlet portal implementation	115
	5.3.3	Compiling the PortalServlet	120
5.4	Applet Portal		120
	5.4.1	Applet portal in action	120
	5.4.2	Applet portal implementation	122
	5.4.3	Compiling the PortalApplet	128
5.5	Chapter Review		130
	5.5.1	API classes and interfaces introduced in this chapter	130

6. **BUILDING A SEARCH ENGINE WITH JAVA**   131

    6.1 The Design   131
    6.2 Core Search Engine/Web Crawler   133
         6.2.1 SearchEngine   133
    6.3 Simple Searching Example   140
         6.3.1 SearchHandler   141
         6.3.2 SimpleSearcher   141
    6.4 A Search Engine Search Engine   145
         6.4.1 WileySearcher   147
    6.5 Chapter Review   151
         6.5.1 API classes and interfaces introduced in this chapter   151

7. **MAIL MINING WITH JAVA**   153

    7.1 The Design   153
         7.1.1 Brief introduction to JavaMail   154
    7.2 Parsing Email Messages   155
         7.2.1 MailParserWrapper   155
    7.3 Email to SMS Example   164
         7.3.1 SMSRelay   167
    7.4 XML in Email   170
    7.5 More Ideas   172
         7.5.1 Web to SMS   172
         7.5.2 Email as a search source   173
         7.5.3 Speaking email   174
    7.6 Chapter Review   175
         7.6.1 API classes and interfaces introduced in this chapter   175

8. **INTRODUCTION TO TEXT MINING**   177

    8.1 The Design   177
    8.2 Basic Text Parsing   180
         8.2.1 WordNet   180
         8.2.2 TextParserWrapper   181
    8.3 Phrase Structure Analysis   190
         8.3.1 Top-down and bottom-up parsing   191
    8.4 Feature Extraction   194
         8.4.1 FeatureExtractor   195
    8.5 Other Text Mining Applications   201
         8.5.1 Indexing   201
         8.5.2 Increasing the search scope   202

8.6   Chapter Review   204
       8.6.1   API classes and interfaces introduced in this chapter   205

9.   INTRODUCTION TO DATA MINING   207

     9.1   The Design   207
     9.2   Fetching Data   209
            9.2.1   CensusDataFetcher   210
            9.2.2   The *Function* class   213
     9.3   Data Mining Techniques   216
            9.3.1   Classification   216
            9.3.2   Association   220
            9.3.3   Clustering   224
     9.4   Chapter Review   228

10. LOOSE ENDS AND LOOKING AHEAD   231

     10.1   Loose Ends: Metadata   231
            10.1.1   Metadata in relational databases   232
            10.1.2   Metadata in HTML pages   233
            10.1.3   Metadata in this book   233
     10.2   Looking Ahead   236
            10.2.1   Resource description framework   236
            10.2.2   XPointer and XPath   237
            10.2.3   Presentation techniques   237
     10.3   Looking Further Ahead   239
            10.3.1   Java data mining API   239
            10.3.2   WebRowSet   240
     10.4   Chapter Review   240

APPENDIX A: SOFTWARE INSTALLATION AND
CONFIGURATION   243

     A.1   Third-Party Software   243
            A.1.1   J2SE SDK installation   244
            A.1.2   JAXP   244
            A.1.3   JavaMail and JAF   244
            A.1.4   Tomcat server   245
     A.2   This Book's Software   245
            A.2.1   Servlet deployment   247

APPENDIX B: JAVADOC EXTRACTS   251

B.1   Overview   251
       B.1.1   Class hierarchy   251
       B.1.2   Interface hierarchy   253
B.2   Chapter 2 Classes   253
       B.2.1   HTTPApplet   254
       B.2.2   SimpleApplet   254
       B.2.3   SimpleServlet   255
B.3   Chapter 3 Classes   255
       B.3.1   WebParser   256
       B.3.2   DOMParserWrapper   256
       B.3.3   HTMLParserWrapper   257
       B.3.4   ProxyAuthenticator   258
       B.3.5   SourceElement   258
       B.3.6   WebParserWrapper   259
       B.3.7   XMLParserWrapper   259
B.4   Chapter 4 Classes   260
       B.4.1   Filter   260
       B.4.2   FilterViewer   261
       B.4.3   Operator   261
       B.4.4   QueryEngine   262
       B.4.5   SqlGui   262
B.5   Chapter 5 Classes   263
       B.5.1   PortalApplet   263
       B.5.2   PortalServlet   264
B.6   Chapter 6 Classes   264
       B.6.1   SearchHandler   264
       B.6.2   SearchEngine   265
       B.6.3   SimpleSearcher   265
       B.6.4   WileySearcher   266
B.7   Chapter 7 Classes   267
       B.7.1   MailParserWrapper   267
       B.7.2   SMSRelay   267
B.8   Chapter 8 Classes   268
       B.8.1   FeatureExtractor   268
       B.8.2   TextParserWrapper   269
B.9   Chapter 9 Classes   269
       B.9.1   CensusDataFetcher   269
       B.9.2   Function   270

APPENDIX C: EARLIER VERSIONS OF JAXP   271

     C.1   Symptoms and Solutions   271
           C.1.1   XMLParserWrapper   271
           C.1.2   DOMParserWrapper   273

APPENDIX D: LICENSE AND COPYRIGHT STATEMENTS   275

     D.1   WordNet License Statement   275
     D.2   Census 1891 Information Copyright   276

APPENDIX E: CENSUS 1891 DATA XML   279

APPENDIX F: SHARE PRICE CLUSTER DATA   287

APPENDIX G: GLOSSARY OF ACRONYMS   291

REFERENCES   295

FURTHER READING   297

     Books   297
     Web sites (technology)   298
     Web sites (data and text mining)   298

INDEX   299

Preface

Data mining is now well-established as a discipline, and text mining is gaining ground. The former is concerned with looking for meaningful patterns in data that is arranged neatly as the rows and columns of a relational database, with each data cell having a defined *format* or *data type*. The latter is concerned with looking for meaningful patterns in data hidden within written documents, obscured by the apparently unstructured nature of the written text.

Web mining takes aspects of data mining and text mining, and brings them together in the context of the world's biggest information resource – the World Wide Web. Some of the data on the web is structured, or at least semi-structured in the form of HTML tables or XML record structures. Some of it is unstructured, in the form of plain text with limited HTML mark-up. So both disciplines are applicable.

If you doubt my claim that the Word Wide Web is the world's biggest information resource, maybe you'll at least agree with me that it's the world's most accessible information resource. As an end user all you need is a web browser, and as a programmer all you need is an understanding of a few well-known communications protocols.

In this book I'll be taking the programmer's point of view. I'll explore some of the techniques for gaining access to the vast amounts of data provided on-line, I'll look at how that data may be decomposed and interpreted, and I'll offer some ideas for re-presenting the data – with added value – via your own web presence.

The title could just as well be 'Web Mining with Java – By Example' because most of the techniques that I describe will be backed up by a real example implemented in Java, with the complete code listed in the book and available for download from the companion web site. So as well as learning some interesting tips, tricks and techniques you'll also have some real Java code to use as the basis of your own applications.

Features and Benefits of the Book

- Where other books discuss *why*, this book shows you *how* to jump on the web-enabled knowledge-based bandwagon.

- It tackles the subject from a practical perspective using the most obvious language for the job – Java.

- It bridges the gap between Java programming books (e.g. 'how to use the XML APIs') and the more academic works on text and data mining theory.

- There are simple but effective code examples for working with HTTP connections, parsing HTML and XML documents, filtering of web data via structured queries, searching, building a portal, and processing incoming email messages.

Who Should Read This Book?

This is essentially a Java programming book that assumes a working knowledge of the Java language, and as such I won't be offering a 'Java-for-beginners' tutorial. If you're not familiar with Java, don't let that put you off just yet. Take a look at the topics that are covered, match these against your requirements, and think about how those requirements might uniquely be satisfied by the Java solutions that I present. That should give you the incentive to learn the language or to hire someone to help you put the theory into practice.

The content is aimed at the following groups – if you belong to one of these groups, read on:

- *e-service providers*; are you developing – or looking to develop – web-based information services, portals, search engines or vertical applications in the knowledge sector? This book will provide practical assistance in getting these applications up and running in the shortest possible time using Java, the language of the web.

- *Java developers*; do you have a working knowledge of Java, a need to understand the key APIs for working with web data, but not enough time to work it all out for yourself? Get a head start through this book's coverage of HTTP communication, HTML and XML Parsing, JavaMail, and other related topics.

- *Data and text mining researchers*; do you have mining algorithms, and maybe even implementations of those algorithms in Java or other languages, but not enough training and testing data to put those algorithms through their paces? This book will help you to create new data sets by gathering data from the world's biggest information resource; the World Wide Web.

Scope and Coverage

The aim is not to give an exhaustive coverage of the Java APIs. That's what the official documentation is for, and it's available for free from http://www.javasoft.com. Nor is it an exhaustive review of data and text mining theory because there are many other good books. The three books that I have used as my main sources of inspiration are:

- *Document Warehousing and Text Mining – Techniques for Improving Business Operations, Marketing and Sales*, Dan Sullivan, Wiley, 2001.

- *Data Mining – Practical Machine Learning Tools and Techniques with Java Implementations*, Ian H. Witten and Eibe Frank, Morgan Kaufman, 2000.

- *Mastering Data Mining – The Art and Science of Customer Relationship Management*, Michael J. A. Berry and Gordon S. Linoff, Wiley, 2000.

My aim is to show, through some simple but effective examples, how Java technologies and APIs may be used in interesting ways to tackle some web mining problems and to provision some novel e-information services. Specifically, we'll make use of the following Java APIs:

- *java.applet* and *javax.swing* packages, for applet development: Chapters 2 and 5.

- *javax.servlet* package, for servlet development: Chapters 2 and 5.

- *java.net* and *java.io* packages, for obtaining data via HyperText Transport Protocol (HTTP): Chapter 2.

- *javax.swing.text.html* package, for parsing HyperText Mark-up Language (HTML) content: Chapter 3.

- *Java API for XML Processing (JAXP)*, for parsing XML content: Chapter 3.

- *JavaMail API*, for mail mining: Chapter 7.

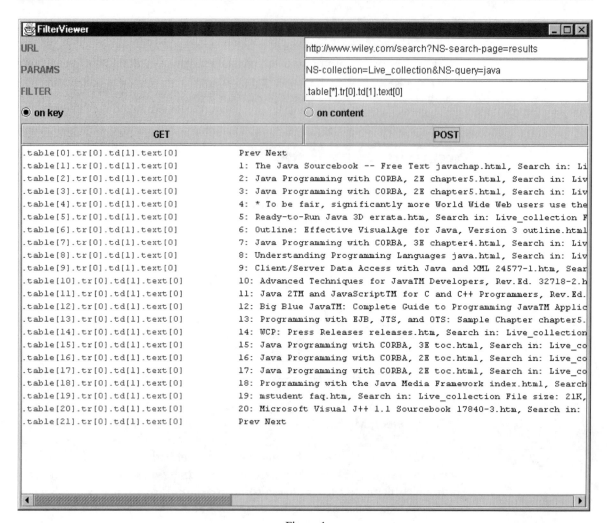

Figure 1

However, it's not just about the APIs themselves. We'll be using those APIs as a foundation on which to build a set of demonstration applications.

Demonstration applications

To whet your appetite I'll introduce some of the applications that we'll build, so that you can get a good idea of the relevance to your needs. These are the applications that I think will capture your imagination, but don't take this list as exhaustive because I'll be introducing many more examples to illustrate the key concepts along the way.

Filtering and querying tool

In Chapter 4 we'll implement a filtering tool that picks out specific HTML or XML elements from any web page, according to the XPath-like positions or content of those elements, as shown in Figure 1.

This idea will subsequently be extended into the realm of SQL queries for web data.

Share price information portal

Chapter 5 will show how a portal could be built, as a servlet or an applet, to combine information from multiple existing web pages into your own integrated information console. Figure 2 shows what this will look like in the servlet version.

Search engine

A customizable search engine/web crawler will be built in Chapter 6, to take a query term and a starting point and to report on the number of times that term appears in the pages leading from the starting page like this:

```
2 hits at http://www.lotontech.btinternet.co.uk/wdbc/help/help.html
2 hits at http://www.lotontech.btinternet.co.uk/wdbc/index.html
3 hits at http://www.lotontech.btinternet.co.uk/wdbc/help/release.html
7 hits at http://www.lotontech.btinternet.co.uk/wdbc.html#bespoke
2 hits at http://www.lotontech.btinternet.co.uk/wdbc/index.html#copyright
7 hits at http://www.lotontech.btinternet.co.uk/wdbc/html#SearchEngine
2 hits at http://www.lotontech.btinternet.co.uk/wdbc/help/help.html#Assist
1 hits at http://www.lotontech.btinternet.co.uk/frontpage.html
7 hits at http://www.lotontech.btinternet.co.uk/wdbc/html
2 hits at http://www.lotontech.btinternet.co.uk/wdbc/index.html#examples
```

Mail miner and SMS relay service

A mail mining application (see in Chapter 7) will retrieve incoming email messages and decompose their contents into a form suitable for the same

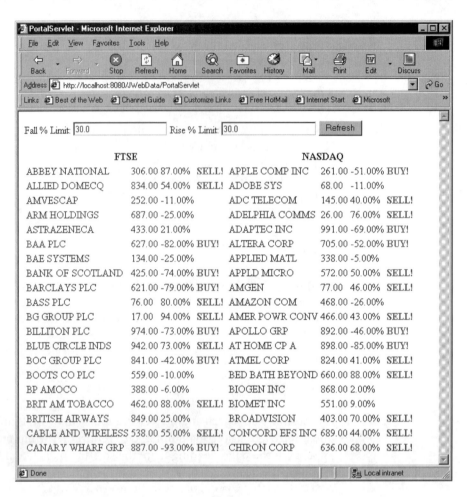

Figure 2

querying and filtering techniques that we will have developed for web pages.

```
.msg[0].subject[0] Web Mining with Java
.msg[0].from[0] "Tony Loton @ LOTONtech" <tony@lotontech.com>
.contentType[0] text/plain;
    charset="iso-8859-1"
.msg[0].body[0] Hi Tony,
.msg[0].body[1]
.msg[0].body[2] Just a short message to congratulate myself on writing the
new book, Web
.msg[0].body[3] Mining with Java.
.msg[0].body[4]
```

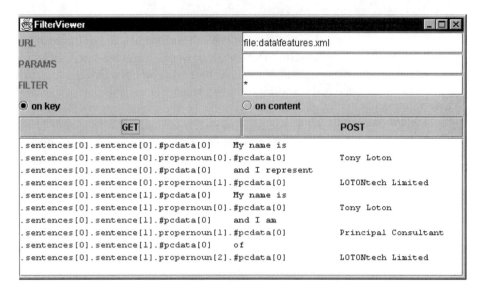

Figure 3

```
.msg[0].body[5] Kind regards,
.msg[0].body[6]
.msg[0].body[7] Tony.
```

As a novel example, we'll use this idea in a service to relay email messages to a mobile phone via the Short Messaging Service (SMS). For which we'll need no SMS knowledge whatsoever as I'll be showing you how to take advantage of an existing web service that provides the required functionality.

Text feature extractor

In Chapter 8 we'll do some parsing of text that is not marked up explicitly with HTML or XML tags, and we'll add some structure based on English parts of speech. In particular we'll look at a simple approach to picking put key features from sentences as shown in Figure 3.

How to Read the Book

We'll be looking at Java code as early as Chapter 2, for which I make no apologies. Serious Java programmers will be interested in the low-level tips, tricks and techniques for working with web data, and in the early chapters we'll be covering some key concepts that will underpin the rest of our work. So if you fit into the serious java programmer category I suggest you read carefully through all of the chapter texts and code listings to gain a thorough end-to-end understanding.

If you're not so serious about the low-level implementations but you do want to use those implementations to build higher-level solutions, you can do that too. There is an escape route through the early chapters, which involves paying more attention to the text than the code listings, and which allows you to take just the main ideas and the final class implementations from each chapter. As a general rule, each chapter will use components from earlier chapters as black-box service providers. So that you can build a portal in Chapter 5, using the query engine from Chapter 4, without knowing too much about the secrets inside. I'll signpost this escape route as we go along.

Tony Loton

About the Author

Tony graduated in 1991 with a BSc. Hons. degree in Computer Science and Management, and prior to launching LOTONtech Limited he gained almost ten years experience as a (managing) consultant, technical architect, course instructor and amateur salesman specializing in Enterprise Java, CORBA , Unified Modeling Language and related technologies.

He launched LOTONtech Limited in 2000 as a vehicle for researching and developing innovative software solutions. Having puzzled for some time on the best way to access web-based information, for a new breed of knowledge-based applications, he developed the WebDataKit; a Java2 solution comprising an API and a Structured Query Language designed specifically for the automatic extraction of HTML and XML data from web sources.

Tony's early Java web mining ideas have been featured previously as:

- *case study* contribution to '*Professional Java Data*' (Wrox Press, 2001), and

- an article at JavaWorld,
  http://www.javaworld.com/javaworld/jw-03-2001/jw-0316-webdb.html

This book takes these ideas much further, with brand new material, and is not directly based on either of these earlier works.

If you're a regular reader of *Java Developer's Journal*, *Java Report*, *JavaWorld* or any other of the popular Java journals, chances are you'll see more of Tony's ideas popping up from time to time. And you can always find out about LOTONtech Limited by visiting us at: http://www.lotontech.com

Acknowledgements

Specifically I would like to thank Simon Plumtree at Wiley for sharing my enthusiasm for this project at an early stage, and for the invaluable assistance he would no doubt have provided if I'd asked more often. Thanks to Sally Mortimore at Wiley for a constructive and enthusiastic first contact that pointed me in Simon's direction. Thanks also to Gaynor Redvers-Mutton for picking up after Simon.

Thanks to my wife, Debbie, for helping to keep the LOTONtech ship afloat by taking some of my workload, for her inspirational contributions, and for proof-reading my 'do not disturb' sign more times than she would have liked. Not to mention all those hours spent indexing.

On the subject of inspiration, I'd like to pass on my thanks to the following authors whose works have helped – without knowing it – to plug the gaps in my knowledge of the accepted data mining wisdom; Michael Berry, Eibe Frank, Gordon Linoff, Dan Sullivan and Ian Witten.

For commenting on the first draft of my complete manuscript I'd like to pass on my thanks to Samir Khobragade, Ron Hitchens, and Stan Ng and Steve Webster.

This has largely been a *lone* work, even a *lonely* work at times. I've been underground for some time, putting all my thoughts down on e-paper, and I've now resurfaced to see the world in all its glory. Though I've been working alone on the book itself, there are many unsung heroes who have contributed to my ideas and knowledge over the past few years, thus making it all possible. Some of them I've met, some I've worked with, and some I've only read about. Thanks, whoever you are, and if you think it's you please get in touch.

Surveying the Scene

From information comes knowledge, and from knowledge comes power. This is a book about getting your hands on the information, turning it into knowledge, and harnessing the power. Using Java. In this introductory chapter we'll survey the scene by looking at:

- Our starting point of web services and web technology.

- My interpretation of the term web mining and its relationship to data mining and text mining.

- Our end-goals (what I've called The Big Picture) and how the book will be structured to take us through to the end result.

- The design notation and code presentation styles that I have adopted to convey the ideas.

1.1 What's it all About?

Let's start by taking a look at what we mean by *web services*, how those services are supported by *web technology*, and how they fit into the context of *web mining*.

1.1.1   The world of web services

Consider the number of web sites and the sheer volume of data that they contain. So many sites, and so much data, that you need a search engine to help you find the sites you want. There are tens – if not hundreds – of search engine interfaces provided on-line, some more popular than others, but which one to choose? Fortunately you don't have to choose because there are also a number of engines to search the search engines. We'll implement a meta search engine, like that in chapter 6.

Once you've narrowed your search to a just few sites, you tend to put the ones you like into your select circle of friends to be visited regularly. These will be the quality sites that provide the latest information on the subject of your choice. If it's a portal site, that means the *subjects* (plural) of your choice. We'll look at building a portal in Chapter 5. *So we'll be looking at how to emulate some of the popular web services such as search engines and portals.*

What do you do with the information at the sites you visit? You read it, print it, and maybe do a screen grab, but you could do so much more with it if only you could get hold of the information in a more usable form; a form that you could manipulate, store, and query. In Chapter 4 we'll implement a filtering and querying mechanism for web data. *So as well as emulating some web services, we'll be using existing web services as a source of data that might be suitable for mining.*

Since the information available on the Internet is not all in the form of web pages, it's worth giving some thought to other data feeds. In many cases these alternative data sources, such as news groups, have been made available via on-line web interfaces, thus making them accessible via a core set of techniques for capturing data from web sites. In other cases, some additional programming effort will be required. I'm thinking here of incoming electronic mail which constitutes a very valuable source of data. In Chapter 5 we'll look at how to capture inbound email messages. *So we'll be extending the scope to incorporate data from a range of sources.*

1.1.2   The world of web technology

The incredible growth of the Internet is in part a product of the technologies that underpin it. The key communications protocols and data representation schemes used on the net are largely based on non-proprietary, open standards, or at least based on *de facto* standards originating from wide adoption. This means it's not too difficult to build web services and applications that are compatible.

In this book we'll be concentrating on four of the open standards:

- HyperText Transfer Protocol (HTTP),
- HyperText Mark-up Language (HTML),
- eXtensible Mark-up Language (XML),
- Post Office Protocol (POP),

and by implication some lower level standards like TCP/IP, though we won't be looking into the details.

From a programming point of view we'll be dealing exclusively with Java, which has become the *de facto* standard language of the web. And, as I'll try to convince you in Chapter 2, it is probably the best option for building the applications that I'll describe.

1.1.3   What is web mining?

The subject we are looking at is *web mining*, which is related to – but not quite the same as – *data mining*. Data mining involves extracting data from in-house corporate databases or data warehouses, processing the data in some way, and then presenting it in more meaningful ways, usually summarized, and possibly in the form of web pages on an internal intranet or the global Internet. This book treats the World Wide Web itself as the ultimate data source, the world's biggest database. We'll gather information from web sources, some of which may have originated in someone's data warehouse and some of which may be destined for our own corporate database. Some of it we'll collect, collate, cross-reference or simply re-present via our own web pages – our portal – in new ways and novel combinations.

Since we'll be dealing mainly with textual data, albeit encoded as HTML or XML, there will be some aspects of text mining but not a complete coverage. Both data mining and text mining have been documented very expertly elsewhere, so rather than compete with those works, my intention is to complement them. You will be able to take the tried and tested algorithms for classification, association, clustering, prediction, natural language processing, which are described in the other texts, and apply them to web-based data with the help of this book.

Web mining itself seems to conjure up two possible definitions: web *usage* mining and web *content* mining. The former is concerned with analysis of how users interact with web site(s), what information they look at, what they buy, and where they go next. That's not the subject of this book unless, by some good fortune, the necessary data is made available as web content that we can mine. From now on whenever I say *web mining* I'll actually mean *web content mining*.

1.2 The Master Plan

Now that we have some idea of the scope we'll look in more detail at what we'll do throughout the chapters, and how we'll do it.

1.2.1 The big picture

The underlying theme of this book is to take information from the world's biggest information resource, add some value by processing the raw information, and then re-present the modified information in novel ways. In most cases you can take the world's biggest information resource to mean the World Wide Web, but I will stray at least once outside the web realm, into email, which falls within the wider definition of the Internet.

When talking about processing the information I'll concentrate more on the technological aspects, particularly the Java programming techniques, than on text and data mining theory. I'll try to give some ideas about how you could combine my Java techniques with the tried and tested data processing and mining algorithms described so well elsewhere.

I'll cover the presentation of data through our own applet and servlet based portal that combines information from two data sources into a single page. I won't take the portal concept through all of the examples, in order to keep them as simple as possible, but you can take this to be a possible front-end to any of the further techniques that we discuss. To demonstrate the diversity of the outgoing delivery channels that we might like to use, I'll suggest a way of presenting summarized information to mobile telephone users in the form of Short Messaging Service (SMS) notifications. And if you're not interested in something quite so exciting you could simply dump the extracted, enhanced, information straight into a conventional database.

Figure 1.1 gives a schematic representation showing:

• The data sources that we have access to via the Internet; static web pages, dynamically generated web content provided through on-line services, and incoming email messages.

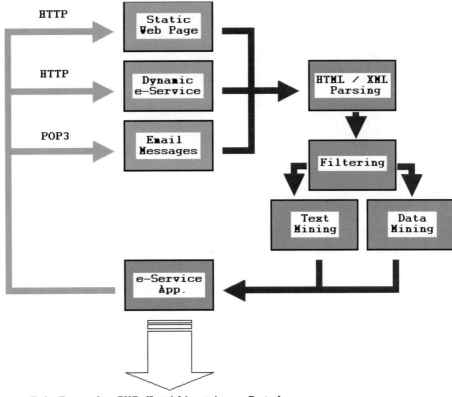

Figure 1.1   The big picture

- The standard protocols that we'll use for connecting to those data sources; HTTP for static and dynamic web content, and POP for email.

- The processing that we shall apply to content; parsing, filtering, text and data mining.

- The possible delivery channels for outgoing content; a portal, an SMS relay service, or a data load into a traditional relational database.

1.2.2   The grand design

Figure 1.2 provides a Unified Modeling Language (UML) overview of the Java applications that we'll develop, arranged into Java packages and labelled with the chapters in which we'll look at their implementations.

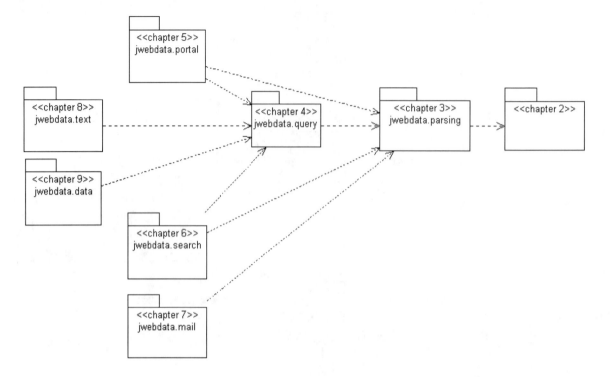

Figure 1.2   Package structure

This provides a road map for the book. Although I've arranged the material in what I think is the most logical order, there may be a more optimum route for you to take according to your needs. The dependencies in Figure 1.2 show what's on the critical path and what is not.

Chapter 2 is essential as an introduction to Java as the language of the web, and Chapter 3 establishes the core parsing techniques on which everything else depends. So those two chapters are mandatory. From Chapter 3 you could go straight to Chapter 7 if your interest is limited to *JavaMail*, but I recommend Chapter 4 as the enabler for all of the remaining chapters. Chapters 5 to 7 can, in principle, be tackled in any order once you've done Chapter 4, but my suggestion is to work numerically. The final chapter (Chapter 10) is not shown in Figure 1.2 as it contains no code examples.

In each individual chapter we'll drill down into the relevant package and I'll present a more detailed UML diagram showing the classes and their relationships for that chapter. For example, when drilling down into the *jwebdata.portal* package (Chapter 5), you will see Figure 1.3.

Though I've used a very limited subset of the UML notation, it's worth a

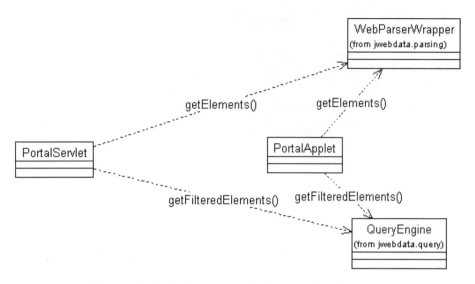

Figure 1.3   UML class diagram for package jwebdata.query

brief clarification of what that notation means so that we're all talking the same language.

1.2.3   UML notation

I've limited myself to one UML diagram type, the class diagram, which shows the static relationships between classes. On the class diagrams I've limited the types of relationships to two; class dependencies and interface implementations. In Figure 1.4 you will see a class dependency example and an interface implementation example.

Class dependency

A dependency is shown as a dashed arrow between two classes, and the nature of the dependency may be labelled. In the general sense a UsingClass *depends* on functionality provided by a UsedClass. A specific example is that of the *filterviewer* class that *depends* on (makes use of) the Filter class, in which you will have seen that I've labelled the relationship with a method name. In that respect, my class diagram is in part playing the role of a collaboration diagram.

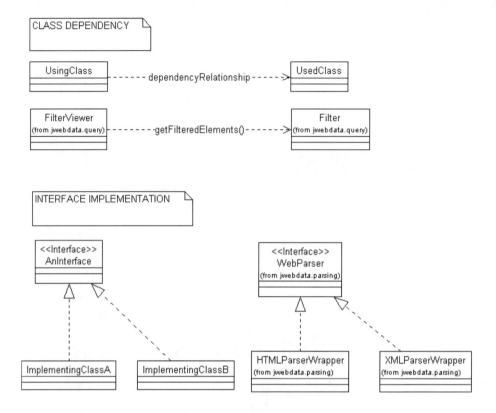

Figure 1.4   UML notation

Interface implementation

Interface implementation is shown as a dashed line with a triangular head. In the general sense, ImplementingClassA and ImplementingClassB both implement AnInterface, withAnInterface being marked with the <<Interface>> stereotype to show that it is a Java interface rather than a class. A specific example is that of the WebParser <<Interface>> that is implemented by the *HTMLParserWrapper* class and the *XMLParserWrapper* class.

There's much more to UML than this, but for our purposes that limited notation will suffice.

1.2.4   Java code presentation

I've tried to keep the Java code examples as simple, logical and easy to read as possible. The code listings correspond exactly with the source code that you can download, so what you read is what you get. Comments have been added, and highlighted, as shown below so that – in many cases – the code will stand as self-explanatory.

```
SourceElement thisElement=(SourceElement)
  sortedElements.elementAt (i);
// -- By default compare the key field of this element --
String compareField=(String) thisElement.getKey();
// -- Compare the content field if required --
if (fieldConstant.equals(CONTENT))
  compareField=(String) thisElement.getContent();
if (compareField!=null)
{
  // -- Add a positive match to the filtered list --
  if (Operator.compare(compareField,operator,compareString))
    filteredElements.addElement(thisElement);
}
```

The in-code comments provide a blow-by-blow account of the example implementations in a form that is concise and related directly to the code. So as not to interrupt the flow of the explanatory text I've not strayed into a detailed description of the Java API classes that we've used. That information is available in the official API documentation, but for convenience at the end of each chapter I've included a list of the Java API classes introduced in that chapter.

Each of the class and method definitions has been prefixed with as *javadoc* style comment like this one:

```
/**
 * Method to get a key/value list of HTML or XML elements at baseURL.
 */
```

which means you can generate the documentation using the *javadoc* tool, as shown in Figure 1.5. For convenience I've included a subset of this documentation in Appendix B, and you can generate the full set yourself with the following command:

```
javadoc -d ./javadocs jwebdata.applet jwebdata.data jwebdata.mail
jwebdata.parsing jwebdata.portal jwebdata.query jwebdata.search
jwebdata.servlet jwebdata.text
```

Finally, I've pre-fixed every code listing with a line like this one so that you're in no doubt as to which source file contains which piece of code:

```
// ** Code taken from jwebdata/parsing/WebParser.java **
```

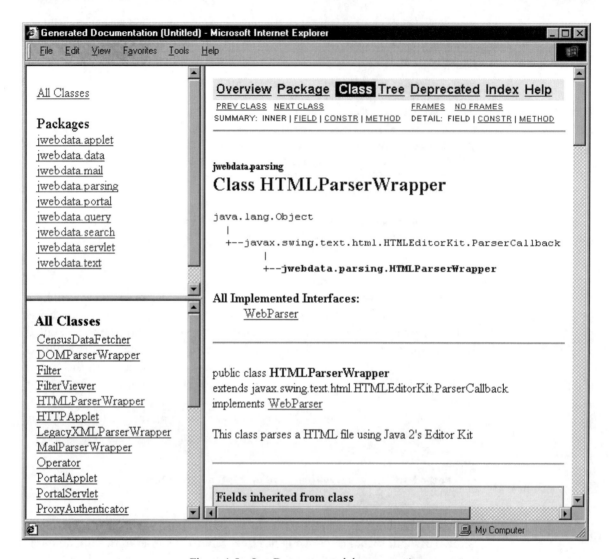

Figure 1.5   JavaDoc generated documentation

1.3   Software Download

All of the source code, binary code, and (where applicable) sample data shown
in this book is available at the companion website:
http://www.lotontech.com/wiley

In addition to my code you will also need some pre-requisite Java SDK software. It's all available for free, with Appendix A telling you where to get it and what to do with it.

1.4   Copyright Implications

Before you read on, a word of warning, while web-based information is readily available, that doesn't necessarily mean it's freely available, and I'm not suggesting that you infringe anyone's copyright. I think it's probably safe to provide new browsing and searching experiences for users, and to collect data for private use – after all, that's why it's published – but I'm not here to give legal or moral advice.

If you intend to collect not generally available data from existing sites, then no matter how much you *add value* to it or combine it with data from other sites, you might need permission from the original data provider in order to re-publish it in your own name via your own portal. However, if you think your portal idea will make you rich you won't mind paying a licence fee to the original author, will you?

I've found a few web pages that discuss the topic of web copyright, and I've provided the links here – but not the content, just in case it's copyrighted – so that you can take a look. Its not very conclusive, I'm afraid.

http://www.templetons.com/brad/copymyths.html
http://www.benedict.com/digital/www/webiss.htm#Top
http://sunsite.berkeley.edu/Imaging/Databases/Fall95papers/fenton.html
http://www.ala.org/acrl/paperhtm/e40.html

Finally, in putting this book together I have been careful enough to use materials mainly taken from web sites owned by myself, my company, or the book's publisher, John Wiley & Sons, Ltd. Where I have strayed slightly onto someone else's territory, I've taken no direct screenshots and I've limited my use of third-party data to very small data sets that are not exclusive to one provider and of no commercial value to me. Where a site provides an explicit copyright statement granting limited rights I've taken advantage of those rights and I've included the original copyright statement as an appendix.

I suggest you tread with caution as I have done.

1.5 Chapter Review

I'll set the standard for the following chapters by including a review of what we've covered in this chapter.

We started by looking briefly at some of the key services and technologies of the web, after which we put the term *web mining* in the context of the related disciplines of *text mining* and *data mining*. We drew the distinction between *web usage mining* (which we won't be considering further) and *web content mining* (which we will).

The scene was set by looking at the 'big picture' for this book, comprising the potential data sources, the access protocols, the processing mechanisms and the final delivery channels. A UML class diagram was used to provide a high-level view of how the Java classes appearing throughout the book will be decomposed into packages. and that diagram served as a road map for the book. To ensure we're all singing from the same song sheet, I included a summary of the UML notation that has been used.

Towards the end of the chapter I described the presentation style for the Java code examples, my use of comments, and the possibility of using the *javadoc* tool to provide a handy navigable overview, in HTML, of the full set of classes.

Finally I highlighted the issue of copyright, which is an important consideration when taking data from the web. Especially if you're intending to re-publish it. Maybe I've been a bit too cautious here, maybe not, as the jury is still out on the copyright implications of information provided on-line. Inadvertently I might have given an impression of this being the book they wouldn't want you to read.

I hope you'll want to read it, and in the next chapter we'll look at some of the features that make Java the ideal choice for taking data from the web and for re-presenting that data back onto the web.

2

Language of
The Web

To be the language of choice for the kind of applications we're looking to build, any candidate language must have capabilities in at least three areas. First, it must provide a communications infrastructure supporting the common Internet protocols, namely HTTP over TCP/IP over sockets, so that we can physically connect to the web data sources. Secondly, it must support the development of applications that are themselves delivered over the web, so that we can create a portal or provide an on-line interface to our applications. Finally, there should be some helper classes or libraries that facilitate the parsing of HTML and XML source data.

Java has all three of these pre-requisite capabilities. Since the very beginning (which in Java terms means the mid 90s) Java has allowed HTTP-based connections to URL data sources, all wrapped up in the neat *java.net* and *java.io* class packages. The language was designed with web delivery of applications in mind, initially as downloadable applets and soon afterwards as Common Gateway Interface (CGI) like servlets too. The more recent (Java 2) releases have included a built-in HTML parser and a Java API for XML Processing (JAXP).

In this chapter I'll cover applets and servlets as the web-based delivery channels for our mining applications, and I'll dig deep into the technicalities of HTTP communication as the mechanism for extracting information via existing web interfaces. Think about that sentence. 'Extracting information via existing web interfaces' means we're on the road to the Holy Grail of computing; a set of solutions based on re-use!

2.1   Web Application Delivery Channels

Some web mining applications will be designed to extract data automatically from a range of web sources, process that information, and then dump it straight into a database or a printed report. There will be no user interface. However, for those situations where we wish to take up to the minute information from various sources, to be re-presented to the user in new combinations with added value, we will need a mechanism for taking input from the user and for providing the results back to the user via our own web-based interfaces. I'm talking about *delivery channels*.

We'll look at two possible delivery channels for Java applications, applets and servlets, not from the point of view of trying to teach those technologies but from a comparative point of view. What are the relative strengths and weaknesses of the two approaches for web mining applications? And it's worth reading through this even if you have a great deal of experience with Java because I'll be sowing the seeds for what will grow out of the remaining chapters.

2.1.1   Applets as a delivery channel

From the very first version (1.0) the Java language and platform provided for the delivery of small applications, applets, into the browsers of web surfers. Thus the applet was the original *delivery channel*, and the one that I'll consider first.

A brief history of applets

The idea was that small applications could be downloaded on demand from web sites with no tedious installation, no restriction on the client hardware or software platform (as long as a Java-enabled web browser was supported), and no costly upgrades necessary for the introduction of new functionality. Each time you launched the applet you could be sure that you were using the latest version.

The first few applets to appear – animated clocks and the like -- looked promising but the more serious applets, the ones that would rival traditional PC-based office applications, never quite materialized for a number of reasons. The applet security model was too restrictive, download time was too long, and browser vendors failed to keep pace with the rapid development of the Java Virtual Machine (JVM). Applets fell out of favour.

Over the years, Java has evolved to address the key problems exhibited by the original applet model. Java Archive (JAR) files were introduced to reduce the download delay, the Java Plug-in was conceived to separate the virtual machine version from the browser version, and a new security model allowed for *trusted* applets within a configurable sandbox.

As of Java 2 all of these pieces are in place. With the Java Plug-in down from 20Mb to a trim 5Mb and with the Java Web-Start technology promising locally installed applications delivered via the web, the tide has begun to turn back towards applets as a viable delivery mechanism.

A simple applet

I'll present a first applet here, which looks simple but is essential to the plot. We'll use it as a comparison between the applet and servlet approaches to web application delivery and, towards the end of the chapter, we'll adapt it to become our first example application for collecting and re-presenting web data. I'm by no means offering a tutorial as I assume you're already programming in Java.

This first applet will provide an input field into which the user may type some search text, as shown in Figure 2.1. Upon pressing the Submit button, the text will be redisplayed in a separate field with the legend 'you searched for:' as shown in Figure 2.2.

I said this would be a simple applet, and it is. It doesn't actually do any searching, we'll implement that later, but it does illustrate the way that an applet user interface works. Once the applet has been downloaded from the server, via its HTML page, it is completely self-sufficient. There is no need to communicate again with the originating server and there is no page refresh between providing the input and receiving the output response. As a Java programmer, you should know that already.

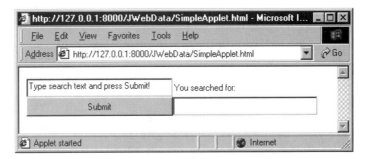

Figure 2.1   SimpleApplet input

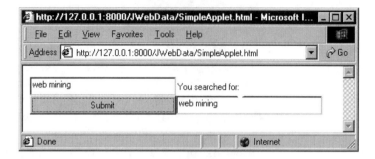

Figure 2.2   SimpleApplet output

Here is the code for SimpleApplet.java, not too taxing I hope:

```java
// ** Code taken from jwebdata/applet/SimpleApplet.java **

package jwebdata.applet;

import java.applet.*;
import java.awt.*;
import java.awt.event.*;

/**
 * A first applet that presents a simple GUI form.
 */
public class SimpleApplet extends Applet implements ActionListener
{
    // -- GUI Components --
    TextField inputText;
    Button submitButton;
    TextField outputText;

    /**
     * Initialization method.
     */
    public void init()
    {
        setLayout(new GridLayout(2,2));

        // -- Set up the input text field --
        inputText=new TextField("Type search text and press Submit!");
        add(inputText);

        // -- Add a simple label --
        Label messageLabel=new Label ("You searched for:");
        messageLabel.setBackground(Color.white);
        add(messageLabel);
```

```
// -- Set up the submit button with a listener for events --
submitButton=new Button("Submit");
submitButton.addActionListener(this);
add(submitButton);

// -- Set up an output text field --
outputText=new TextField ("");
add(outputText);
}

/**
 * Method for responding to the button click.
 */
public void actionPerformed(ActionEvent event)
{
    // -- Process the submission --
    if (event.getSource()==submitButton)
      outputText.setText(inputText.getText());
}
}
```

To launch this applet via a web browser we'll also need a basic HTML file, *SimpleApplet.html*, with the following tag(s):

```
<applet code=jwebdata.applet.SimpleApplet width=400 height=50>
Simple Applet
</applet>
```

Just to set the record straight, when I say that there is no need to communicate with the server again I mean that there is no need to communicate with the same server, and not for the purpose of simply updating the displayed content. This is an important differentiator when looking at the servlet approach. Of course, if our applet were to perform a real search it would need to communicate with a server, somewhere, via the HTTP communication mechanisms that I'll describe later.

To keep it simple I've shown a Java 1.1 applet with its associated HTML tag. This book is based on the Java 2 standard, and any future applets that we implement will be dependent on the Java Plug-in that decouples the Java version from the browser version. In practice this means that the HTML tag for our applets will actually be as follows.

For Internet Explorer:

```
<object
  classid="clsid:8AD9C840-044E-11D1-B3E9-00805F499D93"
  width="500" height="500"
```

```
       codebase="http://java.sun.com/products/plugin/1.2.2/jinstall-
  1_2_2win.cab#Version=1,2,2,0">
    <param NAME="code" VALUE="jwebdata.portal.PortalApplet">
    <param NAME="type" VALUE="application/x-java-applet;version=1.2.2">
    <param NAME="scriptable" VALUE="true">
  </object>
```

For Netscape Navigator:

```
<embed
  type="application/x-java-applet;version=1.2.2"
      width="500"
      height="500" align="baseline"
      code="jwebdata.portal.PortalApplet"
  pluginspage="http://java.sun.com/products/plugin/1.2/plugin-
install.html">
  </embed>
```

It looks more frightening than it is.

Compiling and running the SimpleApplet

You should ensure that your current directory contains these files:

```
SimpleApplet.html
jwebdata/applet/SimpleApplet.java
```

The simplest way to test the *SimpleApplet* is to open the *SimpleApplet.html* file in your browser after compiling the applet with the command:

```
javac jwebdata/applet/SimpleApplet.java
```

If you've set up the Tomcat servlet engine as described in Appendix A you'll also be able to run the *SimpleApplet* in your browser via this URL: http://localhost:8080/JWebData/SimpleApplet.html

Should we use applets for our application delivery?

As I said earlier, applets failed to deliver on what was originally promised and thus they fell out of favour, particularly with regard to the write-once/run-anywhere philosophy. If you're developing solutions based on the Java 2 standard – which we will be – you may find few browsers supporting this standard, and indeed they don't need to because that functionality is provided by the Java 2 Plug-in. In a closed environment such as a corporate intranet, you can ensure that all desktops have the Plug-in installed, but across the wider Internet no such control may be exercised. Any solution provided in the form of a Java 2 applet will require users to have the Plug-in pre-installed or else be willing to perform a one time only download of the required software, about 5Mb of it.

For intranet deployment applets have some significant advantages in behaving like traditional desktop applications, with a degree of interaction and graphical support that cannot be matched by servlets and HTML. For Internet deployment here is what might be the killer argument in favour of applets; there is no alternative for some developers. For an individual developer who is not hosting his own site, and whose web-hosting provider does not support servlets, the only way to deliver any kind of interactive, dynamic content over the Internet with Java is via an applet.

2.1.2   Servlets as a delivery channel

Before you decide on applets as the delivery mechanism of choice, read on as I present the case for servlets.

A brief history of servlets

Servlets were introduced as the original server-side Java components, long before the appearance of Enterprise Java Beans. Not components in the same sense, but rather as the equivalent of CGI scripts that provide interactive applications through a series of HTML forms and pages. Where applets failed, servlets (and other CGI like technologies) succeeded as the lowest common denominator for browser compatibility. The vast majority of on-line interfaces are still based on the HTML standard despite its limitations, which is very good news for web miners!

The servlet API is a standard Java extension supported by stand-alone servlet engines and incorporated into the Java 2 Enterprise Edition SDK. The retention of many of the core features in the latest revision 2.3 of the servlet API specification suggests a high-level of stability and acceptance, yet some of the additional features – such as *filters* – allow for many new possibilities.

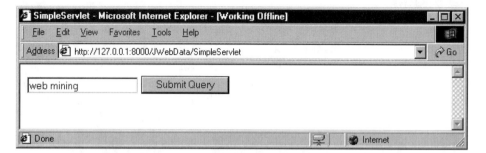

Figure 2.3   SimpleServlet input

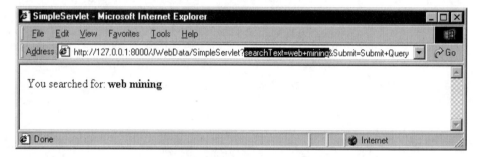

Figure 2.4   SimpleServlet output

A simple servlet

This is a servlet version of the applet that you've just seen. Once again there's an input field to take the search text and a Submit button, as you can see in Figure 2.3, but no sign of where the response will go.

The servlet model requires that user input is supplied via a HTML form that is then *submitted* to the server for processing and formulation of the response. Thus upon pressing the Submit button, a page refresh results in the response which is shown in Figure 2.4.

In the following code for SimpleServlet.java notice, how the initial request (with no parameters), and the form submission (with *searchText* passed with the URL), are both handled by the servlet's *doGet(...)* method shown in this code:

```
// ** Code taken from jwebdata/servlet/SimpleServlet.java **

package jwebdata.servlet;

import javax.servlet.*;
```

```java
import javax.servlet.http.*;
import java.io.*;

/**
 * A first servlet that presents a simple GUI form.
 */
public class SimpleServlet extends HttpServlet
{
    /**
     * Servlet method to process a GET submission.
     */
public void doGet(HttpServletRequest req, HttpServletResponse res)
  throws IOException
{
    // -- Set up the HTTP response --
    res.setContentType("text/html");
    PrintWriter outputWriter = res.getWriter();

    // -- Write the HTML Header --
    outputWriter.println("<html>");
    outputWriter.println("<head><title>SimpleServlet</title></head>");

    // -- Get input searchText if present --
    String searchText=req.getParameter("searchText");

    if (searchText==null)
    {
      // -- Ask the user for search text via a GET form --
      outputWriter.println("<body>");
      outputWriter.println("<form method=get
        action='SimpleServlet'>");
      outputWriter.println("<input type-text name-'searchText'>");
      outputWriter.println("<input type=submit name='Submit'><br>");
      outputWriter.println("</form>");
      outputWriter.println("</body>");
    }
    else
    {

      // -- Process the search text --
      outputWriter.println("<body>");
      outputWriter.println("You searched for: <b>"
        +searchText+"</b>");
      outputWriter.println("</body>");
    }
  {

  /**
   * Servlet method to process a POST submission.
   */
```

```
public void doPost(HttpServletRequest req, HttpServletResponse res)
  throws IOException
{
    doGet(req,res);
}
}
```

Besides showing how we might develop our own on-line user interfaces, this example servlet also highlights some of the issues that we'll have to think about when extracting data from existing web sites. Some sites will be static, comprising a number of hyperlinked HTML files, but many of the sites that we'll be interested in will provide the latest data – such as share prices – as dynamic content.

For dynamic sites the content will have been generated by a servlet much like this one, or by an equivalent technology such as CGI or ASP (Active Server Pages). I really do mean *equivalent* because our interaction with those sites will be the exactly the same regardless of which technology is actually used at the back-end. What all of these technologies have in common is:

• Presentation of information and prompting for input via HTML forms

• Capturing of user input data via HTTP *get* or *post* methods.

What we've seen here is the *get* method in action, which results in user input data being transmitted to the server as part of the URL. Look again at the text that I've highlighted in Figure 2.4. Also look at the HTML version of the form that our servlet presented, with the *get* method highlighted:

```
<html>
<head><title>SimpleServlet</title></head>
<body>
<form method=get action='SimpleServlet'>
<input type=text name='searchText'>
<input type=submit name='Submit'><br>
</form>
</body>
</html>
```

If we changed this form's *get* method to *post* there would be little perceivable difference from the user's point of view except that the data would no longer be transmitted as part of the URL, so we wouldn't see it, but it would still get through to the server; trust me. Our servlet would cope with the change because the *doPost(...)* method passes the request through to our *doGet(...)* method anyway.

Although the user sees little difference, it means that our automated web mining applications will have to support two methods for requesting dynamic content – *get* and *post* – each having an implementation slightly different from the other. I'll tell you more about that later in this chapter.

Compiling, deploying and running the SimpleServlet

You can compile the servlet with the command:

```
javac jwebdata\servlet\SimpleServlet.java
```

If you've not already done so you should now work through the deployment instructions for the Tomcat servlet engine, given in Appendix A.

If all goes according to plan you'll now be able to run the *SimpleServlet* by typing the URL in your browser as shown in Figures 2.3 and 2.4: http://localhost:8080/JWebData/SimpleServlet

Should we use servlets for our application delivery?

Here's some food for thought. If developers had adopted the applet approach *en masse* then the web mining techniques that I'll be describing here would have been rendered completely useless. Web mining relies on the fact that data is provided on the Internet as a set of static hyperlinked text files – encoded as HTML, XML or whatever else – or as dynamic content that may be retrieved via simple HTTP requests. That's not a good enough reason for us to implement *our* user interfaces with servlets unless, of course, we want to open ourselves up to being mined. So what's in it for us if we use servlets?

What we'll lose in terms of user interface functionality, compared with applets, we'll gain in terms of audience reach. HTML and HTTP are still the lowest common denominators for Internet applications. So I can practically guarantee that anyone, anywhere, with a fairly modern browser could use our servlet based applications. I can't make the same guarantee for applets.

Before some of you raise questions like 'what about Java Server Pages?' I'll just say that they're included implicitly in the servlet coverage. I have no doubt that there are some advantages, and disadvantages, of using Java Server Pages (JSPs) rather than hand-coded servlets but the fundamental delivery mechanism is the same.

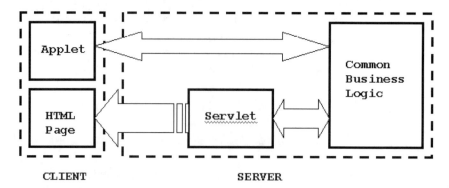

Figure 2.5   Access channels to common business logic

2.1.3   Applets vs. servlets: the verdict

In a nutshell I prefer the servlet approach for Internet deployment except in those situations where no servlet environment is available, or where we can dictate the nature of the client installation, or where HTML simply isn't up to the job. In any event, we should separate the application logic from the user interface aspect sufficiently to allow both kinds of interface to the same application as shown in Figure 2.5.

Remember I said that the *SimpleApplet* and *SimpleServlet* were included as essential to the plot, and not just as a gentle introduction to programming? The relevance will become clear when we consider HTTP communication.

2.2   HTTP Communication

HTTP communication will be the foundation on which all of the other techniques will be built. I've already hinted at how it works in principle; requests for data are submitted using the *get* or *post* method and results are returned in the form of HTML, XML, plain text, or one of a number of more exotic types called Multipurpose Internet Mail Extension (MIME) types.

I'll now show you the code for a modified version of the *SimpleApplet* which I've called *HTTPApplet*. The first modification is the inclusion of two additional import statements:

```
import java.io.*;
import java.net.*;
```

The second modification is a rewritten *actionPerformed(...)* method that passes the user's input text through to the *SimpleServlet*, and then captures the servlet's response, using a HTTP communication channel in *get* or *post* mode. Here it is:

```java
// ** Code taken from jwebdata/applet/HTTPApplet.java **

/**
 * This method POSTs the HTTP request in response to the button click.
 */
public void actionPerformed(ActionEvent event)
{
  if (event.getSource()==submitButton)
  {
    String searchText=inputText.getText();
    String baseURL="http://127.0.0.1:8000/JWebData/SimpleServlet";
    URL targetURL;
    InputStreamReader urlReader;

    try
    {
      if (getParameter("method").equals("get")) // -- GET --
      {
        targetURL=new URL(baseURL+"?searchText="+searchText);
        URLConnection urlConnection=targetURL.openConnection();
        urlReader=
          new InputStreamReader(urlConnection.getInputStream());
      }
      else // -- POST --
      {
        targetURL=new URL(baseURL);
        URLConnection urlConnection=targetURL.openConnection();
        // -- Prepare for input and output --
        urlConnection.setDoInput(true);
        urlConnection.setDoOutput(true);
        urlConnection.setUseCaches(false);

        // -- Write the submission --
        PrintWriter writer=new PrintWriter(new
          BufferedOutputStream(urlConnection.getOutputStream()));
        writer.println("searchText="+searchText);
        writer.close();
        urlReader=new
          InputStreamReader(urlConnection.getInputStream());
      }

      // -- Read the response --
      BufferedReader bufferedReader=new BufferedReader(urlReader);
      String responseText;
```

```
      while ((responseText-bufferedReader.readLine())!-null)
      {
        int boldIndex=responseText.indexOf("<b>");
        if (boldIndex>=0) // -- Very basic HTML parsing --
        {
          responseText=responseText
            .substring(boldIndex+3,responseText.length()-4);
          outputText.setText(responseText);
        }
      }
      bufferedReader.close();
      urlReader.close();
    }
    catch (Exception ex) {ex.printStackTrace();}
  }
}
```

We can switch the *HTTPApplet* to work in *get* or *post* mode by changing the value of the method parameter in the applet's HTML file shown here:

```
<applet code=jwebdata.applet.HTTPApplet width=400 height=50>
<param name=method value=post></param>
Simple Applet
</applet>
```

Our new applet will be used to *drive* an existing web-based interface; in this case our own *SimpleServlet*, but it could easily be adapted to drive someone else's servlet, CGI script, or ASP. Taking a ride on the back of existing web services like this will be a key concept that we'll develop.

All we need to know is the URL, the required HTTP method and expected parameters, and the format of the response. Now imagine that our new service driving applet was a servlet instead, through which we could drive many existing on-line interfaces. What we'd have is the basis of our own *portal*. I'll say a lot more about that in Chapter 5.

2.2.1   Compiling and running the HTTPApplet

You can compile the *HTTPApplet* with the command:

```
javac jwebdata/applet/HTTPApplet.java
```

Assuming you have the Tomcat servlet engine up and running (Appendix A) you will be able to run the *HTTPApplet* via this URL:
http://localhost:8080/JWebData/HTTPApplet.html

If you're wondering what the result looks like when you run this applet, I'm afraid there's nothing new to show you. It looks exactly like Figure 2.2, except that the URL will now have the text *SimpleApplet.html* replaced with *HTTPApplet.html*. However, we've done something quite different behind the scenes in driving an existing web-based service.

Although I've moved rapidly to a point at which we can get hold of dynamic content via existing web interfaces using very little Java code, much of the data that we'll be interested in will be in the form of static HTML files. This code will perform equally well if we assume that all static content will be retrieved using the *get* method, but in reality we can ignore the distinction completely. Due to some trickery on the part of the web server at the back-end, what looks like a static request might in fact return dynamically generated data and what looks like a dynamic request might return a static file from disk. All that matters is that we have a valid URL.

2.2.2   Beyond the proxy and through the firewall

If you're accessing the Internet at work rather than from home, chances are that you will not be doing so directly. There will probably be a firewall and a proxy server standing in the way of your direct HTTP communication. As the code stands at the moment it could fail, unless we tell the JVM about the proxy and unless (in some cases) we provide a valid username and password to get us through to the outside world.

When running as an applet via the Java 2 Plug-in no code changes will be required. The Plug-in Properties dialog allows proxy server settings to be specified explicitly or inherited from the browser that launches the Plug-in, as shown in Figure 2.6. Windows users can launch the Plug-in Properties dialog from the Windows Control Panel.

When running as a Java application we have to specify the required settings on the command line or from within the code. The JVM picks up the values of three properties: *proxySet*, *proxyHost* and *proxyPort* (usually 80) that we can set on the command line like this:

```
java -DproxySet=true -DproxyHost=thehost
   -DproxyPort=theport TheApplicationClass
```

Or we can set them in code with these statements:

```
System.getProperties().put("proxySet", "true");
System.getProperties().put("proxyHost", theHost);
System.getProperties().put("proxySet", thePort);
```

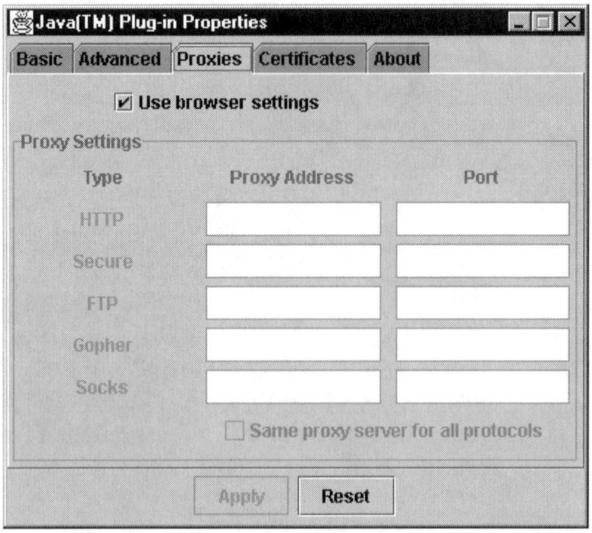

Figure 2.6   Plug-in proxy settings

So far so good, but what about the username and password that I was telling you about? If we must give these details in order to break through to the outside world the simplest way is to use the Java 2 *Authenticator*. We can create our own simple class – *ProxyAuthenticator* – that extends *java.net.Authenticator*, and which takes a user name and password in its constructor. It will then give up these details on demand from the JVM, via the *getPasswordAuthentication(...)* method. Here is the code, which will be placed in the *jwebdata.parsing* package in preparation for the next chapter.

```java
// ** Code taken from jwebdata/parsing/ProxyAuthenticator.java **

/**
 * A Java 2 Authenticator to provide the proxy/firewall password.
 */
public class ProxyAuthenticator extends java.net.Authenticator
{
    private String user;
    private String password;

    /**
     * Constructor to take the username and password.
     */
    public ProxyAuthenticator(String user, String password)
    {
        this.user=user;
        this.password=password;
```

```
    }

    /**
      * Method to give up the username and password if requested.
      */
    protected java.net.PasswordAuthentication getPasswordAuthentication()
    {
        return new java.net.PasswordAuthentication(user
          ,password.toCharArray());
    }
}
```

To capture the authentication information in the first place I propose that we introduce two new properties of our own; *proxyUser* and *proxyPassword*. We'll read those properties, use them to construct an instance of our *ProxyAuthenticator*, and set that as the default authenticator. Thus any application will need these few lines of code inserting before we do any HTTP work:

```
// -- Look for user and password properties --
try
{
  String user=System.getProperty("proxyUser");
  String password=System.getProperty("proxyPassword");
  Authenticator.setDefault(new ProxyAuthenticator(user,password));
}
catch (Exception ex) {}
```

The full command line for our applications will now be:

```
java -DproxySet=true -DproxyHost=thehost -DproxyPort=theport
    -DproxyUser=username -DproxyPassword=password TheApplicationClass
```

Remember that we don't strictly need that code, or those extra properties, if we're accessing the Internet directly. As it won't do any harm I think it's better to add it anyway, as a contingency for all situations.

2.3 Performance Implications

You might now have preference for the applet or servlet approach for the delivery of web applications that fetch data via HTTP. Maybe you want to appeal to the largest possible user base by using servlets, maybe you need the

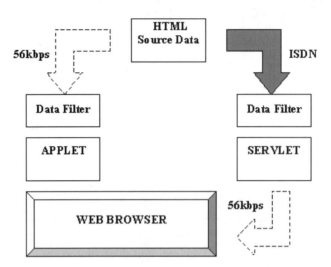

Figure 2.7   Applet/servlet performance implications

advanced graphical and interactive capabilities of applets, or maybe your ISP
simply does not provide servlet support. Before you make up your mind you
should also consider the performance implications of HTTP communication
between applets and servlets.

Take a look at Figure 2.7 which summarizes the point I'll make next.

We'll be taking content from existing web pages and, as I'll show you in
Chapter 4, we'll be filtering the content for presentation to our users.

Figure 2.7 shows that if we take the applet route, the entire HTML content
will be downloaded over the user's dial-up connection (maximum speed
56kbps) for local filtering by the applet running in the client browser. Thus
we're at the mercy of the dial-up connection. If we take the servlet route, only
the filtered content – possibly a very small subset – will be transmitted onward
to the client browser after server-side filtering. The full content will have been
retrieved over our own ISDN Internet connection.

2.4 Chapter Review

In this chapter we've looked at applets and servlets as an alternative delivery
channel for our web applications. We've contrasted the two approaches and
discovered how our applications – whether applets or servlets – can retrieve
static or dynamic web content by submitting a HTTP request. Probably to

someone else's servlet. We've considered the problem of accessing content from behind a firewall/proxy and implemented a solution to this problem.

Any HTTP request that we submit using *get* or *post* will result in some data being returned as a response, the content of which may be HTML data, XML data, plain text or some other MIME type. Prior to reading the response we can determine the content type, which will typically be one of the following;

- text/plain,
- text/HTML,
- application/XML.

In the next chapter, I'll discuss how we'll process the different kinds of content, in particular HTML and XML.

2.4.1   API classes and interfaces introduced in this chapter

The following Java API classes and interfaces have been introduced for the first time in this chapter's code examples:

- *java.applet.Applet* is extended by any applet that is to be embedded in a web page, providing a standard interface between the applet and its environment.

- *java.awt.Button* represents a graphical component in the form of a labelled button that triggers actions when pushed.

- *java.awt.Label* represents a graphical component in the form of a read-only text label that has no interactive capabilities.

- *java.awt.TextField* represents a graphical component in the form of a text component that allows for the editing of a single line of text.

- *java.awt.event.ActionEvent* may be generated by a component in response to a user interacting with that component. Events are passed to objects that implement the *ActionListener* interface and which are registered as listeners of the component.

- *java.awt.event.ActionListener* should be implemented by any class that wishes to receive action events from a component.

- *java.io.BufferedReader* is used to read text from a character input stream in buffered fashion.

- *java.io.InputStreamReader* reads bytes and translates them into characters according to a specified character encoding.

- *java.io.PrintWriter* prints formatted representations of objects to a text output stream.

- *java.lang.String* is the Java representation of a character string.

- *java.net.URL* represents a URL that addresses a resource on the World Wide Web.

- *java.net.URLConnection* represents a communications link between an application and a URL, allowing the resource at that URL to be written to or read from.

- *java.net.Authenticator* is used to obtain authentication information – for example a username and password – for a network connection.

- *java.net.PasswordAuthentication* is a holder for user name and password information used by an *Authenticator*.

- *javax.servlet.http.HttpServlet* should be extended by any servlet that provides dynamic content in response to a HTTP request.

- *javax.servlet.http.HttpServletRequest* represents an incoming HTTP request to a servlet.

- *javax.servlet.http.HttpServletResponse* represents the servlet's response to a HTTP request.

HTML and XML Parsing

Having established what kind of content we're dealing with, and assuming that it will be HTML or XML, we'll want to discover the structure and arrangement of the constituent HTML or XML elements. Understanding the structure and arrangement of elements presented as text means *parsing*, so in this chapter we'll implement a parser.

3.1 The Design

We will implement two parsers, called *HTMLParserWrapper* and *XMLParserWrapper* respectively. I've tagged the suffix *wrapper* onto each because we'll be *wrapping* parser functionality provided by the Java SDK. We'll implement a *WebParserWrapper* as our entry point, which will decide on the most appropriate parser for the given content, HTML or XML. The two parser wrappers may be used interchangeably thanks to a generic *WebParser* interface that they will both implement. How the classes for this chapter will fit together is shown in Figure 3.1.

Three classes then, plus an interface and an additional class that I've not yet told you about. The extra class – to be called *DOMParserWrapper* – will be an alternative implementation of the *XMLParserWrapper*, based on the Document Object Model (DOM) approach rather than the Simple API for XML (SAX) approach to XML parsing.

3.1.1 SAX and DOM

I'll offer just one approach to parsing HTML content, unless you count my

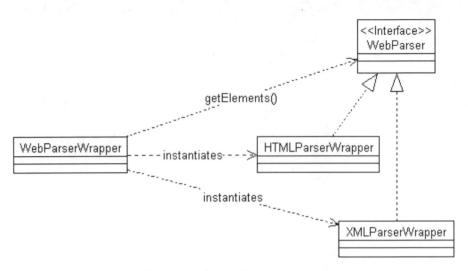

Figure 3.1   UML class diagram for package jwebdata.parsing

discussion of XHTML at the end of the chapter. For XML parsing I'll present two different approaches; one based on the SAX APIs and one based on the DOM APIs.

The SAX approach allows XML source data to be parsed in streaming fashion, via a call back mechanism that notifies the presence of XML elements as they are encountered. The DOM approach allows XML source data to be parsed into a tree structure representing a complete XML document. The SAX and DOM APIs are pulled together in the Java SDKs as the Java API for XML Processing (JAXP), which you should have downloaded by following the instructions in Appendix A.

When you read through the XML related code examples you'll notice that the JAXP support classes do not all come from standard Java packages (prefixed with *java*) or Java extension packages (prefixed with *javax*), because they're Java implementations of API specifications controlled by independent organizations such as the World Wide Web Consortium (http://www.w3c.com). Look out for import statements beginning with *org.xml* or *org.w3c*, and if you examine the API help documentation for JAXP classes you'll come across some statements like this: *This module, both source code and documentation, is in the Public Domain, and comes with NO WARRANTY*.

Note that if you're using an IDE or a J2EE implementation prior to version 1.3 you might need to make some changes in order to make the examples work. This is due to some API changes between SAX version 1 and SAX version 2, and I've given some hints as to what you can do in Appendix C.

Escape Route

In the coverage that follows there's quite a bit of code to get through, which will be invaluable if you're a serious Java programmer wanting to understand some of the intricacies of HTML and XML parsing. If you are more interested in what these parsers can do rather than how they work, I suggest you skip through the text of this chapter to pick up the main points, ignoring the code listings, and then take the resulting class implementations through – in black-box fashion – to the next chapter where we'll put them to good use.

3.2   Generic Parsing

In this section I'll tell you about the aspects of parsing that we'll treat as generic and independent of the data format, whether HTML or XML.

3.2.1   WebParserWrapper and WebParser

Our first class – *WebParserWrapper* – will submit a HTTP request, determine the content type of the response, and run the correct parser for that content. For simplicity we'll assume that the HTML parser will be used for all content unless the content description contains the word *XML*. Take a look at the code and then I'll tell you a bit more about it:

```
// ** Code taken from jwebdata/parsing/WebParserWrapper.java **

package jwebdata.parsing;

import java.util.*;
import java.net.*;
import java.io.*;

/**
 * Entry point for all web access, delegates to HTMLParserWrapper
 * or XMLParserWrapper according to the content type.
 */
public class WebParserWrapper
{
    public static final String GET="WITHGET";
    public static final String POST="WITHPOST";
```

```java
/**
 * Method to get a key/value list of HTML or XML elements at baseURL.
 */
public Vector getElements(String baseURL, String params
  , String method) throws Exception
{
    Vector elements=new Vector();
    URLConnection urlConnection;

    // -- Look for user and password properties --
    try
    {
      String user=System.getProperty("proxyUser");
      String password=System.getProperty("proxyPassword");
      Authenticator.setDefault(new ProxyAuthenticator(user,password));
    }
    catch (Exception ex) {}

    try
    {
      URL targetURL=new URL(baseURL);

      if (method.equals(GET)) // -- GET --
      {
        if (params.length()>0)
          largeURL=new URL(baseURL+"?"+params);
        else
          targetURL=new URL(baseURL);
        urlConnection=targetURL.openConnection();
      }
      else // -- POST --
      {
        targetURL=new URL(baseURL);
        urlConnection=targetURL.openConnection();
        urlConnection.setDoInput(true);
        urlConnection.setDoOutput(true);
        urlConnection.setUseCaches(false);

        // -- Write the submission --
        PrintWriter writer=new PrintWriter(new
          BufferedOutputStream(urlConnection.getOutputStream()));
        writer.println(params);
        writer.close();
      }

      // -- See what type the content is --
      String contentType=urlConnection.getContentType();

      WebParser webParser=new HTMLParserWrapper();
      try
      {
```

```
            if (contentType.toLowerCase().indexOf("xml")>=0)
            {
              webParser=(WebParser) Class.forName(
                "jwebdata.parsing.XMLParserWrapper").newInstance();
            }
          }
          catch (Throwable ex) {webParser=new HTMLParserWrapper();}

          // -- Run the correct parser --
          elements=webParser.getElements(baseURL, urlConnection);
        }
        catch (Exception ex2){throw new Exception(ex2.toString());}

        return elements;
     }
```

Did you notice the code that set the default authenticator, which I introduced in the previous chapter? It's not required in all situations but is quite harmless and will have no effect as long as we don't set the properties. By putting it in this class – which will handle all HTTP connections – we have removed the burden from our application programs and other classes that will use the parser(s).

If you have read the previous chapter the *get* and *post* submissions will need no further explanation, but you will want to know more about the action we're taking according to the content type. Whatever the content, we'll want to get hold of a suitable parser that has a *getElements(...)* method for returning the structured HTML or XML elements. This common behaviour is defined in a *WebParser* interface that each of our parsers will implement, and it has the following definition:

```
// ** Code taken from jwebdata/parsing/WebParser.java **

package jwebdata.parsing;

import java.io.*;
import java.net.*;
import java.util.*;

/**
 * Generic Parser interface implemented by HTMLParserWrapper and
 * XMLParserWrapper.
 */
public interface WebParser
{
    public Vector getElements(String baseURL, URLConnection urlConnection)
      throws Exception;
}
```

Back in *WebParserWrapper* we're creating an instance of class *HTMLParserWrapper* or *XMLParserWrapper* and in either case casting to interface *WebParser*. However, you are probably wondering why there are two kinds of instantiation in this code; why have I not instantiated the XML parser with code like this?

```
webParser=new XMLParserWrapper();
```

The fact is that your Java 2 Standard Edition SDK will certainly include the support classes – which I'll describe next – for HTML parsing. However, the support classes for XML parsing may not be present in your SDK because the JAXP classes were supplied originally as a separate download or as part of the Java 2 Enterprise Edition version 1.3. By taking the approach that I have, I've allowed for compiling and running of the HTML parser with a Java 2 Standard Edition SDK, with no dependence on the Enterprise Edition unless you want XML support.

3.3 Parsing HTML

We now have a generic *WebParserWrapper* that submits our HTTP request, figures out what kind of content is contained in the response, and invokes the correct parser for that content. For HTML content it will invoke the *HTMLParserWrapper*.

3.3.1 HTMLParserWrapper

I'll begin by describing what our HTML parser will do and what the end result will be. Then I'll take you through the code. If it any point it starts to look complicated, remember that it will all be hidden behind the *WebParserWrapper*.

The HTML parsing process

Figure 3.2 presents a simple web page as an example of a page that we might wish to parse. I say simple, but this page does contain enough complexity to demonstrate some important principles.

Figure 3.2   Simple HTML page

I've listed the source for that page below, with some strategic indentation that distinguishes those HTML tags that could serve to determine the structure of the text content from those tags that merely determine how the text is rendered. The *<table>>*, *<tr>* and *<td>* tags are what we'll define as structural tags, whereas the *<b>* (bold) tag is not.

```
<html>
<body>
Latest share prices at 16:00 GMT
<table BORDER=1 CELLSPACING=2 CELLPADDING=0 WIDTH="100%">
  <tr>
    <td VALIGN=TOP>LSE</td>
    <td VALIGN=TOP>London</td>
    <td>
      <table BORDER=1 WIDTH="100%">
        <tr>
          <td>ABC Industries</td>
          <td ALIGN=RIGHT><b>247</b></td>
        </tr>
        <tr>
          <td>DEF Technology</td>
          <td ALIGN=RIGHT ><b>103</b ></td>
        </tr>
        <tr>
          <td>GHI Financial</td>
          <td ALIGN=RIGHT><b>52</b></td>
        </tr>
      </table>
    </td>
  </tr>
  <tr>
    <td VALIGN=TOP>NYSE</td>
    <td VALIGN=TOP>New York</td>
```

```
<td>
  <table BORDER=1 WIDTH="100%" >
    <tr>
      <td>JKL Publishing</td>
      <td ALIGN=RIGHT><b>66</b></td>
    </tr>
    <tr>
      <td>MNO Financial</td>
      <td ALIGN=RIGHT><b>112</b></td>
    </tr>
  </table>
</td>
</tr>
</table>
</body>
</html>
```

From that listing I could say that the text 'London' has a unique position within the HTML source, which in plain English could be phrased thus: The 2nd table data (*<td>*) element of the 1st row (*<tr>*) of the 1st table (*<table>*). Reading the other way, and assuming that indexes will begin at 0, its position would be table 0 (*table[0]*), row 0 (*tr[1]*), table data 1 (*td[1]*).

We could label every element like that and, because most web authors will not have laid out the HTML in a neat hierarchic fashion as I have, I envisage a simple GUI application that presents the HTML data as a tree structure like the one shown in Figure 3.3. Notice how the index values are shown for each of the hierarchic elements, consistent with my description in the previous paragraph.

Any item prefixed with @ is a HTML attribute belonging to the parent tag, and in most cases we'll ignore the attributes. Some exceptions will include images and (hyper-) links, for which the attributes contain important information.

Now look at the listing below to see how I've presented exactly the same information in the form of a list rather than a tree. I prefer this representation because it takes less space, makes for a less cumbersome GUI, and helps a great deal with the filtering and querying that I'll describe in the next chapter. We've lost none of the information and we could still visualize and navigate in tree fashion if we really wanted to.

```
.text[0]=Latest share prices at 16:00 GMT
.table[0].@border[0]=1
.table[0].@cellspacing[0]=2
.table[0].@cellpadding[0]=0
.table[0].@width[0]=100%
```

```
.table[0].tr[0].td[0].@valign[0]=top
.table[0].tr[0].td[0].text[0]=LSE
.table[0].tr[0].td[1].@valign[0]=top
.table[0].tr[0].td[1].text[0]=London
.table[0].tr[0].td[2].table[0].@border[0]=1
.table[0].tr[0].td[2].table[0].@width[0]=100%
.table[0].tr[0].td[2].table[0].tr[0].td[0].text[0]=ABCIndustries
.table[0].tr[0].td[2].table[0].tr[0].td[1].@align[0]=right
.table[0].tr[0].td[2].table[0].tr[0].td[1].text[0]=247
.table[0].tr[0].td[2].table[0].tr[1].td[0].text[0]=DEFTechnology
.table[0].tr[0].td[2].table[0].tr[1].td[1].@align[0]=right
.table[0].tr[0].td[2].table[0].tr[1].td[1].text[0]=103
.table[0].tr[0].td[2].table[0].tr[2].td[0].text[0]=GHIFinancial
.table[0].tr[0].td[2].table[0].tr[2].td[1].@align[0]=right
.table[0].tr[0].td[2].table[0].tr[2].td[1].text[0]=52
.table[0].tr[1].td[0].@valign[0]=top
.table[0].tr[1].td[0].text[0]=NYSE
.table[0].tr[1].td[1].@valign[0]=top
.table[0].tr[1].td[1].text[0]=NewYork
.table[0].tr[1].td[2].table[0].@border[0]=1
.table[0].tr[1].td[2].table[0].@width[0]=100%
.table[0].tr[1].td[2].table[0].tr[0].td[0].text[0]=JKLPublishing
.table[0].tr[1].td[2].table[0].tr[0].td[1].@align[0]=right
.table[0].tr[1].td[2].table[0].tr[0].td[1].text[0]=66
.table[0].tr[1].td[2].table[0].tr[1].td[0].text[0]=MNOFinancial
.table[0].tr[1].td[2].table[0].tr[1].td[1].@align[0]=right
.table[0].tr[1].td[2].table[0].tr[1].td[1].text[0]=112
```

When I said '. . . see how I've presented exactly the same information in the form of a list . . .' the implication was that I'd done some studious typing at my keyboard. Actually, I didn't produce that list myself. The HTML parser did it for me, and now we'll see how.

HTMLParserWrapper code

The Java 2 Software Development Kit has a HTML Parser built-in, so rather than implement or buy our own it makes sense to use that. Since the parser was originally developed to support the rendering of HTML files with the Swing *JEditorPane* you will find the parser classes within the *javax.swing* package, and to use this parser at its simplest level you need to understand just two classes; *javax.swing.text.html.HTMLEditorKit.ParserCallback* and *javax.swing.text.html.parser.ParserDelegator*.

ParserCallback is a class that should be extended and provided to the parser

Figure 3.3   HTML tree structure

as a handler for HTML tokens. Every time the parser encounters a tag or text token it calls a method on the call back object, which may be one of:

```
public void handleStartTag(HTML.Tag tag, MutableAttributeSet attributes
  , int pos);
public void handleEndTag(HTML.Tag tag, int pos);
public void handleSimpleTag(HTML.Tag tag, MutableAttributeSet attributes
```

```
    , int pos);
public void handleEmptyTag(HTML.Tag tag, int pos);
public void handleText(char data, int pos);
```

The easiest way to invoke a parser to drive the call back object is via the *ParserDelegator* class. This class does what its name suggests and delegates the parsing task to a concrete parser implementation that extends the *javax.swing.text.html.parser.Parser* interface, which by default will be *javax.swing.text.html.parser.DocumentParser*.

To put this theory into practice we'll implement the *HTMLParserWrapper*, to be invoked from within the *WebParserWrapper*. The basic definition for this class will be:

```
// ** Code taken from jwebdata/parsing/HTMLParserWrapper.java **

package jwebdata.parsing;

import javax.swing.text.*;
import javax.swing.text.html.*;
import javax.swing.text.html.HTMLEditorKit.*;
import javax.swing.text.html.parser.*;

import java.io.*;
import java.net.*;

import java.util.*;

/**
  * This class parses a HTML file using the Java 2 Editor Kit
  */
public class HTMLParserWrapper extends HTMLEditorKit.ParserCallback
  implements WebParser
{
    private Vector tagHistory=new Vector();
    private Vector countHistory=new Vector();
    private Vector elements=new Vector();
    private URL currentURL;
    String runningText="";
}
```

Notice that we're extending *javax.swing.text.html.HTMLEditorKit.Parser-CallBack* – so as to receive parser events – and implementing the *WebParser* interface that we defined earlier. As we receive the parser events relating to the HTML tags, we will effectively be traversing a tree that reflects the hierarchic structure of the HTML data. We'll use the *tagHistory* member variable as a stack on which to record our current position in the tree, the *countHistory* variable to record the count of each tag type at each level, and the *elements* variable to contain the final results.

You might remember that our *WebParserWrapper* has code to invoke this *HTMLParserWrapper* (or the *XMLParserWrapper*) via a *getElements(...)* method, which we'll define as:

```
// ** Code taken from jwebdata/parsing/HTMLParserWrapper.java **

/**
  * Method to get a key/value list of HTML elements at baseURL.
  */
public Vector getElements(String baseURL, URLConnection urlConnection)
  throws Exception
{
    // -- Initialise the member variables --
    tagHistory=new Vector();
    countHistory=new Vector();
    countHistory.addElement(new Hashtable());
    elements=new Vector();
    currentURL=new URL(baseURL);
    // -- Run the parser on the HTML content --
    InputStreamReader urlReader=new InputStreamReader(urlConnection
      .getInputStream());
    new ParserDelegator().parse(urlReader,this,true);
    urlReader.close();

    return elements;
}
```

Did you see how the *ParserDelegator* was used to kick-start the parsing process, and how this was supplied as the call back object via the second argument? Now that we've started the parser running with our *HTMLParser-Wrapper* object itself as the handler for events, we'll need to give our class some proper implementations of the *handleXXXTag(...)* methods as required by the *ParserCallBack* interface.

handleStartTag(...) and handleEndTag(...)

We'll use the HTML tags as markers for breaking the text into distinct chunks, and for arranging the textual elements into a hierarchic structure. As we encounter each tag we'll first determine whether it's one we're interested in, which means we'll take note of structure tags – *<table>*, *<tr>*, *<td>*, *<title>*, *<form>* and so on – and ignore the formatting tags – such as *<b>* – that would break the text unnecessarily.

For each start tag that we receive, the following actions will be performed:

• Add a result element for any text accumulated since the last (structural) start- or end- tag.

- Update the count for this tag type at this level.

- Add this tag to the current tag history.

- If the tag has attributes, add one or more attribute elements to the results.

At any time, the *tagHistory* vector will grow and shrink to reflect our current position within the HTML source. The *countHistory* vector will tell us how many of each type of tag we have so far encountered at the current level, so that we can insert the index values into the square brackets. Table 3.1 gives an example of how the contents of these variables might change as we encounter the start- and end- tags in sequence.

Table 3.1   How the contents of the variables change as we encounter the start and end tags in sequence

Next Tag	tagHistory Position	tagHistory Content	countHistory Content	Cumulative tagKey
<table>	0	table	table=0	.table[0]
<tr>	0	table	table=0	
	1	tr	tr=0	.table[0].tr[0]
<td>	0	table	table=0	
	1	tr	tr=0	
	2	td	td=0	.table[0].tr[0].td[0]
</td>	0	table	table=0	
	1	tr	tr=0	.table[0].tr[0]
			td=0	
<td>	0	table	table=0	
	1	tr	tr=0	
	2	td	td=1	.table[0].tr[0].td[1]
</td>	0	table	table=0	
	1	tr	tr=0	.table[0].tr[0]
			td=1	
<td>	0	table	table=0	
	1	tr	tr=0	
	2	td	td=2	.table[0].tr[0].td[2]
<table>	0	table	table=0	
	1	tr	tr=0	
	2	td	td=2	
	3	table	table=0	.table[0].tr[0].td[2] .table[0]

For simplicity I've implied that the *countHistory* vector contains only one entry at each position. In fact, each position holds a *Hashtable* containing a set of counts, one for each tag type. A table – for example – may contain several rows, some text, and a few attributes all at the same level.

Having read the description, you'll want to see the implementation in code. Here is the *handleStartTag(...)* method:

```java
// ** Code taken from jwebdata/parsing/HTMLParserWrapper.java **

/**
 * Parser callback method.
 */
public void handleStartTag(HTML.Tag tag, MutableAttributeSet
  attributes, int pos)
{
    // -- Ignore any tag that is not one of these --
    if ( !(
        tag==HTML.Tag.TABLE || tag==HTML.Tag.TR || tag==HTML.Tag.TH
        || tag==HTML.Tag.TD || tag==HTML.Tag.TITLE
        || tag==HTML.Tag.A || tag==HTML.Tag.FRAME
        || tag==HTML.Tag.FORM || tag==HTML.Tag.SELECT
        || tag==HTML.Tag.OPTION || tag==HTML.Tag.INPUT
        || tag==HTML.Tag.IMG || tag==HTML.Tag.META
      ) ) return;

    // -- Add any cumulative text --
    addText(runningText);
    runningText="";

    // -- Update the count of this tag at this level --
    int tagCountInt=-1;
    Hashtable tagCounts=(Hashtable)
      countHistory.elementAt(tagHistory.size());
    Integer tagCountInteger=(Integer) tagCounts.get(tag);
    if (tagCountInteger!=null) tagCountInt=tagCountInteger.intValue();
    tagCountInt=tagCountInt+1;
    tagCounts.remove(tag);
    tagCounts.put(tag,new Integer(tagCountInt));

    // -- Put this tag on the stack and start some new counts --
    tagHistory.addElement(tag+"["+tagCountInt+"]");
    countHistory.addElement(new Hashtable());

    // -- Process the attributes for this start tag --
    for (Enumeration attributeNames=attributes.getAttributeNames();
      attributeNames.hasMoreElements();)
    {
        Object attKey=attributeNames.nextElement();
        String attributeName=(String) attKey.toString();
```

```
        String attributeValue=attributes.getAttribute(attKey)
          .toString().trim();

        // -- Make any relative URL absolute.
        if (attributeName.toLowerCase().equals("href")
            || attributeName.toLowerCase().equals("src")
            || attributeName.toLowerCase().equals("action")
            )
        {
            try { attributeValue=
              new URL(currentURL,attributeValue).toString(); }
            catch (Exception ex) {}
        }

        // -- Add this attribute --
        String tagKey="";
        for (int i=0; i<tagHistory.size(); i++)
          tagKey=tagKey+"."+tagHistory.elementAt(i);

        elements.addElement(new SourceElement(tagKey+".@"
          +attributeName+"[0]",attributeValue));
    }
}
```

As Newton said, every action has an equal and opposite reaction, and so it is with HTML tags. For every start tag that we encounter we will also encounter a matching end tag, although it might not actually have been present in the input text. I understand that the SDK parser will attempt to match end tags to start tags in any badly formed HTML file, to the extent of inserting phantom end tags where necessary. On the subject of badly formed HTML, here's what the Java SDK help documentation says:

'Unfortunately there are many badly implemented HTML parsers out there, and as a result there are many badly formatted HTML files. This parser attempts to parse most HTML files. This means that the implementation sometimes deviates from the SGML specification in favor of HTML.'

Assuming the SDK parser does its job and inserts an end tag even if there isn't one, we'll get a call back into this *handleEndTag(...)* method:

```
// ** Code taken from jwebdata/parsing/HTMLParserWrapper.java **

/**
  * Parser callback method.
  */
public void handleEndTag(HTML.Tag tag, int pos)
{

    // -- Ignore any tag that is not one of these --
```

```
if ( !(
    tag==HTML.Tag.TABLE || tag==HTML.Tag.TR || tag==HTML.Tag.TH
    || tag==HTML.Tag.TD || tag==HTML.Tag.TITLE
    || tag==HTML.Tag.A || tag==HTML.Tag.FRAME
    || tag==HTML.Tag.FORM || tag==HTML.Tag.SELECT
    || tag==HTML.Tag.OPTION || tag==HTML.Tag.INPUT
    || tag==HTML.Tag.IMG || tag==HTML.Tag.META
  ) ) return;

// -- Add any cumulative text --
addText(runningText);
runningText="";

// -- Pop the tag off the stack --
if (tagHistory.size()>0)
{
  tagHistory.remove(tagHistory.size()-1);
  countHistory.remove(countHistory.size()-1);
}
{
```

handleSimpleTag(...) and handleEmptyTag(...)

A simple tag is one that stands alone with no matching end tag and no interstitial text, but in order to reuse some of the code that has already been written we'll pretend that a simple tag is in fact a start tag / end tag combination. So our implementation of the *handleSimpleTag(...)* method will call *handleStartTag(...)* and *handleEndTag(...)* like this:

```
// ** Code taken from jwebdata/parsing/HTMLParserWrapper.java **

/**
  * Parser callback method.
  */
public void handleSimpleTag(HTML.Tag tag, MutableAttributeSet attributes
  , int pos)
{
    // -- For a simple tag, pretend it's a start/end combination.
    handleStartTag(tag, attributes, pos);
    handleEndTag(tag, pos);
}
```

For every empty tag that we encounter we'll do nothing:

```
// ** Code taken from jwebdata/parsing/HTMLParserWrapper.java **

/**
```

```
 * Parser callback method.
 */
public void handleEmptyTag(HTML.Tag tag, int pos)
{
    // -- Do nothing --
}
```

In between each set of tags will be plain text, which the parser tells us about by invoking the *handleText(...)* method.

handleText(...)

Each chunk of text that we encounter will not be added immediately to the results. So as to ignore the effect of formatting tags – like *<b>* and *<font>* – we'll concatenate all of the text items that we receive into a single string until we hit the next *structural* tag. The *handleText(...)* method therefore simply accumulates text in a *runningText* variable until it is processed by the *handleStartTag(...)* and *handleEndTag(...)* methods.

```
// ** Code taken from jwebdata/parsing/HTMLParserWrapper.java **


/**
  * Parser callback method.
  */
public void handleText(char data, int pos)
{
    // -- Add these (printable) characters to cumulative text --
    String thisText="";
    for (int i=0; i<data.length; i++)
    {
      if (((int)data[i])==160) thisText=thisText+" ";
      else thisText=thisText+data[i];
    {
    runningText=runningText+" "+thisText.trim();
    runningText=runningText.trim();
}
```

I know it's not very efficient to use string concatentation for the *runningText* in that code. I've kept it like that because I think it looks more intuitive and, to be honest, it's a personal weakness of mine. Feel free to use a *StringBuffer* instead.

You will have noticed that when the *handleStartTag(...)* and *handleEndTag(...)* methods do decide to add a new text element to the results, they do so via an *addText(...)* method that completes the implementation of our *HTMLParserWrapper* class. It adds a new text element to the final results (the elements variable) and pushes a new *text* tag onto the tag history, then pops it off again so that we stay at the current level.

```
// ** Code taken from jwebdata/parsing/HTMLParserWrapper.java **

/**
 * Method to add a new text element.
 */
private void addText(String text)
{    if (text.length()<=0) return;

     String tag="text";

     // -- Update the count of this (text) tag at this level --
     int tagCountInt=-1;
     Hashtable tagCounts=(Hashtable) countHistory
       .elementAt(tagHistory.size());
     Integer tagCountInteger=(Integer) tagCounts.get(tag);
     if (tagCountInteger!=null) tagCountInt=tagCountInteger.intValue();
     tagCountInt=tagCountInt+1;
     tagCounts.remove(tag);
     tagCounts.put(tag,new Integer(tagCountInt));

     // -- Put this text tag on the stack and start a new count --
     tagHistory.addElement(tag+"["+tagCountInt+"]");
     countHistory.addElement(new Hashtable());

     // -- Add the text element --
     String tagKey="";
     for (int i=0; i<tagHistory.size(); i++)
       tagKey=tagKey+"."+tagHistory.elementAt(i);
     elements.addElement(new SourceElement(tagKey,text));

     // -- Pop the text tag off the stack --
     tagHistory.remove(tagHistory.size()-1);
     countHistory.remove(countHistory.size()-1);
}
```

Every new element that we add to the final results, i.e. into the *elements* vector, is of type *SourceElement*. The *SourceElement* class holds a simple key/value combination and has this definition:

```
// ** Code taken from jwebdata/parsing/SourceElement.java **

package jwebdata.parsing;

/**
 * An instance of this class is created for every HTML or XML element.
 */
public class SourceElement
```

```
{
    public SourceElement(String key, String content)
    {
        this.key=key;
        this.content=content;
    }

    /**
     * Each element is addressed via a unique key.
     */
    public String getKey() {return key;}
    public void setKey(String key) {this.key=key;}

    /**
     * Each element has content.
     */
    public String getContent() {return content;}

    private String key;
    private String content;
}
```

At the end of the HTML parsing process we'll have a vector of *SourceElement* elements that when printed will look like this (yes, you've seen it before):

```
.text[0]=Latest share prices at 16:00 GMT
.table[0].@border[0]=1
.table[0].@cellspacing[0]=2
.table[0].@cellpadding[0]=0
.table[0].@width[0]=100%
.table[0].tr[0].td[0].@valign[0]=top
.table[0].tr[0].td[0].text[0]=LSE
.table[0].tr[0].td[1].@valign[0]=top
.table[0].tr[0].td[1].text[0]=London
.table[0].tr[0].td[2].table[0].@border[0]=1
.table[0].tr[0].td[2].table[0].@width[0]=100%
.table[0].tr[0].td[2].table[0].tr[0].td[0].text[0]=ABC Industries
.table[0].tr[0].td[2].table[0].tr[0].td[1].@align[0]=right
.table[0].tr[0].td[2].table[0].tr[0].td[1].text[0]=247
.table[0].tr[0].td[2].table[0].tr[1].td[0].text[0]=DEF Technology
.table[0].tr[0].td[2].table[0].tr[1].td[1].@align[0]=right
.table[0].tr[0].td[2].table[0].tr[1].td[1].text[0]=103
.table[0].tr[0].td[2].table[0].tr[2].td[0].text[0]=GHI Financial
.table[0].tr[0].td[2].table[0].tr[2].td[1].@align[0]=right
.table[0].tr[0].td[2].table[0].tr[2].td[1].text[0]=52
.table[0].tr[1].td[0].@valign[0]=top
.table[0].tr[1].td[0].text[0]=NYSE
.table[0].tr[1].td[1].@valign[0]=top
.table[0].tr[1].td[1].text[0]=New York
```

```
.table[0].tr[1].td[2].table[0].@border[0]=1
.table[0].tr[1].td[2].table[0].@width[0]=100%
.table[0].tr[1].td[2].table[0].tr[0].td[0].text[0]=JKL Publishing
.table[0].tr[1].td[2].table[0].tr[0].td[1].@align[0]=right
.table[0].tr[1].td[2].table[0].tr[0].td[1].text[0]=66
.table[0].tr[1].td[2].table[0].tr[1].td[0].text[0]=MNO Financial
.table[0].tr[1].td[2].table[0].tr[1].td[1].@align[0]=right
.table[0].tr[1].td[2].table[0].tr[1].td[1].text[0]=112
```

Our HTML parser is complete and towards the end of this chapter I'll show you how to take it for a test drive. If you can't wait, feel free to skip ahead to Section 3.5 now but don't forget to come back.

3.4 Parsing XML

XML is set to replace HTML as a more flexible way of transmitting structured information across the web. Where HTML has a closed set of tag types – *<table>*, *<tr>* and so on – XML supports an open set of tags that may be user-defined. Our *XMLParserWrapper* will do for XML data what our *HTMLParserWrapper* does for HTML data.

3.4.1 XMLParserWrapper

Thanks to the SAX implementation provided with the JAXP there is an approach to parsing XML files that is almost identical to that presented for HTML, only the names have changed. *ParserCallback* becomes *DefaultHandler*, and *ParserDelegator* becomes *SAXParserFactory*.

XMLParserWrapper Code

It will implement the same *WebParser* interface and will be fronted by the same *WebParserWrapper* class. The basic shell will be almost identical to *HTMLParserWrapper*, it will contain a very similar *getElements(...)* method, and it will look like this:

```
// ** Code taken from jwebdata/parsing/XMLParserWrapper.java **

package jwebdata.parsing;
```

```
import javax.xml.parsers.*;
import org.xml.sax.*;

import java.io.*;
import java.net.*;
import java.util.*;

/**
  * This class parses an XML file using SAX.
  */
public class XMLParserWrapper extends org.xml.sax.helpers.DefaultHandler
  implements WebParser
{
    private Vector tagHistory=new Vector();
    private Vector countHistory=new Vector();
    private Vector elements=new Vector();

/**
  * Method to get a key/value list of XML elements at baseURL.
  */
public Vector getElements(String baseURL, URLConnection uurlConnection)
  throws Exception
{
    // -- Initialise the member variables --
    tagHistory=new Vector();
    countHistory=new Vector();
    countHistory.addElement(new Hashtable());
    elements=new Vector();

    // -- Run the parser on the XML content --
    InputSource inputSource=new InputSource(urlConnection
      .getInputStream());
    inputSource.setSystemId(baseURL);
    SAXParser parser=SAXParserFactory.newInstance().newSAXParser();
    parser.parse(inputSource,this);
    urlConnection.getInputStream().close();

    return elements;
  }
}
```

In that *getElements(...)* method we're using the *javax.xml.parsers.SAXParserFactory* in pretty much the same way that we previously used the *javax.swing.text.html.parser.ParserDelegator*. The similarities don't end there. Our *XMLParserWrapper* has a *startElement(...)* method that is the direct equivalent of the *startTag(...)* method of our *HTMLParserWrapper*, an *endElement (...)* method equivalent to the *endTag(...)* method, and a *characters(...)* method equivalent to the *handleText(...)* method.

startElement(...)

There should be no surprises in this code apart from the fact that we'll not be choosing to ignore certain tags. This is XML with its limitless tag types, not HTML with its finite set, so we have no idea what tags we'll find until we find them.

```java
// ** Code taken from jwebdata/parsing/XMLParserWrapper.java **

/**
 * Parser callback method.
 */
public void startElement(java.lang.String uri, java.lang.String
  localName, java.lang.String qName, Attributes attributes)
{
    String tag=localName.toString();

    // -- Update the count of this tag at this level --
    int tagCountInt=-1;
    Hashtable tagCounts=(Hashtable) countHistory
      .elementAt(tagHistory.size());
    Integer tagCountInteger=(Integer) tagCounts.get(tag);
    if (tagCountInteger!=null) tagCountInt=tagCountInteger.intValue();
    tagCountInt=tagCountInt+1;
    tagCounts.remove(tag);
    tagCounts.put(tag,new Integer(tagCountInt));

    // -- Put this tag on the stack and start a new count--
    tagHistory.addElement(tag+"["+tagCountInt+"]");
    countHistory.addElement(new Hashtable());

    int attCount=attributes.getLength();
    for (int i=0; i<attCount; i++)
    {
        String attributeName=attributes.getLocalName(i);
        String attributeValue=attributes.getValue(i);

        // -- Add this attribute --
        String tagKey="";
        for (int ti=0; ti<tagHistory.size(); ti++)
          tagKey=tagKey+"."+tagHistory.elementAt(ti);
        elements.addElement(new SourceElement(tagKey+".@"
          +attributeName+"[0]",attributeValue));
    }
}
```

endElement(...)

Once again every action has a reaction, every *startElement* has a corresponding *endElement*.

```
// ** Code taken from jwebdata/parsing/XMLParserWrapper.java **
/**
 * Parser callback method.
 */
public void endElement(java.lang.String uri, java.lang.String
  localName, java.lang.String qName)
{
   // -- Pop the tag off the stack --
   if (tagHistory.size()>0)
   {
     tagHistory.remove(tagHistory.size()-1);
     countHistory.remove(countHistory.size()-1);
   }
}
```

characters(...)

This time we're not accumulating text between *structural* tags because we have no pre-conception of which tags might be structural and which might not. We simply add each chunk of text as a new element as soon as we encounter it, via the *characters(...)* call back method:

```
// ** Code taken from jwebdata/parsing/XMLParserWrapper.java **

/**
 * Parser callback method.
 */
public void characters(char data, int start, int length)
{    String thisText="";

   // -- Add these (printable) characters to cumulative text --
   for (int i=start; i<(start+length); i++)
   {
     if (((int)data[i])==160) thisText=thisText+" ";
     else thisText=thisText]data[i];
   }

   if (thisText.length()>0) thisText=thisText.trim();

   // -- Add the text element --
   String tagKey="";
   for (int ti=0; ti<tagHistory.size(); ti++)
     tagKey=tagKey+"."+tagHistory.elementAt(ti);
   elements.addElement(new SourceElement(tagKey+".#pcdata[0],thisText));
}
```

XML parsing result

XML parsing wasn't so bad once we'd done all the hard work for HTML, and this is the kind of result we'd expect to see (end portion only):

```
.PLAY[0].ACT[4].SCENE[3].SPEECH[49].SPEAKER[0].#pcdata[0]=VALENTINE
.PLAY[0].ACT[4].SCENE[3].SPEECH[49].LINE[0].#pcdata[0]=I warrant you, my
lord, more grace than boy.
.PLAY[0].ACT[4].SCENE[3].SPEECH[50].SPEAKER[0].#pcdata[0]=DUKE
.PLAY[0].ACT[4].SCENE[3].SPEECH[50].LINE[0].#pcdata[0]=What mean you by
that saying?
.PLAY[0].ACT[4].SCENE[3].SPEECH[51].SPEAKER[0].#pcdata[0]=VALENTINE
.PLAY[0].ACT[4].SCENE[3].SPEECH[51].LINE[0].#pcdata[0]=Please you,
I'll tell you as we pass along,
.PLAY[0].ACT[4].SCENE[3].SPEECH[51].LINE[1].#pcdata[0]=That you will
wonder what hath fortuned.
.PLAY[0].ACT[4].SCENE[3].SPEECH[51].LINE[2].#pcdata[0]=Come, Proteus; 'tis
your penance but to hear
.PLAY[0].ACT[4].SCENE[3].SPEECH[51].LINE[3].#pcdata[0]=The story of your
loves discovered:
.PLAY[0].ACT[4].SCENE[3].SPEECH[51].LINE[4].#pcdata[0]=That done, our day
of marriage shall be yours;
.PLAY[0].ACT[4].SCENE[3].SPEECH[51].LINE[5].#pcdata[0]=One feast, one
house, one mutual happiness.
.PLAY[0].ACT[4].SCENE[3].STAGEDIR[4].pcdata[0]=Exeunt
```

That was based on the freely available *two_gent.xml* file. I've listed a very limited extract here, comprising the first and final few lines that correspond directly with the results displayed above.

```
<?xml version="1.0"?>
<!DOCTYPE PLAY SYSTEM "play.dtd">

<PLAY>
<TITLE>The Two Gentlemen of Verona</TITLE>

<FM>
<P>Text placed in the public domain by Moby Lexical Tools, 1992.</P>
<P>SGML markup by Jon Bosak, 1992-1994.</P>
<P>XML version by Jon Bosak, 1996-1998.</P>
<P>This work may be freely copied and distributed worldwide.</P>
</FM>

<PERSONAE>
<TITLE>Dramatis Personae</TITLE>
. . .
<SPEAKER>VALENTINE</SPEAKER>
```

```
<LINE>I warrant you, my lord, more grace than boy.</LINE>
</SPEECH>

<SPEECH>
<SPEAKER>DUKE</SPEAKER>
<LINE>What mean you by that saying?</LINE>
</SPEECH>

<SPEECH>
<SPEAKER>VALENTINE</SPEAKER>
<LINE>Please you, I'll tell you as we pass along,</LINE>
<LINE>That you will wonder what hath fortuned.</LINE>
<LINE>Come, Proteus; 'tis your penance but to hear</LINE>
<LINE>The story of your loves discovered:</LINE>
<LINE>That done, our day of marriage shall be yours;</LINE>
<LINE>One feast, one house, one mutual happiness.</LINE>
</SPEECH>

<STAGEDIR>Exeunt</STAGEDIR>
</SCENE>
</ACT>
</PLAY>
```

That's the XML parser completed, and as with the HTML parser you may skip ahead and take it for a test drive now. Otherwise read on to find out about an alternative technique for parsing XML data, using our *DOMParser Wrapper*.

3.4.2 DOMParserWrapper

I described XML parsing in terms of the call back model provided by the SAX API, so as to be consistent with the HTML parser. There is another way to parse XML that does not drive events through a call back object, and which presents the entire parsed content as an object tree. This second way uses the Document Object Model (DOM) API.

Purely for illustration I'll show you a version of the XML Parser that uses DOM rather than SAX, so that you can work with that approach if you want to. I'll call it *DOMParserWrapper*, and with that name in mind I suppose I should really have called the other one *SAXParserWrapper*. However, I'll stick with the original name – *XMLParserWrapper* – for the original parser because it will be our default implementation.

To create the *DOMParserWrapper* class, you can rename the original *XMLParserWrapper* (the SAX version) then retrofit the import statements and the *getElements(...)* method that follows. Notice that although we're taking

the DOM approach this time, we retain the original SAX import statements
and provide these two import statements in addition.

```
import org.xml.sax.helpers.*;
import org.w3c.dom.*;
```

The new *getElements(...)* method starts off in the same way as the one it
replaces but this time round the XML data will be parsed completely, behind
the scenes, before we get our hands on any of the data. Contrast this with the
SAX approach that provides us with each data element as it is discovered. In
the code that follows the *javax.xml.parsers.DocumentBuilderFactory* is used
to obtain a *javax.xml.parsers.DocumentBuilder*, which parses the XML and
produces an *org.w3c.dom.Document*.

```
// ** Code taken from jwebdata/parsing/DOMParserWrapper.java **


/**
 * Method to get a key/value list of XML elements at baseURL.
 */public Vector getElements(String baseURL, URLConnection urlConnection)
throws Exception
{
    // -- Initialise the member variables --
    tagHistory=new Vector();
    countHistory=new Vector();
    countHistory.addElement(new Hashtable());
    elements=new Vector();


    InputSource inputSource=new InputSource(urlConnection
      .getInputStream());
    inputSource.setSystemId(baseURL);


    // -- Run the parser on the XML content --
    DocumentBuilderFactory dbf =
        DocumentBuilderFactory.newInstance();
    DocumentBuilder db = null;
    Document doc = null;
    try
    {
        db = dbf.newDocumentBuilder();
        doc = db.parse(inputSource);
    }
    catch (Exception ex)
    {
    }
```

```
    urlConnection.getInputStream().close();

    // -- Now traverse the DOM tree to drive our own call backs --
    traverse(doc);

    return elements;
}
```

Towards the end of that listing you'll see that a new method, *traverse(...)*, is invoked with the *org.w3c.dom.Document* provided as a parameter. We'll use this method to traverse the DOM tree representing the structure of the parsed elements. The document contains the DOM tree, which itself represents the root node of that tree. This is possible because interface *org.w3c.dom.Document* extends *org.w3c.dom.Node*. We'll invoke the *traverse(...)* method with the root node and this method will then call itself – recursively – with each subsequent node.

To cut down on the amount of extra work we need to do, and to fit into our existing scheme, we'll use this tree traversal to drive call backs through our existing call back methods as shown here:

```
// ** Code taken from jwebdata/parsing/DOMParserWrapper.java **

/**
 * Method to traverse the DOM tree and drive our callback methods.
 */
private void traverse(Node n)
{
    int type = n.getNodeType();

    switch (type)
    {
      case Node.ELEMENT—NODE:

        // -- For simplicity, ignore the attributes --
        // NamedNodeMap atts = n.getAttributes();

        // -- startElement(...) CALLBACK --
        this.startElement(n.getNamespaceURI(),n.getLocalName()
          ,n.getLocalName(),new AttributesImpl());
        break;

      case Node.TEXT—NODE:

        String value=n.getNodeValue().trim();
        char data=value.toCharArray();

        // -- characters(...) CALLBACK --
        this.characters(data, 0, data.length);
        break;
```

```
    }

    // -- Recursion to handle the child nodes --
    for (Node child = n.getFirstChild(); child != null;
      child = child.getNextSibling())
    {
        traverse(child);
    }

    switch (type)
    {
        case Node.ELEMENT-NODE:
          // -- endElement(...) CALLBACK --
          this.endElement(n.getNamespaceURI(),n.getLocalName()
            ,n.getLocalName());
          break;
    }
}
```

That was an easy way for me to demonstrate the DOM approach as an alternative to the SAX approach, but I'm not advising you to use DOM simply to drive SAX like call backs. Particularly as an XML Parser based on the *DOMParserWrapper* that we've just implemented takes noticeably more time to achieve exactly the same result.

3.5 Compiling and Running the Parsers

You might already have been here if you took my earlier advice to skip ahead. If so, welcome back!

If you want to take the HTML parser or the XML parser for a spin you will need to add the following *main(...)* method to *WebParserWrapper*:

```
// ** Code taken from jwebdata/parsing/WebParserWrapper.java **
/**
  * A main() method for testing.
  */
public static void main(String args)
{
    try
    {
      WebParserWrapper webParser=new WebParserWrapper();

      //Vector elements=webParser
```

```
// .getElements("file:data/ShareData.html","","WITHGET");

Vector elements=webParser
  .getElements("file:data/two-gent.xml","","WITHGET");

for (int i=0; i<elements.size(); i++)
{
    SourceElement thisElement
      =(SourceElement) elements.elementAt(i);
    System.out.println(thisElement.getKey()+"="
      +thisElement.getContent());
}
}
catch (Exception ex) {ex.printStackTrace();}
}
```

The code that you have downloaded from the companion web site will
contain the following files:

```
jwebdata/parsing/DOMParserWrapper.java (not strictly needed)
jwebdata/parsing/HTMLParserWrapper.java
jwebdata/parsing/ProxyAuthenticator.java
jwebdata/parsing/SourceElement.java
jwebdata/parsing/WebParser.java
jwebdata/parsing/WebParserWrapper.java
jwebdata/parsing/XMLParserWrapper.java
```

You can compile all of those classes by typing the command:

```
javac jwebdata/parsing/*.java
```

You can now test the parser(s) by running the *WebParserWrapper*'s
main(...) method with the command:

```
java jwebdata.parsing.WebParserWrapper
```

If you look back at the code for that *main(...)* method you'll see that you
have the option of interchanging the *two_gent.xml* with the *ShareData.xml*
file to test both parsers.

3.5.1   Introducing XHTML

In the future we might not need the HTML parser at all. XML parsing could
ultimately replace HTML parsing altogether by using an XHTML Document

Type Definition (DTD) to define a HTML page using XML.

We could turn the simple HTML page that I showed you at the start of this chapter into a XHTML page by giving it an *.xml* extension and by inserting the following header at the beginning:

```
<?xml version="1.0"?>
<!DOCTYPE HTML SYSTEM "xhtml1-transitional.dtd">
```

This requires the *xhtml1-transitional.dtd* file, freely available from http://www.w3.org/TR/xhtml1/#dtds, to be present in the same directory as our XHTML source file. At which point, a word of warning: the use of this DTD with our SAX-based XML parser is much stricter than the HTML parser provided with the Java SDK's Swing package. When I first tried to parse the file as XHTML, rather than straight HTML, I was rewarded with the following error message:

```
java.lang.Exception: org.xml.sax.SAXParseException: Value must be quoted.
at jwebdata.parsing.WebParserWrapper.getElements(WebParserWrapper.java:71)
```

To fix it I had to carefully quote each attribute value that was carelessly, but previously allowably, unquoted in the original source. For example *<td VALIGN=TOP>LSE</td>* now reads *<td VALIGN=TOP>LSE</td>* now read *<td VALIGN="TOP">LSE</td>* (spot the new quotes).

This is annoying, but not too intellectually challenging, and I was soon rewarded with the result shown in Figure 3.4. Let me clarify what this means. I have now parsed a HTML file using the XML parser.

However, I don't think it's wise to throw away the HTML parser just yet.

If you're only ever going to deal with HTML data, you might want to keep the HTML parser and do away with the XML parser instead. For pure HTML work we can take advantage of the fact that there is a closed set of tags, and we know what they all are. Our HTML parser ignores many of the tags that are encountered, even some structural tags like *<html>* and *<body>*, because – in my opinion – they add little value and increase the key lengths unnecessarily (see what I mean by looking back at Figure 3.4). In contrast, our XML parser handles all XML files in a uniform way and considers all element tags to be equally important.

If you're going to deal with HTML *and* XML data I think both parsers are needed in order to cover all eventualities. It will be some time before all HTML files are prefixed with the XML header, so we need to be able to handle old style HTML files and new ones.

```
.html[0].body[0].#pcdata[0]
.html[0].body[0].#pcdata[0]
.html[0].body[0].#pcdata[0]                            Latest share prices at 16:00 GMT
.html[0].body[0].#pcdata[0]
.html[0].body[0].table[0].@BORDER[0]       1
.html[0].body[0].table[0].@CELLSPACING[0]                        2
.html[0].body[0].table[0].@CELLPADDING[0]                        0
.html[0].body[0].table[0].@WIDTH[0]        100%
.html[0].body[0].table[0].tr[0].td[0].@VALIGN[0]                 TOP
.html[0].body[0].table[0].tr[0].td[0].@rowspan[0]                1
.html[0].body[0].table[0].tr[0].td[0].@colspan[0]                1
.html[0].body[0].table[0].tr[0].td[0].#pcdata[0]                 LSE
.html[0].body[0].table[0].tr[0].td[1].@VALIGN[0]                 TOP
.html[0].body[0].table[0].tr[0].td[1].@rowspan[0]                1
.html[0].body[0].table[0].tr[0].td[1].@colspan[0]                1
.html[0].body[0].table[0].tr[0].td[1].#pcdata[0]                 London
.html[0].body[0].table[0].tr[0].td[2].@rowspan[0]                1
.html[0].body[0].table[0].tr[0].td[2].@colspan[0]                1
.html[0].body[0].table[0].tr[0].td[2].#pcdata[0]
.html[0].body[0].table[0].tr[0].td[2].#pcdata[0]
.html[0].body[0].table[0].tr[0].td[2].#pcdata[0]
.html[0].body[0].table[0].tr[0].td[2].table[0].@BORDER[0]    1
.html[0].body[0].table[0].tr[0].td[2].table[0].@WIDTH[0]     100%
.html[0].body[0].table[0].tr[0].td[2].table[0].tr[0].td[0].@rowspan[0]        1
.html[0].body[0].table[0].tr[0].td[2].table[0].tr[0].td[0].@colspan[0]        1
.html[0].body[0].table[0].tr[0].td[2].table[0].tr[0].td[0].#pcdata[0]         ABC Industries
.html[0].body[0].table[0].tr[0].td[2].table[0].tr[0].td[1].@ALIGN[0]          RIGHT
.html[0].body[0].table[0].tr[0].td[2].table[0].tr[0].td[1].@rowspan[0]        1
.html[0].body[0].table[0].tr[0].td[2].table[0].tr[0].td[1].@colspan[0]        1
.html[0].body[0].table[0].tr[0].td[2].table[0].tr[0].td[1].b[0].#pcdata[0]    247
.html[0].body[0].table[0].tr[0].td[2].table[0].tr[1].td[0].@rowspan[0]        1
.html[0].body[0].table[0].tr[0].td[2].table[0].tr[1].td[0].@colspan[0]        1
.html[0].body[0].table[0].tr[0].td[2].table[0].tr[1].td[0].#pcdata[0]         DEF Technology
```

Figure 3.4   XHTML parsing results

3.6 Chapter Review

In this chapter we've looked at how to build custom HTML and XML parsers, what I've called *Wrappers*, based on the parser implementations provided with the Java 2 SDKs. In the case of XML I've presented SAX as the preferred approach, and DOM as an alternative. Finally I've introduced XHTML as a kind of XML meets HTML.

Along the way we've developed a hierarchic structure for marked-up elements comprising content values and unique keys. The value in doing that will become apparent in the next chapter.

Now that you have the ability to parse HTML and XML data, what will you do with it?

3.6.1   API classes and interfaces introduced in this chapter

The following Java API classes and interfaces have been introduced for the first time in this chapter's code examples:

- *java.lang.Integer* is an object wrapper for a value of primitive type *int*.

- *java.lang.Object* is the superclass for all other Java classes.

- *javax.swing.text.MutableAttributeSet* provides an interface to a to a collection of unique attributes.

- *javax.swing.text.html.HTMLEditorKit.ParserCallback* should be extended and supplied to the parser in order to receive parser-generated events.

- *javax.swing.text.html.HTML.Tag* defines all known HTML tags as static final variables.

- *javax.swing.text.html.parser.ParserDelegator* is used to invoke a *DocumentParser* via the *parse(...)* method.

- *java.util.Enumeration* generates a series of elements via calls to its *nextElement(...)* method.

- *java.util.Hashtable* holds a collection of key-value pairs.

- *java.util.Vector* provides an array of objects that can grow and shrink as elements are added and removed.

- *javax.xml.parsers.DocumentBuilder* defines the API to obtain DOM document instances from an XML document.

- *javax.xml.parsers.DocumentBuilderFactory* allows applications to obtain a parser that produces DOM object trees from XML documents.

- *javax.xml.parsers.SAXParser* defines the API that wraps an *XMLReader* implementation class for parsing XML content.

- *javax.xml.parsers.SAXParserFactory* allows applications to configure and obtain a SAX based parser for XML content.

- *org.w3c.dom.Document* represents a complete HTML or XML document and provides access to the document's data.

- *org.w3c.dom.Node* represents a single node in the document tree that is the DOM is the primary data type for the entire DOM.

- *org.xml.sax.Attributes* is an interface for a list of XML attributes.

- *org.xml.sax.helpers.DefaultHandler* is the default base class for SAX2 event handlers that receive events through call back methods.

- *org.xml.sax.InputSource* allows encapsulates information about an input source in a single object.

4

Data Filters and Structured Queries

In this chapter we'll look at how we could apply filters and structured queries in order to pick out particular HTML or XML elements, according to their content or positions within the mark-up structure. How about picking out just the images from a web page, or the contents of a particular HTML table? Returning to the *Two Gentlemen of Verona*, how would you like to pick out only Act II or all the lines spoken by Valentine? Taking this to its logical conclusion, could the industry standard SQL be used to extract information from a web page as though selecting from a relational database table?

4.1 The Design

Any kind of filtering implies comparison, so we'll start gently with an *Operator* class that supports straightforward numeric and lexical comparisons of data items. A *Filter* class, which makes use of *Operator*, will be our implementation of a filter that I described in the introduction. In order to view the filtered results, and as an aid to formulating valid filters, there will be a *FilterViewer* graphical application.

The filter idea will be extended further in the form of a *QueryEngine* class, an enabler for structured queries. To move us closer to the ambition of SQL-based web queries, we'll put together a simple *SqlGui* application.

Figure 4.1 shows the five new classes along with the original *WebParserWrapper* from Chapter 3.

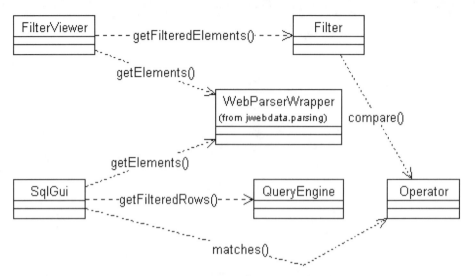

Figure 4.1   UML class diagram for package jwebdata.query

4.2 Filtering

In this section we'll look at how to implement a handy filter for picking out specified HTML or XML elements individually or in groups.

To start with, all filtering and querying tasks will depend on our ability to compare data items with literal values or with other data items. We'll implement a class, called *Operator*, which handles all comparison operations and which is therefore fundamental to the process.

4.2.1 Operator

The basic definition of the class will be:

```
// ** Code taken from jwebdata/query/Operator.java **

package jwebdata.query;

import java.util.*;

/**
  * A class to perform simple numeric and lexical comparisions.
  */
public class Operator
{
}
```

Comparison operations

It will come as no surprise that the principal method, listed next, will be called *compare(...)* and we'll make it static so that we can call it whenever and from wherever we want.

compare(...)

This method will allow us to pass two string values and a comparison operator as arguments. The comparison operators that I have in mind are:

=   The numeric or string values must be equivalent.

>   The first item must be numerically or lexically greater then the second.

<   The second item must be numerically or lexically less than the second.

matches The first item must match the wildcard string value of the second.

To keep it simple I've omitted compound comparison operators like >= (greater than or equal to) on the assumption that we can test both conditions by calling the *compare(...)* method twice if necessary. However, I will allow any operator to be preceded by '!' (not) in order to reverse the sense. To make it even simpler you will see that the following code implements greater than but not less than, so there's an exercise up for grabs if you want it. Or, if that's too much like hard work, you could just take a look in the downloadable version of the code!

```
// ** Code taken from jwebdata/query/Operator.java **
```

```java
/**
 * Compares two values according to the supplied operator.
 */
public static boolean compare(String realContent, String operator
  , String compareContent)
{
    boolean negative=false;
    boolean result=false;

    // -- Reverse the sense if necessary --
    if (operator.startsWith("!"))
    {
      operator=operator.substring(1,operator.length());
      negative=true;
    }

    if (operator.toLowerCase().equals("matches")) // -- MATCHES --
    {
      result=Operator.matches(realContent,compareContent);
    }
    else if (operator.equals("=")) // -- EQUALS --
    {
      // -- Try a numeric comparison first --
      try
      {
        Double realDouble=Double.valueOf(realContent);
        Double compareDouble=Double.valueOf(compareContent);
        result=realDouble.equals(compareDouble);
      }
      catch (Exception ex)
      {
        // -- Compare as strings --
        result=realContent.equals(compareContent);
      }
    }
    else if (operator.equals(">")) // -- GREATER --

      // -- Try a numeric comparison first --
      try
      {
        Double realDouble=Double.valueOf(realContent);
        Double compareDouble=Double.valueOf(compareContent);
        result=(realDouble.doubleValue()
          >compareDouble.doubleValue());
      }
      catch (Exception ex)
      {
        // -- Compare as strings --
        if (realContent.compareTo(compareContent)>0) result=true;
```

```
      else result=false;
    }
  {

  if (negative) result=!result;
  return result;
```

Although the values are passed in as strings, those strings might in fact contain numeric values. So for all operators except *matches* we are first attempting a numeric comparison. If the numeric comparison fails with a Java exception, because one or both values contain non-numeric characters, we are performing a lexical comparison.

We can perform a wildcard string comparison by invoking the *compare(...)* method with the '*matches*' operator. This triggers a call to another method on the *Operator* class, the *matches(...)* method.

matches(...)

This method allows asterisks to be used as wildcards anywhere within the comparison string, to match zero or more characters – any characters – leading up to the next specified text within the string.

```java
// ** Code taken from jwebdata/query/Operator.java **

/**
 * Performs a wildcard comparison of two strings.
 */
public static boolean matches(String realString, String wildCardString)
{
    int pos=0;
    boolean sameFlag=true;

    StringTokenizer matchTokens
      =new StringTokenizer(wildCardString,"*",true);
    while (matchTokens.hasMoreTokens())
    {
        String thisToken=matchTokens.nextToken();
        if (thisToken.equals("*"))
        {

          // -- Get the text that follows the * --
          if (matchTokens.hasMoreTokens())
          {
            String matchText=matchTokens.nextToken();
            // -- It must be found somewhere, else no match --
            int foundAt=realString.indexOf(matchText,pos);
            if (foundAt>=0)
              pos=pos+matchText.length();
```

```
        else
        {
          // -- No match --
          sameFlag=false;
          break;
        }
      }
    }
    else
    {
      // -- Text not preceded by a * so must match here --
      int foundAt=realString.indexOf(thisToken,pos);
      if (foundAt==pos)
        pos=pos+thisToken.length();
      else
      {
        sameFlag=false;
        break;
      }
    }
  }
  return sameFlag;
}
```

4.2.2 Filter

Now that we are able to compare values we have the basis on which to implement a simple filter for HTML or XML elements. You might be surprised to see how straightforward it now is. Here is the shell of the *Filter* class:

```
// ** Code taken from jwebdata/query/Filter.java **

package jwebdata.query;

import java.util.*;
import jwebdata.parsing.*;

/**
 * Utility class to filter HTML or XML elements by key or content.
 */
public class Filter
{
    public static final String KEY="key";
    public static final String CONTENT="content";
}
```

We'll use the *key* and *content* constant values to tell the filter whether to compare the key field or content field of each element. The elements in question will come straight out of our *WebParserWrapper* and will be filtered using the *getFilteredElements(...)* method.

getFilteredElements(...)

This method should be quite easy to understand. It completes the *Filter* class and allows us to apply the kinds of filters that I'll show you next in my discussion of the *FilterViewer* visualization GUI.

```
// ** Code taken from jwebdata/query/Filter.java**

/**
 * Static method for applying a filter to a set of elements.
 */
public static Vector getFilteredElements(Vector sortedElements
  , String fieldConstant, String operator, String compareString)
{
    Vector filteredElements=new Vector();
    for (int i=0; i<sortedElements.size(); i++)
    {
      SourceElement thisElement=(SourceElement)
        sortedElements.elementAt(i);

      // -- By default compare the key field of this element --
      String compareField=(String) thisElement.getKey();

      // -- Compare the content field if required --
      if (fieldConstant.equals(CONTENT))
        compareField=(String) thisElement.getContent();

      if (compareField!=null)
      {
        // -- Add a positive match to the filtered list --
        if (Operator.compare(compareField,operator,compareString))
          filteredElements.addElement(thisElement);
      }
    }
    return filteredElements;
}
```

4.2.3   FilterViewer

What is needed now is a simple graphical application that will allow us to experiment with filters. The *FilterViewer* will provide a limited web browsing capability, tailored to show the structure of marked-up HTML and XML content. A URL, optional parameters and an optional filter – on *key* or *content*

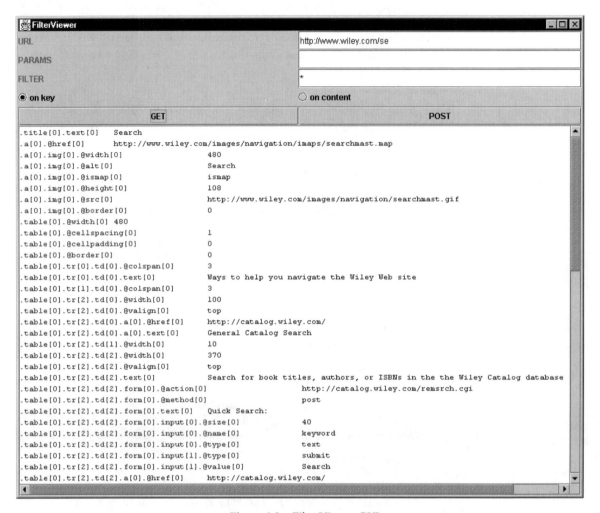

Figure 4.2   FilterViewer GUI

– will be collected as input and we'll be able to specify *get* or *post* as the submission method. Figure 4.2 shows what the application will look like.

Contrast that view with the traditional browser rendering of the same page, as shown in Figure 4.3. What we lose in terms of aesthetic appeal we'll gain in usefulness, as I'll demonstrate.

By applying a suitable filter it is possible, for example, to pick out only those elements that comprise HTML forms within the page. The wildcard filter text for forms, which will be applied using the *matches* operation, will be '*form[*]*'. The result is given in Figure 4.4.

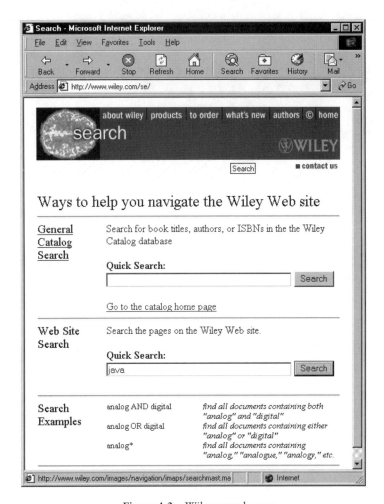

Figure 4.3   Wiley search page

The application of this filter makes things look somewhat clearer, believe it or not, and it helps a lot with what I now want to demonstrate. It's no accident that I've chosen form elements as my example.

Suppose we wanted to automate a search submission and capture the results into Java program. We can see from Figure 4.4 that the second form, corresponding with Web Site Search in Figure 4.3, has the following action and method:

```
.table[0].tr[4].form[0].@action[0] http://www.wileysearch.com/search?NS-
search-page=results
.table[0].tr[4].form[0].@method[0] post
```

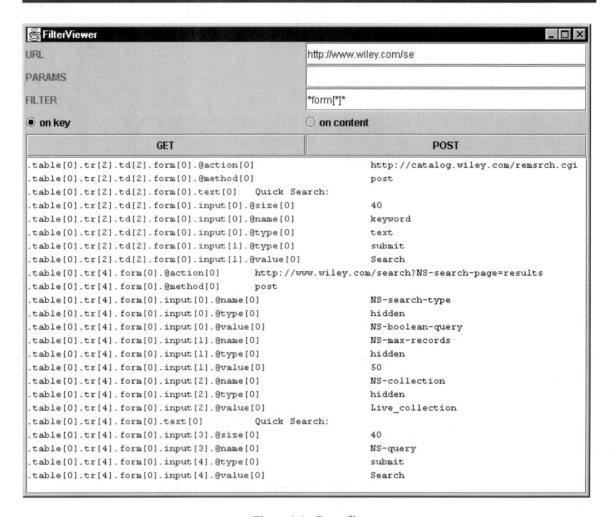

Figure 4.4 Form filter

This means that to simulate the action of this form we need to use the *WebParserWrapper* to *post* a submission to URL http://www.wileysearch.com/search?NS-search-page=results. Not only that, but we can – in fact *must* – supply the parameters that are indicated by the various *input* elements such as:

```
.table[0].tr[4].form[0].input[2].@name[0] NS-collection
.table[0].tr[4].form[0].input[2].@value[0] Live-collection
```

From the information provided by the *FilterViewer* and with a little trial and error, I can formulate a submission that simulates the action of posting this

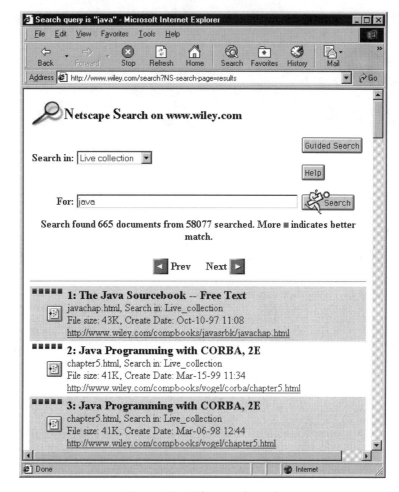

Figure 4.5   Wiley search results

form. A valid submission would combine URL

```
http://www.wiley.com/search?NS-search-page=results
```

with posted parameters.

```
NS-collection-Live_Collection&NS-query-java
```

Without the *FilterViewer* it would be considerably more difficult to construct such a submission. In a standard browser, the URL box will give no clues about the required parameters for any form that uses the *post* method, as you

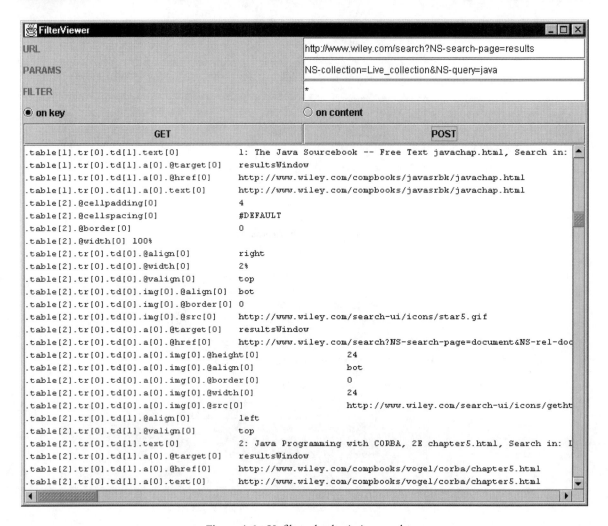

Figure 4.6   Unfiltered submission results

can see from the result shown in Figure 4.5.

So the *FilterViewer* will help a lot with the task of formulating valid form submissions, particularly those that require parameters to be posted. However, it will also be very useful for determining what kinds of filters we could apply to the content that results from a submission. Look at Figure 4.6 which shows what happens when we issue a search submission on the Wiley site via the *FilterViewer*. Then look at Figure 4.7 which shows what happens when I issues the same submission with a simple filter – *.table[*].tr[0].td[1].text[0]* – applied to the elements keys.

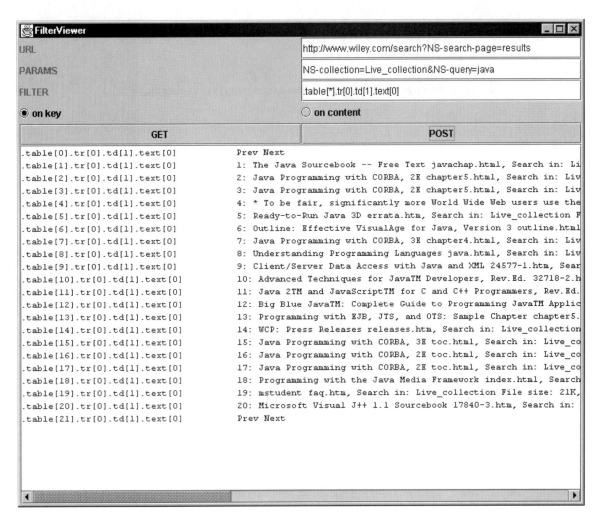

Figure 4.7   Filtered submission results

That's much more useful, isn't it, so having sold the idea of the *FilterViewer* to you all that's left now is to actually implement it.

FilterViewer code

The basic class will have a few member variables to hold the list of source elements and for the interactive GUI components, plus a *main(...)* method so that we can run it from the command line. It will implement *ActionListener* so as to receive events from the buttons, *ListCellRenderer* so that we can display the elements in our own style, and *ListSelectionListener* so that we can respond to list selections.

```java
// ** Code taken from jwebdata/query/FilterViewer.java **

package jwebdata.query;

import java.awt.*;
import java.awt.event.*;
import javax.swing.*;
import javax.swing.event.*;
import java.util.*;

import jwebdata.parsing.*;

/**
 * GUI application for visualising a filter.
 */
public class FilterViewer extends JFrame implements ActionListener
  , ListCellRenderer, ListSelectionListener
{
    Vector elements=new Vector();

    // -- GUI Components --
    private JTextField urlText;
    private JTextField paramsText;
    private JTextField filterText;
    private JRadioButton keyFilterButton;
    private JRadioButton contentFilterButton;
    private JButton getButton;
    private JButton postButton;

    JList elementList;

    public static void main(String args)
    {
      FilterViewer thisViewer=new FilterViewer("FilterViewer");

      thisViewer.addWindowListener(new WindowAdapter() {
        public void windowClosing(WindowEvent event) ·System.exit(0);}
        });

      thisViewer.setVisible(true);
    }
}
```

FilterViewer(...) Constructor

The constructor will instantiate the various GUI widgets and add the *Filter-Viewer* itself as the *ActionListener* on the *get* and *post* buttons.

```java
// ** Code taken from jwebdata/query/FilterViewer.java **
```

```java
/**
 * Constructor to create the GUI.
 */
public FilterViewer(String title)
{
    super(title);
    getContentPane().setLayout(new BorderLayout());

    JPanel topPanel=new JPanel();
    topPanel.setLayout(new GridLayout(5,2));

    // -- Text Fields --

    topPanel.add(new JLabel("URL"));
    topPanel.add(urlText=new JTextField());

    topPanel.add(new JLabel("PARAMS"));
    topPanel.add(paramsText=new JTextField());

    topPanel.add(new JLabel("FILTER"));
    topPanel.add(filterText=new JTextField("*"));

    // -- Radio Buttons --

    keyFilterButton=new JRadioButton("on key",true);
    contentFilterButton=new JRadioButton("on content");
    ButtonGroup filterGroup=new ButtonGroup();
    filterGroup.add(keyFilterButton);
    filterGroup.add(contentFilterButton);
    topPanel.add(keyFilterButton);
    topPanel.add(contentFilterButton);

    // -- Standard Buttons --

    topPanel.add(getButton=new JButton("GET"));
    topPanel.add(postButton=new JButton("POST"));

    // -- Set the Action Listeners --
    getButton.addActionListener(this);
    postButton.addActionListener(this);

    // -- Build the GUI --
    getContentPane().add(topPanel,BorderLayout.NORTH);
    elementList=new JList();
    elementList.setCellRenderer(this);
    elementList.setBackground(Color.white);
    elementList.addListSelectionListener(this);

    getContentPane().add(new JScrollPane(elementList)
      ,BorderLayout.CENTER);

    setSize(500,500);
}
```

actionPerformed(...)

Upon receiving events from the button, through the *actionPerformed(...)* method given below, we perform the following actions:

- Issue the submission using *get* or *post*, and parse the results.

- Filter the elements according to the user-supplied wildcard filter text.

- Set the filtered elements as the data model for our JList.

```
// ** Code taken from jwebdata/query/FilterViewer.java **

/**
 * Method to respond to the button click by applying the filter.
 */
public void actionPerformed(ActionEvent event)
{
    WebParserWrapper webParser=new WebParserWrapper();
    Vector elements=new Vector();

    try
    {
      setCursor(new Cursor(Cursor.WAIT-CURSOR));

      if (event.getSource()==getButton)
      {
        // -- GET Submission --
        elements=webParser.getElements(urlText.getText()
          ,paramsText.getText(),WebParserWrapper.GET);
      }
      else if (event.getSource()==postButton)
      {
        // -- POST Submission --
        elements=webParser.getElements(urlText.getText()
          ,paramsText.getText(),WebParserWrapper.POST);
      }

      if (keyFilterButton.isSelected())
      {
        // -- KEY Filter --
        elements=Filter.getFilteredElements(elements,Filter.KEY
          ,"MATCHES",filterText.getText());
      }
      else
      {
        // -- CONTENT Filter --
        elements=Filter.getFilteredElements(elements,Filter.CONTENT
          ,"MATCHES",filterText.getText());
      }
```

```
        elementList.setListData(elements);
    }
    catch (Exception ex)
    { ex.printStackTrace(); }

    setCursor(new Cursor(Cursor.DEFAULT-CURSOR));
}
```

The *elementList* (JList) will be redrawn automatically to reflect the new
content. As each individual entry in the list is drawn, or *rendered*, the *Filter-
Viewer* will get a nudge – a call back – through the *getListCellRendererCom-
ponent(...)* method.

getListCellRendererComponent(...)

This is our chance to determine exactly how the elements are displayed, by
returning our own custom component. We won't be too adventurous though.
Element *keys* will be rendered blue, padded to achieve a degree of alignment.
Element *contents* will be rendered black.

```
// ** Code taken from jwebdata/query/FilterViewer.java **

/**
  * Swing method to display each filtered element in our own style.
  */
public Component getListCellRendererComponent(JList list, Object value
  , int index, boolean isSelected, boolean cellHasFocus)
{
    Font labelFont=new Font("Courier",Font.PLAIN,11);

    // -- Get Element Key and Content --
    SourceElement thisElement=(SourceElement) value;
    String key=thisElement.getKey();
    String content=thisElement.getContent();

    JPanel elementPanel=new JPanel();
    elementPanel.setLayout(new BorderLayout());
    elementPanel.setBackground(Color.white);

    // -- Construct the KEY Label --
    int keyLength=key.length();
    String padding=new String("
      .substring(0,20-(keyLength%20));
    JLabel keyLabel=new JLabel(key]padding);
    keyLabel.setForeground(Color.blue);
    keyLabel.setFont(labelFont);
    elementPanel.add(keyLabel,BorderLayout.WEST);

    // -- Construct the CONTENT Label --
```

```
JLabel contentLabel=new JLabel(content);
contentLabel.setForeground(Color.black);
contentLabel.setFont(labelFont);
elementPanel.add(contentLabel,BorderLayout.CENTER);


    return elementPanel;
}
```

Once we've viewed a page using the simple '*' filter text we'll probably want to adjust the filter text to pick out certain elements according to their key values, like I showed you in Figure 4.7. To save typing a lengthy key value into the filter box, we'll respond to a list selection – via the *valueChanged(...)* method – by transferring the key value of the selected element into the *filterText* field as the basis of a new filter.

valueChanged(...)

```
// ** Code taken from jwebdata/query/FilterViewer.java **


/**
  * Transfer the clicked element to the filter box, for convenience.
  */
public void valueChanged(ListSelectionEvent event)
{
    // -- Transfer the selected key value to the filter box --
    int selectedIndex=elementList.getSelectedIndex();
    SourceElement selectedElement
      =(SourceElement) elements.elementAt(selectedIndex);
    filterText.setText(selectedElement.getKey());
}
```

That completes the *FilterViewer* implementation, but we won't stop there. After giving you a chance to try it out we'll then extend the idea into the realm of *structured queries*.

Compiling and running the FilterViewer

The following files are included in the code download:

```
jwebdata/query/Filter.java
jwebdata/query/FilterViewer.java
jwebdata/query/Operator.java
```

You can compile the code then run the *FilterViewer* by issuing these commands:

```
javac jwebdata/query/*.java
java jwebdata.query.FilterViewer
```

To practice using it, you might like to try reproducing Figures 4.2, 4.4, 4.6 and 4.7 above and Figure 4.9 below.

4.3   Structured Queries

Applying a filter lets us capture a subset of the parsed elements into a single-column list, thus allowing us to take a vertical – or horizontal – slice through the data. Look at Figure 4.8 which has data arranged in table rows and columns, and from which we could take a vertical slice (e.g. the share names) as shown in Figure 4.9.

Just for the record, we could also take a horizontal slice by applying the wildcards (*) to the table data elements, .td[*], rather than to the table row elements. For example, if you look back at Figure 4.8 we could pick the name and share price of DEF Technology with a filter like this:

```
.table[0].tr[0].td[2].table[0].tr[1].td[*].text[0]
```

to give

```
.table[0].tr[0].td[2].table[0].tr[1].td[0].text[0] DEF Technology
.table[0].tr[0].td[2].table[0].tr[1].td[1].text[0] 103
```

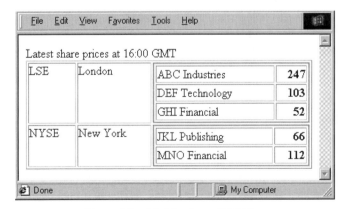

Figure 4.8   Multi-column HTML page

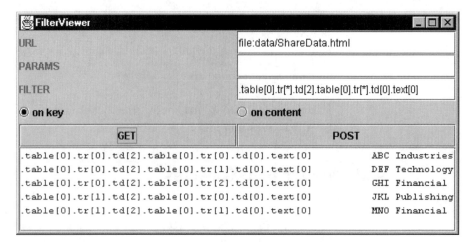

Figure 4.9   Share names filter

Notice how the columns have been turned into rows.

I won't go any further down that route now, but it means we can do something with a HTML table that is not so easy with a traditional relational database table – read across the table columns rather than down the table rows. Oh, and my mention of *relational database tables* in that sentence is no accident since that's the topic I'd like to turn to next.

What I'd really like to do now is to combine the results of the *share name* filter (*.table[0].tr[*].td[0].tr[*].td[0].text[0]*) with the results of a *share price* filter (*.table[0].tr[*].td[0].tr[*].td[1].text[0]*) to capture complete table rows into a Java program. To make things even more interesting I'd like to throw in the results of an *exchange name* filter, with exchange names repeated as necessary to form complete meaningful rows like this:

    LSE|ABC Industries|247|
    LSE | DEF Technology| 03 |
    LSE | GHI Financial| 52 |
    NYSE | JKL Publishing| 66|
    NYSE | MNO Financial| 112

It's not quite as easy as it sounds. Since we'll be applying the filters separately, there will be some work to do in matching up the selected elements from one filter with those selected elements from another filter that belong in the same target row. This is compounded by the fact that the *exchange name* filter will produce only two result elements, LSE and NYSE, compared with five result elements from each of the other two filters.

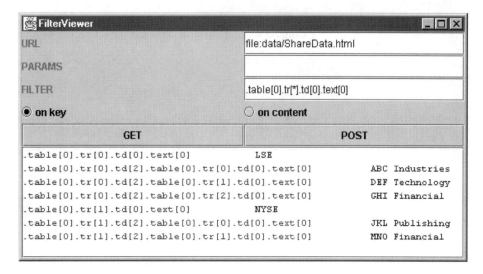

Figure 4.10   Exchange name filter

4.3.1   QueryEngine

Filtering revisited

First we need to solve a little problem. Our existing *Filter* class works correctly but not in quite the way that we need for this task. To see what I mean, take a look at my attempt at filtering exchange names in Figure 4.10.

To my surprise I got more than I bargained for, but if you think about it a key like *.table[0].tr[0].td[2].table[0].tr[0].td[0].text[0]* really does match the wildcard text *.table[0].tr[*].td[0].text[0]*.

We'll fix that problem by implementing the first two methods of our new *QueryEngine* class.

matchesKey (...) and getPaddleKey (...)

For this *matchesKey(...)* method key values should match *exactly* with the filter text with the one concession that any index value – between the [and] brackets – may match a wildcard *. Here is the *QueryEngine* class with the *matchesKey(...)* method:

```
// ** Code taken from jwebdata/query/QueryEngine.java **

package jwebdata.query;
import java.util.*;
import jwebdata.parsing.*;
```

```java
/**
 * A class for combining filters into structured queries.
 */
public class QueryEngine
{
    private boolean matchesKey(String key, String filter)
    {
        // -- Get key and filter padded to 5-digit indexes --
        key=getPaddedKey(key);
        filter=getPaddedKey(filter);

        if (filter.length()!=key.length()) return false;

        // -- Move along side-by side, replacing *s with digits --
        int pos=0;
        while (pos<filter.length())
        {
          char char1=filter.charAt(pos);
          if (char1=='*' || char1=='?')
          {
            char char2=key.charAt(pos);
            filter=filter.substring(0,pos)+char2
              +filter.substring(pos]1,filter.length());
          }
          pos++;
        }

        if (filter.equals(key)) return true;
        return false;
    }
```

All we're doing here is moving along a *key* string and a *filter* string character-by-character, replacing any wildcard *s (or ?s) in the filter with the corresponding concrete index digits from the key. At the end of the process, the (new) filter text and the key should match exactly:

```
Key Text:          .table[00000].tr[00000].td[00000].text[00000]
Filter Text:       .table[00000].tr[*****].td[00000].text[00000]
(New) Filter Text: .table[00000].tr[00000].td[00000].text[00000]
```

For the character by character replacement to work, it's crucial that we first pad out each index – with leading zeros or extra *s as required – to exactly five digits. That's the reason for the *getPaddedKey(...)* method invocations that you might have noticed in the previous code. For completeness, I'll list the *getPaddedKey(...)* method here:

```
// ** Code taken from jwebdata/query/QueryEngine.java **

/**
  * Returns a version of a key padded to 5 characters.
  */
private String getPaddedKey(String key)
{
    // -- Pad the key or filter text to 5-digit indexes --
    String paddedKey="";
    StringTokenizer st=new StringTokenizer(key,".");
    while (st.hasMoreTokens())
    {
      String thisToken=st.nextToken();
      int openPos=thisToken.indexOf("[");
      int closePos=thisToken.indexOf("]");

      if ((closePos>openPos) && (openPos>=0))
      {
        String index=thisToken.substring(openPos+1,closePos);
        if (index.startsWith("*")) index="*****";
        else if (index.startsWith("?")) index="?????";
        while (index.length()<5) index="0"+index;
        paddedKey=paddedKey+"."+thisToken.substring(0,openPos+1)
          +index]thisToken.substring(closePos,thisToken.length());
      }
      else paddedKey=paddedKey+"."+thisToken;
    }
    return paddedKey;
}
```

getFilteredElements(...) Revisted

Next we'll take the *getFilteredElements(...)* method from our *Filter* class and include it in this *QueryEngine* class, modified to call the new *matchesKey(...)* method rather than *Operator.compare(...)*.

```
// ** Code taken from jwebdata/query/QueryEngine.java **

/**
  * Returns a set of elements matching a particular filter.
  */
private Vector getFilteredElements(Vector sortedElements
  , String filter)
{
    Vector filteredElements=new Vector();

    for (int i=0; i<sortedElements.size(); i++)
    {
      SourceElement thisElement=(SourceElement)
        sortedElements.elementAt(i);
```

```
    // -- By default compare the key field of this element --
    String key=(String) thisElement.getKey();

    // -- Add a positive match to the filtered list --
    if (matchesKey(key,filter))
        filteredElements.addElement(thisElement);
    }
    return filteredElements;
}
```

We've solved the problem that I highlighted, so we're now well placed to achieve our wider objective. In case you've forgotten, that objective is to combine multiple filters into a single selection that produces sensible rows of data.

From filters to rows

A *getFilteredRows(...)* method will be our main entry point into the *QueryEngine* class. It will take in a list of elements, which we will have got from the *WebParserWrapper*, along with a vector containing the wildcard filter texts to be applied for each *column* in our final row set.

getFilteredRows(...)

```
// ** Code taken from jwebdata/query/QueryEngine.java **
/**
  * Entry point to this class, returns a set of rows comprising
  * elements selected by the supplied filters.
  */
public Vector getFilteredRows(Vector elements, Vector filters)
{
    Vector columns=new Vector[filters.size()];

    for (int filterIndex=0; filterIndex<filters.size(); filterIndex++)
    {
      // -- Get matching elements for this filter --
      String filterText=(String) filters.elementAt(filterIndex);
      Vector filteredElements=getFilteredElements(elements, filterText);

      // -- Add the filtered elements as data for a new column --
      columns[filterIndex]=filteredElements;
    }

    Vector rows=getValidRows(columns,filters);
    return rows;
}
```

Each *vector* of filtered elements is recorded as an entry in the columns array. The data in each column vector is at this stage unrelated to the data in other columns, and the columns may well contain different numbers of elements resulting from the separate filters. To make sense of it all, we invoke the *getValidRows(...)* method as shown above and defined next.

getValidRows(...)

This method combines every element in each column with every element in each other column, in all possible combinations to form candidate rows. Then it removes the combinations that don't make sense. Here's the code:

```
// ** Code taken from jwebdata/query/QueryEngine.java **

/**
 * Combines elements from separate filter columns into meaningful rows.
 */
private Vector getValidRows(Vector columns, Vector filters)
{
    int columnCount=columns.length;
    Vector rows=new Vector();

    // -- To start, copy the column 0 elements into "rows" --
    Vector column0=columns[0];
    for (int colPos=0; colPos<column0.size(); colPos++)
    {
      SourceElement thisRow=new SourceElement[columnCount];
      thisRow[0]=(SourceElement) column0.elementAt(colPos);
      rows.addElement(thisRow);
    }

    // -- Now do all the other columns --
    for (int c=1; c<columnCount; c++)
    {
      Vector newRows=new Vector();

      // -- For every item in column c, duplicate all rows --
      Vector thisColumnElements=columns[c];

      int thisColumnNumElements=0;
      if (thisColumnElements!=null)
        thisColumnNumElements=thisColumnElements.size();

      for (int colPos=0; colPos<thisColumnNumElements; colPos++)
      {
        for (int rowPos=0; rowPos<rows.size(); rowPos++)
        {
          SourceElement thisRow=(SourceElement)
            ((SourceElement)rows.elementAt(rowPos)).clone();
```

```
        thisRow[c]=(SourceElement)
         thisColumnElements.elementAt(colPos);

      if (consistentRow(thisRow,filters))
         newRows.addElement(thisRow);
    }
  }
  rows=newRows;
 }
 return rows;
}
```

To clarify what's going on here imagine we have three filters for three columns. For each column, its filter picks out a few matching items. In this example the filter for column 1 picks out two items (C1A and C1B), the filter for column 2 picks out two items (C2A and C2B), and the filter for column 3 picks out three items (C3A, C3B and C3C):

Column 1	Column 2	Column 3
C1A	C2A	C3A
C1B	C2B	C3B
		C3C

Remember that at this stage the data in each column is unrelated to the data in the other columns, they're just three separate lists. What the above code will do is combine every element with every other element to product a row set of all possible combinations, like this:

Row	Column 1	Column 2	Column 3
1	C1A	C2A	C3A
2	C1B	C2A	C3A
3	C1A	C2B	C3A
4	C1B	C2B	C3A
5	C1A	C2A	C3B
6	C1B	C2A	C3B
7	C1A	C2B	C3B
8	C1B	C2B	C3B
9	C1A	C2A	C3C
10	C1B	C2A	C3C
11	C1A	C2B	C3C
12	C1B	C2B	C3C

So we have a set of all possible candidate rows, but not all of those combinations are valid, which is why earlier I said '. . . then it removes the combinations that don't make sense'. Actually it never adds the nonsensical rows in the first place. Whenever the call to *consistentRow(...)* in the previous code reports false for a candidate row, we discount that row before ever adding it to the final set.

consistentRow(...)

The *consistentRow(...)* method establishes a *context* for each element in the candidate row and determines the validity of the whole row by comparing the *contexts* of the individual elements. A candidate row is valid, or consistent, if the context of each element is consistent with the context of every other element in the row. The cross checking of every element context with every other element context is the reason for the nested loops in the code that follows.

```java
// ** Code taken from jwebdata/query/QueryEngine.java **

/**
  * Determines if the supplied candidate row is valid.
  */
private boolean consistentRow(SourceElement thisRow, Vector filters)
{
    boolean consistent=true;

    // -- Check the consistency of every element combination --
    for (int c1=0; c1<thisRow.length; c1++)
    {
      for (int c2=0; c2<thisRow.length; c2++)
      {
        SourceElement element1=(SourceElement) thisRow[c1];
        SourceElement element2=(SourceElement) thisRow[c2];

        if ( (element1==null) || (element2==null))
            break;

        // -- Get a context for this pair of elements --
        String element1Context
          =getContext(element1,(String) filters.elementAt(c1));
        String element2Context
          =getContext(element2,(String) filters.elementAt(c2));
        if (!consistentElements(element1Context,element2Context))
            return false;
      }
    }
    return consistent;
}
```

Now I need to tell you what I mean by *context*, and how we get the context for each element.

Elements in context

First of all, remember that the elements extracted by the filters will not be of the form 'C1A' or 'C3B', but of this form representing unique elements keys – their positions – within the source HTML or XML text:

```
.table[0].tr[0].td[2].table[0].tr[1].td[0].text[0]
```

For any element in that form, we can discover its context via a call to a new *getContext(...)* method.

getContext(...)

In a nutshell it will form the *negative* of the filter that produced the element, by replacing any concrete indexes in the filter with wildcards (*) and any wildcards (*) with concrete indexes.

```
// ** Code taken from jwebdata/query/QueryEngine.java **

/**
 * Get the context of an element by negating its key.
 */
private String getContext(SourceElement element, String filter)
{
    String key=element.getKey();

    String paddedKey=getPaddedKey(key);
    String paddedFilter=getPaddedKey(filter);

    // -- Now reverse the sense of the *s to make the context --

    String context=paddedFilter;
    int pos=0;
    while (pos<context.length())
    {
      char char1=context.charAt(pos);
      if (char1=='*')
      {
        char char2=paddedKey.charAt(pos);
        context=context.substring(0,pos)+char2
          +context.substring(pos+1,context.length());
      }
      else if ( (char1>='0' && char1<='9') || char1=='?')
```

```
      {
        context=context.substring(0,pos)+"*"
          +context.substring(pos+1,context.length());
      }
      pos++;
    }

    // -- replace final type with content[ so final indexes must match --
    int lastDotIndex=context.lastIndexOf(".");
    int lastBracketIndex=context.lastIndexOf("[");

    context=context.substring(0,lastDotIndex)
      +".content"+context.substring(lastBracketIndex,context.length());

    return context;
}
```

To see why we do this, I'll present this dry run of the context matching process. Suppose we'll be applying these three filters:

.table[0].tr[*].td[2].table[0].tr[*].td[0].text[0] **for share names.**

.table[0].tr[*].td[2].table[0].tr[*].td[1].text[0] **for share prices.**
.table[0].tr[*].td[0] **for exchange names.**

For the first two filters, some typical selected elements – and their contexts – will be:

Element .table[0].tr[0].td[2].table[0].tr[0].td[0].text[0] **ABC Industries selected with filter** .table[0].tr[*].td[2].table[0].tr[*].td[0].text[0] **has context** .table[*****].tr[00000].td[*****].table[*****].tr[00000] .td[*****].text[*****]

and

Element .table[0].tr[0].td[2].table[0].tr[0].td[1].text[0] **247 selected with filter** .table[0].tr[*].td[2].table[0].tr[*].td[1].text[0] **has context** .table[*****].tr[00000].td[*****].table[*****].tr[00000] .td[*****].text[*****]

Those two elements are in the same context so may be selected into the same row, whereas the following element is in a different context and therefore does not belong in the same row.

Element .table[0].tr[0].td[2].table[0].tr[1].td[1].text[0] **103**

selected with filter .table[0].tr[*].td[2].table[0].tr[*]
.td[1].text[0]
has context .table[*****].tr[00000].td[*****].table[*****].tr[00001]
.td[*****].text[*****]

If you look back at Figure 4.8 you'll see that this makes sense so far, and when we apply the final filter – for exchange names – you'll see that this falls within the same context (as far as it goes) as all of those elements.

Element .table[0].tr[0].td[0].text[0] **LSE**
selected with filter .table[0].tr[*].td[0]
has context .table[*****].tr[00000].td[*****]

Back in the *consistentRow(...)* method you will have seen that after obtaining the context for a pair of elements we invoked *consistentElements(...)* to test the validity of those elements.

consistentElements(...)

Here's where we do the real context matching that I've just described, by checking that any concrete index values in one element context are identical to the equivalent index values in the other context:

```
// ** Code taken from jwebdata/query/QueryEngine.java **

/**
 * Determines if two elements have matching context, i.e. belong in
 * the same row.
 */
private boolean consistentElements(String element1Context, String
element2Context)
{
    // -- step through the tokens in each context --
    StringTokenizer st1=new StringTokenizer(element1Context,".");
    StringTokenizer st2=new StringTokenizer(element2Context,".");

    boolean consistent=true;
    while (st1.hasMoreTokens() && st2.hasMoreTokens())
    {
      String token1=st1.nextToken();
      String token2=st2.nextToken();

      String type1=token1.substring(0,token1.indexOf("["));
      String index1=token1
        .substring(token1.indexOf("[")+1,token1.length()-1);
      String type2=token2.substring(0,token2.indexOf("["));
      String index2=token2
```

```
       .substring(token2.indexOf("[")+1,token2.length()-1);

    // -- If the types are different, the context is consistent --
    if ( !type1.equals(type2) )
    {
        consistent=true;
        break;
    }

    // -- Same types but different indexes means inconsistent --
    if ( (type1.equals(type2)) && !(index1.equals(index2)) )
    {
        consistent=false;
        break;
    }
  }
  return consistent;
}
```

With all that code under our belts, we just need some way of testing it.

Compiling and running the QueryEngine

We'll add *main(...)* method to the *QueryEngine*, solely for the purpose of taking it for a spin. I've thrown in an extra filter for good measure:

```
// ** Code taken from jwebdata/query/QueryEngine.java **
/**
 * A main() method to test it.
 */
public static void main(String args)
{
    try
    {
      String url="file:data/ShareData.html";
      Vector filters=new Vector();
      filters.addElement(".table[0].tr[*].td[0].text[0]");
      filters.addElement(".table[0].tr[*].td[1].text[0]");
      filters.addElement(
        ".table[0].tr[*].td[2].table[0].tr[*].td[0].text[0]");
      filters.addElement(
        ".table[0].tr[*].td[2].table[0].tr[*].td[1].text[0]");

      // -- Parse the elements at URL --
      WebParserWrapper webParser=new WebParserWrapper();
      Vector elements=webParser
        .getElements(url,"",WebParserWrapper.GET);
```

```
// -- Get rows that satisfy the filters ---
QueryEngine queryEngine=new QueryEngine();
Vector rows=queryEngine.getFilteredRows(elements,filters);

// -- Print them out --
for (int r=0; r<rows.size(); r++)
{
    SourceElement thisRow=(SourceElement) rows.elementAt(r);
    for (int c=0; c<thisRow.length; c++)
    {
      SourceElement thisElement=thisRow[c];
      System.out.print(thisElement.getContent()+"|");
    }
    System.out.println();
  }
}
catch (Exception ex) {ex.printStackTrace();}
}
```

You can now compile and run the *QueryEngine* by issuing the following commands:

```
javac jwebdata/query/QueryEngine.java
java jwebdata.query.QueryEngine
```

On your screen you should see this resulting output:

```
> java jwebdata.query.QueryEngine


LSE | London | ABC Industries | 247 |
LSE | London | DEF Technology | 103 |
LSE | London | GHI Financial | 52 |
NYSE | New York | JKL Publishing | 66 |
NYSE | New York | MNO Financial | 112 |
```

For my next trick, I'll form the link with the industry standard SQL via a new application called *SqlGui*.

4.3.2 SqlGui

We've been taking data *from* a URL in the same way that we might take data *from* a relational database table. The *QueryEngine* has allowed us to apply filters to *select* data elements into meaningful columns within rows. It's beginning to sound like SQL already, and if we add some easier to read column aliases (with the *as* keyword) as well as a simple *where* clause, we can conceive a SQL-like GUI application that fronts the *QueryEngine* as shown in Figure 4.11.

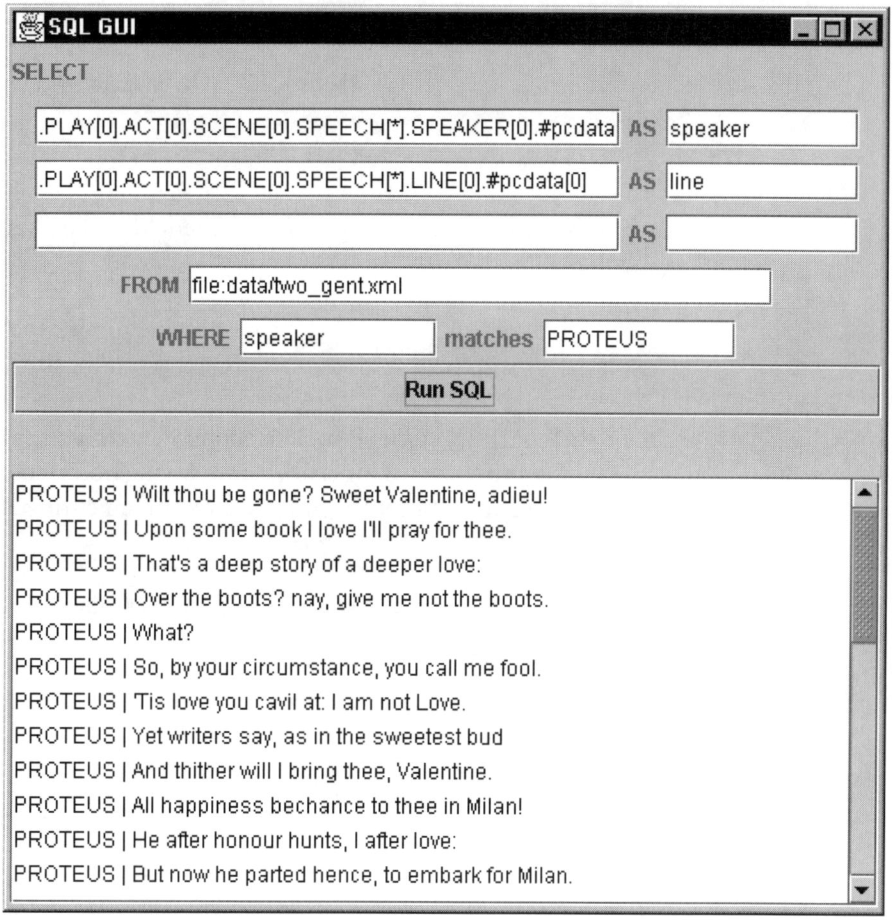

Figure 4.11 SqlGui

It's equally applicable to HTML and XML content, but the reason I've used XML for the example is because data supplied to client programs in the form of XML will very often have originated in a relational database. The individual XML elements will reflect the record structures of the original database, and querying these structures is therefore – in a sense – equivalent to querying the original database as you can see in Figure 4.12. Quite a powerful concept if you think about it.

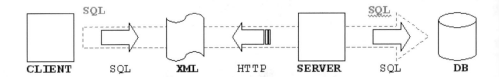

Figure 4.12   SQL through XML

Let's implement the *SqlGui* and then I'll take this SQL idea a little bit further.

SqlGui code

The shell of the *SqlGui* class is listed below with its constructor that initializes the GUI components. This is not a Java Swing book, so I won't give you a blow by blow account, but notice that we're implementing *ActionListener* so as to receive events from *runButton*.

```java
// ** Code taken from jwebdata/query/SqlGui.java **

package jwebdata.query;

import java.awt.*;
import java.awt.event.*;
import javax.swing.*;
import javax.swing.event.*;
import java.util.*;
import jwebdata.parsing.*;

/**
 * GUI application to demonstrate web access via SQL.
 */
public class SqlGui extends JFrame implements ActionListener
{
    // -- GUI Components --

    private JTextField select1Text;
    private JTextField select2Text;
    private JTextField select3Text;

    private JTextField select1Alias;
    private JTextField select2Alias;
    private JTextField select3Alias;
```

```java
private JTextField fromText;

private JTextField whereAlias;
private JTextField whereWildcard;

private JButton runButton;

private JList resultsList;

/**
 * Constructor to create the GUI.
 */
public SqlGui(String title)
{
    super(title);

    // -- Construct the GUI --

    JLabel selectLabel=new JLabel("SELECT");

    JPanel selectPanel1=new JPanel();
    selectPanel1.setLayout(new FlowLayout());
    selectPanel1.add(select1Text=new JTextField(30));
    selectPanel1.add(new JLabel("AS"));
    selectPanel1.add(select1Alias=new JTextField(10));

    JPanel selectPanel2=new JPanel();
    selectPanel2.setLayout(new FlowLayout());
    selectPanel2.add(select2Text=new JTextField(30));
    selectPanel2.add(new JLabel("AS"));
    selectPanel2.add(select2Alias=new JTextField(10));

    JPanel selectPanel3=new JPanel();
    selectPanel3.setLayout(new FlowLayout());
    selectPanel3.add(select3Text=new JTextField(30));
    selectPanel3.add(new JLabel("AS"));
    selectPanel3.add(select3Alias=new JTextField(10));

    JPanel fromPanel=new JPanel();
    fromPanel.setLayout(new FlowLayout());
    fromPanel.add(new JLabel("FROM"));
    fromPanel.add(fromText=new JTextField(30));

    JPanel wherePanel=new JPanel();
    wherePanel.setLayout(new FlowLayout());
    wherePanel.add(new JLabel("WHERE"));
    wherePanel.add(whereAlias=new JTextField(10));
    wherePanel.add(new JLabel("matches"));
    wherePanel.add(whereWildcard=new JTextField(10));

    JPanel topPanel=new JPanel();
    topPanel.setLayout(new GridLayout(8,1));
    topPanel.add(selectLabel);
```

```
         topPanel.add(selectPanel1);
         topPanel.add(selectPanel2);
         topPanel.add(selectPanel3);
         topPanel.add(fromPanel);
         topPanel.add(wherePanel);
         topPanel.add(runButton=new JButton("Run SQL"));
         runButton.addActionListener(this);

         getContentPane().setLayout(new GridLayout(2,1));
         getContentPane().add(topPanel);
         getContentPane().add(new JScrollPane(resultsList=new JList()));
      setSize(500,500);
    }
}
```

The real action takes place in the *actionPerformed(...)* method, which is invoked in response to the user pressing the button.

actionPerformed(...)

The only new concept in the following method is the way we're using the *Operator.matches(...)* method to check each row against the *where* clause.

```
// ** Code taken from jwebdata/query/SqlGui.java **

/**
 * Method to run the query in response to the button press.
 */
public void actionPerformed(ActionEvent event)
{
    // -- Instantiate a web parser and a query engine --

    WebParserWrapper webParser=new WebParserWrapper();
    QueryEngine queryEngine=new QueryEngine();

    try
    {
      setCursor(new Cursor(Cursor.WAIT_CURSOR));

      if (event.getSource()==runButton)
      {
        Vector filters=new Vector();
        if (select1Text.getText().trim().length()>0)
            filters.addElement(select1Text.getText());
        if (select2Text.getText().trim().length()>0)
            filters.addElement(select2Text.getText());
        if (select3Text.getText().trim().length()>0)
            filters.addElement(select3Text.getText());

        // -- Invoke the Parser --
```

```
Vector elements=webParser.getElements(fromText.getText()
  ,"",WebParserWrapper.GET);

// -- Run the SELECT query --
Vector rows=queryEngine.getFilteredRows(elements,filters);

// -- Which field for the WHERE clause? --
int whereIndex=-1;
if (whereAlias.getText().equals(select1Alias.getText()))
   whereIndex=0;
if (whereAlias.getText().equals(select2Alias.getText()))
   whereIndex=1;
if (whereAlias.getText().equals(select3Alias.getText()))
   whereIndex=2;
if (whereAlias.getText().trim().length()==0)
   whereIndex=-1;
Vector rowStrings=new Vector();

// -- Loop through the rows --
for (int r=0; r<rows.size(); r++)
{
    SourceElement thisRow

      =(SourceElement) rows.elementAt(r);

    boolean includeRow=true;

    // -- Check for a match with the WHERE clause --
    if (whereIndex>=0)
    {
      includeRow=false;
      String whereValue=thisRow[whereIndex].getContent();
      if (Operator.matches(whereValue,whereWildcard
        .getText()))
      {
          includeRow=true;
      }
    }

    // -- Create a row data string --
    String rowString="";
    if (thisRow.length>0)
      rowString=rowString+thisRow[0].getContent();
    if (thisRow.length>1)
      rowString=rowString+" | "+thisRow[1].getContent();
    if (thisRow.length>2)
      rowString=rowString+" | "+thisRow[2].getContent();

    // -- Should we display this row? --
    if (includeRow) rowStrings.addElement(rowString);
}
```

```
      resultsList.setListData(rowStrings);
    }
  }
  catch (Exception ex)
  { ex.printStackTrace(); }

  setCursor(new Cursor(Cursor.DEFAULT-CURSOR));
}
```

For completeness, here's the *main(...)* method that launches the GUI in the first place.

```
// ** Code taken from jwebdata/query/SqlGui.java **

/**
 * A main() method to run it.
 */
public static void main(String args)
{
    SqlGui sqlGui=new SqlGui("SQL GUI");

    sqlGui.addWindowListener(new WindowAdapter() {
      public void windowClosing(WindowEvent event) {System.exit(0);}
      });

    sqlGui.setVisible(true);
}
```

Compiling and running the SqlGui

You can compile and run the *SqlGui* by issuing these commands:

```
javac jwebdata/query/SqlGui.java
java jwebdata.query.SqlGui
```

As a test you could try reproducing my results from Figure 4.11.

SQL commercial implementation

I've presented the SQL idea here in the simplest way that I can think of, with code examples that are not too horrendous. A complete implementation of a SQL engine for web data would be too unwieldy to present in this book, but if you're interested there is a case study describing an early version of my company's commercial implementation included as a chapter in *Professional Java Data* (Wrox Press, 2001). Latest information about the commercial implementation, the WebDataKit, is available online at http://www.lotontech.com/wdbc.html.

To give you a taste of what can be achieved I'll say that it's possible to implement a parser for SQL statements so that queries may be submitted in the same way as through a traditional SQL command interface, i.e. not through a GUI screen. The syntax can be brought into line with conventional SQL by allowing selections from, and joins between, multiple tables (in our case, multiple URLs). Look at this query syntax supported by the commercial implementation.

```
SELECT site1.table[1].tr[*].td[0].text[0] AS site1.planet
,site1.table[1].tr[*].td[1].text[0] AS site1.distance
,site2.table[0].tr[0].td[1].table[1].tr[*].td[2].a[?].text[0] AS
site2.moon
,site2.table[0].tr[0].td[1].table[1].tr[*].td[0].a[0].text[0] AS
site2.planet

FROM http://tqjunior.thinkquest.org/3504/ AS site1
,http://freespace.virginnet.co.uk/solar.system/datatext.html AS site2

WHERE site1.moons>=0 AND NOT site1.planet='Sun' AND NOT
site2.planet='Planet' AND site1.planet=site2.planet

ORDER BY site1.distance
```

That's not a hypothetical example. It's a real example that fetches data from two different web sites, combines the results with a SQL join, applies a *where* clause, and finally sorts the results according to the *order by* clause. The proof of the pudding is in Figure 4.13.

As food for thought I'll tell you that not only is it possible to use SQL for querying web data, but it's also possible to wrap the *QueryEngine* that we've implemented in something quite similar to a JDBC driver. Thus allowing data from web sources to be accessed from within a Java program in exactly the same way as data from any other source.

4.4 Chapter Review

We've covered quite a bit of ground in this chapter. First we looked at the idea of filtering HTML or XML elements to pick out just the ones we want. I then

SQL Results			
site1.planet	site1.distance	site2.moon	site2.planet
Earth	1	The Moon	Earth
Mars	1.5	Phobos	Mars
Mars	1.5	Deimos	Mars
Jupiter	5.2	Ganymede	Jupiter
Jupiter	5.2	Callisto	Jupiter
Jupiter	5.2	Io	Jupiter
Jupiter	5.2	Europa	Jupiter
Saturn	9.5	Titan	Saturn
Saturn	9.5	Rhea	Saturn
Saturn	9.5	Iapetus	Saturn
Saturn	9.5	Dione	Saturn
Saturn	9.5	Tethys	Saturn
Saturn	9.5	Enceladus	Saturn
Saturn	9.5	Mimas	Saturn
Uranus	19.2	Titania	Uranus
Uranus	19.2	Oberon	Uranus
Uranus	19.2	Umbriel	Uranus
Uranus	19.2	Ariel	Uranus
Uranus	19.2	Miranda	Uranus
Neptune	30.1	Triton	Neptune
Neptune	30.1	Nereid	Neptune
Pluto	39.5	Charon	Pluto

Figure 4.13   Commercial SQL example

presented the *FilterViewer* graphical application as a tool for visualizing the effect of filters, and in particular for helping with the difficult task of formulating URL/parameter combinations to drive HTML forms.

Next we explored the concept of combining individual filters into structure queries, with hierarchic elements flattened into valid row sets according to the contexts of individual elements. Finally, the link was made with the idea of using industry standard SQL as a mechanism for extracting information from web sources.

You might like to put these new filtering and querying mechanisms to good use, and what better use than your own portal? Which is what we'll look at next.

4.4.1   API classes and interfaces introduced in this chapter

The following Java API classes and interfaces have been introduced for the first time in this chapter's code examples:

- *java.awt.BorderLayout* lays out a graphical container with components arranged into regions: north, south, east, west, and centre.

- *java.awt.FlowLayout* lays out a graphical container with components arranged in a left to right flow.

- *java.awt.GridLayout* lays out a graphical container with components arranged in a rectangular grid.

- *java.awt.Color* is a class to represent colours.

- *java.awt.Component* provides a graphical representation that can be displayed, and which can respond to user actions.

- *java.awt.Cursor* represents the mouse cursor as a bitmap.

- *java.awt.Font* represents a font for rendering characters.

- *java.awt.event.WindowAdapter* should be extended by any class wishing to receive windows events.

- *java.awt.event.WindowEvent* is event which indicates that the status of a window has changed.

- *java.io.StringTokenizer* allows a text string to be broken down into tokens that are separated by delimiters.

- *java.lang.Double* is an object wrapper for a value of type *double*.

- *javax.swing.ButtonGroup* creates scope for a set of buttons that are mutually exclusive.

- *javax.swing.JFrame* is the Swing component that replaces *java.awt.Frame* as a top level window with a title and a border.

- *javax.swing.JLabel* is a display area for a short text string or an image, which does not react to input events.

- *javax.swing.JList* displays a list of items from which the user can select.

- *javax.swing.JRadioButton* displays an item whose state may be changed by user action.

- *javax.swing.JScrollPane* manages a scrollable view on a graphical component.

- *javax.swing.JTextField* is a graphical component that allows a single line of text to be edited.

- *javax.swing.ListCellRenderer* is implemented in order to allow the custom rendering of items in a JList.

- *javax.swing.event.ListSelectionListener* is an interface that should be implemented by any class wishing to receive user selection events from a displayed list.

- *javax.swing.event.ListSelectionEvent* is an event that specifies a change in the current selection of a displayed list.

Building a Portal with Java

In this chapter we'll look at how the query mechanisms described in Chapter 4 could be used as a basis on which to build a portal. Our portal will collect data from more than one source page, add some value to the data, and present it as a single page at our site. We'll implement the portal first as a servlet and then as an applet, so that we can compare the two approaches that I first described in Chapter 1.

5.1 The Design

The example will be a simple but useful one and will be based on an application that is one of the most popular among portal providers. What we're talking about here is a Share Price Information Portal.

I'll start with the servlet approach and use this as the vehicle for describing the functionality, then we'll implement the same thing in the style of an applet. In Figure 5.1 you will see the two new classes, *PortalServlet* and *PortalApplet*, which make use of the *WebParserWrapper* and *QueryEngine* from Chapters 3 and 4.

5.2 Data Sources

Of course, we'll need some data sources. I first wrote and tested the code with a view to using data sourced from the Yahoo!Finance site. That fact adds some

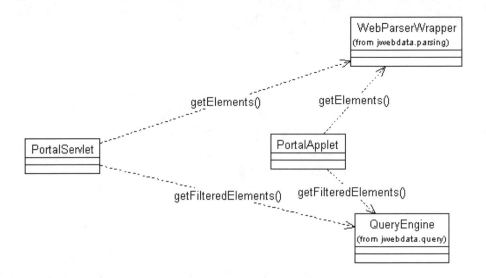

Figure 5.1   UML class diagram for package jwebdata.portal

credibility, I think, but it also gives me a problem. By the time you read this, the format of that site may have changed so the code won't run. For convenience I've included in the software download my own servlet that simulates the same kind of data, thus allowing you to test the approach with a stable data source and (coincidently) without the need for an active Internet connection.

5.2.1   Yahoo!Finance data source

Before telling you about the *ShareServlet* sample data source I'll just clarify that at the time of writing it is possible to substitute the following URLs into the code that follows:

> http://uk.finance.yahoo.com/q?s=+^FTSE+@UKX.L&f=snlcvi (for FTSE data)

> http://uk.finance.yahoo.com/q?s=+^NDX+@NASDQ.L&f=snlcvi (for NASDAQ data)

In which case you would also need to transplant these lines of code at the appropriate place:

```
filters.addElement (".table[5].tr[0].td[0].table[0].tr[*].td[1].text[0]");
filters.addElement (".table[5].tr[0].td[0].table[0].tr[*].td[3].text[0]");
filters.addElement (".table[5].tr[0].td[0].table[0].tr[*].td[5].text[0]");
```

If that doesn't work, don't blame me. It's inevitable that sites will change over time though not necessarily as often as you might think. In my experience a particular set of URLs and filter specifications typically holds out for about six months before it breaks. The beauty of this approach is that those URLs and filter specifications could be stored in text files or as properties, to be loaded into your program(s) at run-time. Which means you could supply update patches to your users, as sites change, rather than providing a new code release.

5.2.2 ShareServlet data source

Really keen readers will be able to use the *FilterViewer* from Chapter 4 to get the code up and running with a live web site, not necessarily the one I chose, but if you'd like to take the easy route for now then help is at hand thanks to my *ShareServlet*. Having followed the instructions in Appendix A for installing and configuring the software you should be able to open a browser window and execute the *ShareServlet* via the following URLs:

http://localhost:8080/JWebData/ShareServlet?exchange=FTSE
(for FTSE sample data)
http://localhost:8080/JWebData/ShareServlet?exchange=NASDAQ
(for NASDAQ sample data)

Figure 5.2 shows what you should see, and you can use the browser Refresh button to update the same share prices. Note that although presented as a single figure, this actually represents two separate browser windows pointed at two different web pages.

The source code for the ShareServlet is not essential to the plot as it is merely a simulation of an Internet based data source. So I'm not providing a code listing here but it is available in the download if you'd like to take a look at it.

Now that we have a sample data source we can move on to the portal implementations, starting with the servlet implementation.

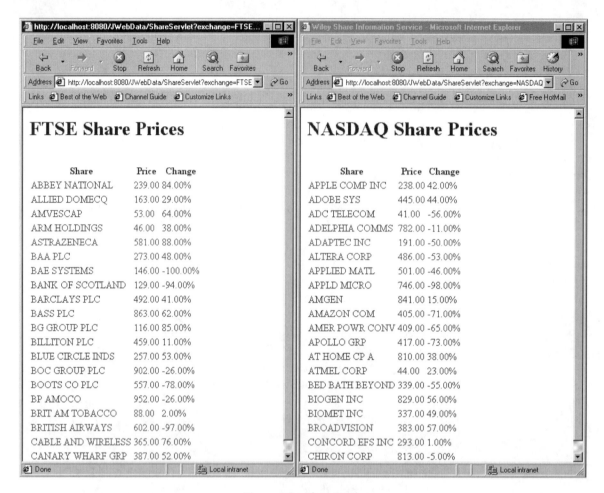

Figure 5.2   ShareServlet

5.3 Servlet Portal

I'd be quite surprised to see any portal development in Java that was not based to some extent on servlets, so the servlet approach will be our first port of call for the development of our own portal.

5.3.1 Servlet portal in action

Our portal will present information in the form shown in Figure 5.3. This page

Figure 5.3   Servlet portal

collects raw share price information from a suitable web source that provides FTSE (London) data, and displays it alongside information gathered from a separate web source – i.e. a different web page – that provides NASDAQ (New York) data.

Our first piece of added value is to pull the separate London and New York exchange data together into one page. Our second piece of added value will be to issue a *buy*, *sell*, or *hold* (not shown) recommendation for each share according to the percentage rise or fall for that share outside a specified range. This is new information that is unlikely to be provided by the original web sources.

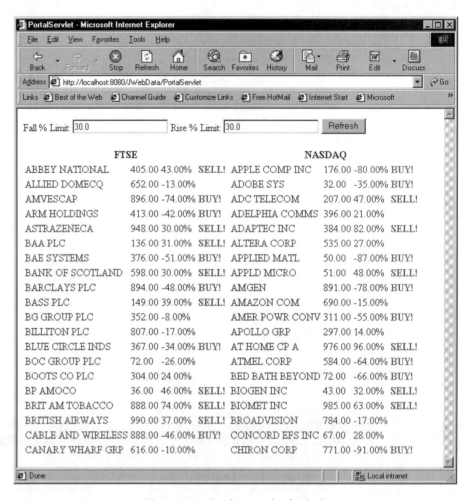

Figure 5.4   Servlet portal refreshed

In addition to the share price information, the portal page has a Refresh button that the user can press at any time to see the latest prices and recommendations. Figure 5.4 gives a sample of what the page might look like following a refresh. Look closely and you'll spot the differences.

To complete the picture I'll tell you about how the recommendations will be decided. My original idea was that if a share fell by a significant percentage it could be bought cheaply and then sold later when the price recovered. Conversely, any share that increases by a significant percentage should be sold to take the instant profit. As an example, let's say that we'll buy any shares that have fallen 30 per cent and sell any shares (if we own them) that have risen 30 per cent. These values may be set via the input fields – comprising a simple

HTML form – shown in Figure 5.3 and 5.4. New values will take effect each time the form is submitted via the Refresh button, at which point I should warn you not to confuse the form Refresh button with the browser Refresh button!

You may have noticed that in Figures 5.3 and 5.4 my simulation is for a very active trading day with prices varying by as much as 100 per cent. A day-trader's dream, I'm sure, but probably not reflecting reality. So if you adapt it to work with a live web site be prepared to specify lower limits or expect to see far fewer recommendations.

5.3.2   Servlet portal implementation

The servlet implementation of our portal will consist of a single class, *Portal-Servlet*, having the following definition:

```java
// ** Code taken from jwebdata/portal/PortalServlet.java **

package jwebdata.portal;

import javax.servlet.*;
import javax.servlet.http.*;
import java.io.*;
import java.util.*;

import jwebdata.parsing.*;
import jwebdata.query.*;

/**
  * Portal implementation as an servlet.
  */
public class PortalServlet extends HttpServlet
{
}
```

The methods

All incoming messages, in response to user actions, will arrive via the servlet's *doGet(...)* and *doPost(...)* methods.

doGet(...) and doPost(...)
The servlet's *doGet(...)* method, listed below, first extracts the values for any *lowerLimit* and *upperLimit* parameters encoded into the servlet submission. The first time in, these parameters will not be present and so the limits will each be set by default to 10.

After setting up the HTTP response we write out the tags for a simple HTML form comprising two text fields (to take the lower and upper limits) and a Refresh button. When the user submits this form via the Refresh button, the same servlet will be invoked again. This time with the parameters I mentioned above.

The share price information itself will immediately follow the form, so now we'll collect that information and write it out as HTML. I'll tell you more about that after you've taken a look at the listing that follows.

```java
// ** Code taken from jwebdata/portal/PortalServlet.java **

/**
 * Servlet method to process a GET submission.
 */
public void doGet(HttpServletRequest req, HttpServletResponse res)
  throws IOException
{
    float lowerLimit;
    float upperLimit;

    // -- Get submitted values for limits if possible --
    try
    {
        lowerLimit=Float.parseFloat(req.getParameter("lowerLimit"));
        upperLimit=Float.parseFloat(req.getParameter("upperLimit"));
    }
    catch (Exception ex)
    {
        lowerLimit=10;
        upperLimit=10;
    }

    // -- Set up the HTTP response --
    res.setContentType("text/html");
    PrintWriter outputWriter = res.getWriter();

    // -- Write the HTML Header --
    outputWriter.println("<html>");
    outputWriter.println("<head><title>PortalServlet</title></head>");
    outputWriter.println("<body>");

    // -- Write the HTML Form --
    outputWriter.println("<form method=post action='PortalServlet'>");
    outputWriter.println(" Fall % Limit: ");
    outputWriter.println("<input type=text name='lowerLimit' value="
      +lowerLimit+">");
    outputWriter.println(" Rise % Limit: ");
    outputWriter.println("<input type=text name='upperLimit' value="
```

```
                        |upperLimit|">");
        outputWriter.println(
          "<input type=submit name='Refresh' value='Refresh'><br>");
        outputWriter.println("</form>");

        try
        {
            WebParserWrapper webParser=new WebParserWrapper();
            QueryEngine queryEngine=new QueryEngine();

            Vector filters=new Vector();
            filters.addElement(".table[4].tr[*].td[1].text[0]");
            filters.addElement(".table[4].tr[*].td[3].text[0]");
            filters.addElement(".table[4].tr[*].td[5].text[0]");

            // -- Run the FTSE Query --
            Vector elements=webParser.getElements(
              "http://localhost:8080/JWebData/ShareServlet?exchange=FTSE",""
              ,WebParserWrapper.GET);

            // -- Get rows that satisfy the filters --
            Vector ftseRows=queryEngine.getFilteredRows(elements,filters);

            // -- Run the NASDAQ Query --
            elements=webParser.getElements(
              "http://localhost:8080/JWebbData/ShareServlet?exchange=NASDAQ"
              ,"",WebParserWrapper.GET);

            // -- Get rows that satisfy the filters ---
            Vector nasdaqRows=queryEngine.getFilteredRows(elements
              ,filters);

            // -- Base the table size on the biggest row set --
            int tableRows=ftseRows.size();
            if (nasdaqRows.size()>ftseRows.size())
                tableRows=nasdaqRows.size();

            outputWriter.println("<table>");
            outputWriter.println("<tr>");
            outputWriter.println("<th colspan=5><b>FTSE</b></th>");
            outputWriter.println("<th colspan=5><b>NASDAQ</b></th>");

            // -- Print the row sets side-by-side --
            for (int r=0; r<tableRows; r++)
            {
              outputWriter.println("<tr>");
              if (r<ftseRows.size())
                printRow(outputWriter, (SourceElement)
                  ftseRows.elementAt(r), lowerLimit, upperLimit);
              else
              {
                outputWriter.println("<td></td><td></td><td></td>");
```

```
        outputWriter.println("<td></td><td></td>");
      }

      if (r<nasdaqRows.size())
        printRow(outputWriter, (SourceElement)
          nasdaqRows.elementAt(r), lowerLimit, upperLimit);
      else
      {
        outputWriter.println("<td></td><td></td><td></td>");
        outputWriter.println("<td></td><td></td>");
      }

      outputWriter.println("</tr>");
    }

    outputWriter.println("</table>");
  }
  catch (Exception ex)
  {
    ex.printStackTrace();
    outputWriter.println(ex.toString());
  }

  outputWriter.println("<body>");
}
```

In the second part of the *doGet(...)* method above we initialize a *WebParser-Wrapper* and a *QueryEngine*. For each data source, the *WebParserWrapper* is used to extract the data and the *QueryEngine* is used to apply the filters: first for the FTSE data, then for the NASDAQ data. Although the data will come from two separate source pages, they are identical in format, so the vector of filters is created once and used twice. Finally the side by side table of information is written as output, with the overall length of the table being determined by the longer of the two row sets.

If you look back at the code for the HTML form you will see that the submission method is *post*, but it will work just as well if we change this to *get*. For our servlet the two submission methods are interchangeable because the following *doPost(...)* method simply invokes *doGet(...)* as shown here:

```
// ** Code taken from jwebdata/portal/PortalServlet.java **

/**
 * Servlet method to process a POST submission.
 */
public void doPost(HttpServletRequest req, HttpServletResponse res)
  throws IOException
{
    doGet(req,res);
}
```

I said that I'd tell you more about writing out the share price information as HTML, and that's the responsibility of the *printRow(...)* method.

printRow(...)

To ensure that the *doGet(...)* method is not too unwieldy I factored the code to print each share instance with its BUY or SELL recommendation out into a *printRow(...)* method, shown next:

```
// ** Code taken from jwebdata/portal/PortalServlet.java **

/**
  * Method to print a row of share information.
  */
private void printRow(PrintWriter outputWriter, SourceElement row
  , float lowerLimit, float upperLimit)
{
    // -- Print the share, price and change --
    String share=row[0].getContent().trim();
    String price=row[1].getContent().trim();
    String change=row[2].getContent().trim();
    outputWriter.println("<td>"+share+"</td><td>"+price+"</td><td>"
      +change+"</td>");

    if (change.endsWith("%")) change=change.substring(0
      ,change.length()-1);
    float changeFloat=Float.parseFloat(change);

    // -- Print BUY or SELL if change is outside the limits --
    if (changeFloat>=upperLimit)
    {
        outputWriter.println(
          "<td><b><font color='#FF0000'>SELL!</font></b></td><td></td>");
    }
    else if (changeFloat<=-lowerLimit)
    {
        outputWriter.println(
          "<td><b><font color='#009900'>BUY!</font></b></td><td> </td>");
    }
    else
        outputWriter.println(<td></td><td></td>");
}
```

That listing shows how we are picking out the share name, price and percentage change from the row and then taking any '%' sign off the end of the *change* string to convert it to a *float* value. Depending where that value falls outside the range that has been set, we write out a *buy* or *sell* recommendation in bold and in colour.

5.3.3.   Compiling the PortalServlet

If you've followed the installation and configuration instructions in Appendix A you'll be able to invoke the *PortalServlet*, in a browser, via this URL: http://localhost:8080/JWebData/PortalServlet

5.4   Applet Portal

Now we'll implement the same functionality in the form of a Java 2 applet. Note that it's Java 2, which means Java version 1.2 or 1.3 or later, and not Java 1.1. Therefore, the applet won't run in a browser as it stands and any users of our portal would need to have installed the Java 2 plug-in. This will be too much for some people and our target audience will therefore be limited to the more enthusiastic users.

So there's an immediate disadvantage, but there must also be advantages otherwise I wouldn't implement it this way, would I? If you think back to what I said in Chapter 2, applets provide for allow a truly application like look and feel that is difficult (if not impossible) to replicate using servlets and HTML. Also, the applet approach allows us to provide interactive applications with dynamic content in the absence of servlet support at the web host. Disappointingly, very few Internet Service Providers (ISPs) provide servlet support.

I'm actually quite keen on providing both kinds of interface, from amongst which the users themselves can choose. Why not offer a servlet interface to the widest possible audience and an all singing all dancing applet interface for the keener users? Plus maybe a scaled down WAP version for people on the move? We might have to be a bit more disciplined about factoring out the common functionality into a set of components that are reusable across these delivery channels, but that's no bad thing. On which subject, you might wish to refer back to Figure 2.11 in Chapter 2.

5.4.1   Applet portal in action

You won't see a Refresh button in Figure 5.5. There is a button, but it's marked Set Limits and it need never be pressed at all unless the user wishes to alter the range for the *buy* and *sell* recommendations. In this example the prices will be refreshed automatically (Figure 5.6) without the need for the user to repeatedly press a Refresh button, all thanks to a Java Thread.

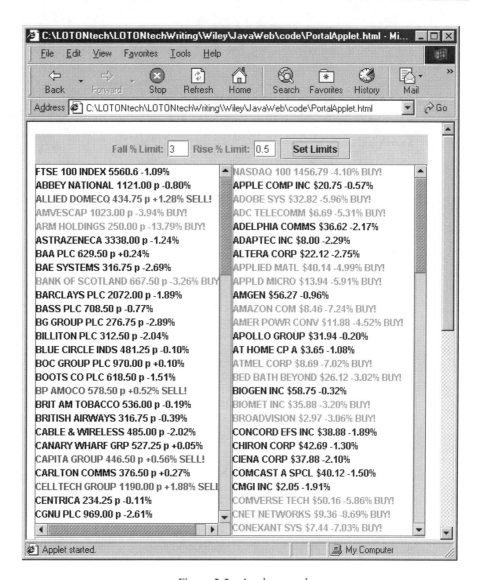

Figure 5.5   Applet portal

On the subject of the recommendations, and the range that determines them, I can tell you that – in data mining terminology – we've implemented a simple *classification*. Each share has been classified as *buy*, *sell* or *hold* (not shown) according to the value of the share's percentage change attribute. We could classify the shares in many other ways but in all cases this will be *classification* – rather than *clustering* – because there will be a fixed set of classes, with distinct labels, that we have decided upon in advance.

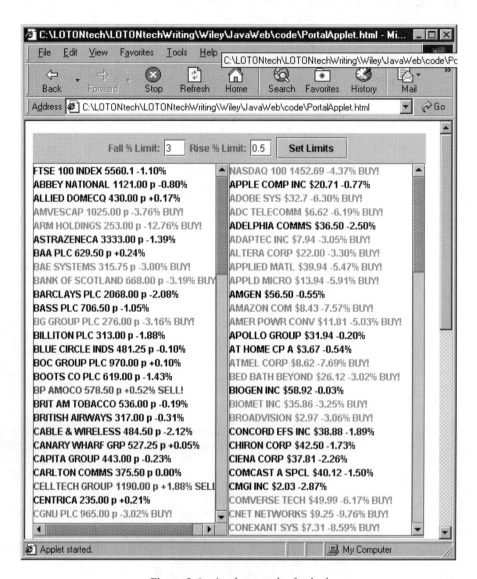

Figure 5.6   Applet portal refreshed

5.4.2   Applet portal implementation

The *PortalApplet* will be the direct counterpart of *PortalServlet*. This class will extend *JApplet*, which is the Java 2/Swing version of applet. It will implement *ActionListener* (to receive events from the button), *Runnable* (for our automatic refresh thread) and *ListCellRenderer* (so that we can specify how list elements are displayed).

```java
// ** Code taken from jwebdata/portal/PortalApplet.java **

package jwebdata.portal;

import java.applet.*;
import java.awt.*;
import java.awt.event.*;
import javax.swing.*;

import java.util.*;

import jwebdata.parsing.*;
import jwebdata.query.*;

/**
 * Portal implementation as an applet.
 */
public class PortalApplet extends JApplet implements ActionListener,
Runnable, ListCellRenderer
{
    // -- GUI Components --
    JTextField lowerLimitText;
    JTextField upperLimitText;
    JButton limitsButton;
    JList ftseList;
    JList nasdaqList;

    // -- Default limit values --
    float lowerLimit=10;
    float upperLimit=10;
}
```

The five GUI components should need no explanation, although this time we're presenting the FTSE and NASDAQ data each within it's own scrollable list-a Swing JList. We'll set the lower and upper limits to 10 by default.

The methods

Our class will operate via the following methods.

init(...)
The entry point for *PortalApplet* will be an *init(...)* method, which constructs the GUI and starts the automatic refresh thread. Points to look out for in this

code are the call to *addActionListener(...)* on the *limitsButton*, the call to *setCellRenderer(...)* on the *ftseList* and *nasdaqList*, and the starting of the refresh thread. Note that in all cases we are passing this as the relevant handler, which means everything will be handled within this one self-contained class.

```java
// ** Code taken from jwebdata/portal/PortalApplet.java **

/**
 * Initialization method.
 */
public void init()
{
    getContentPane().setLayout(new BorderLayout());

    JPanel topPanel=new JPanel();
    getContentPane().add(topPanel,BorderLayout.NORTH);

    // -- Text Fields --
    topPanel.add(new JLabel("Fall % Limit:"));
    topPanel.add(lowerLimitText=new JTextField(""+lowerLimit));
    topPanel.add(new JLabel("Rise % Limit:"));
    topPanel.add(upperLimitText=new JTextField(""+upperLimit));

    // -- Button --
    limitsButton=new JButton("Set Limits");
    limitsButton.addActionListener(this);
    topPanel.add(limitsButton);

    JPanel mainPanel=new JPanel();
    mainPanel.setLayout(new GridLayout(1,2));
    getContentPane().add(mainPanel,BorderLayout.CENTER);

    // -- Lists --
    ftseList=new JList();
    ftseList.setCellRenderer(this);
    mainPanel.add(new JScrollPane(ftseList));
    nasdaqList=new JList();
    nasdaqList.setCellRenderer(this);
    mainPanel.add(new JScrollPane(nasdaqList));

    // -- Start the refresh thread --
    Thread refreshThread=new Thread(this);
    refreshThread.start();
}
```

Starting the refresh thread within the applet's *init(...)* method triggers an invocation of the *run(...)* method listed next.

run(...)

This code will look very familiar to you if you analysed the servlet version, except that this time we're accessing the data sources repeatedly within an endless loop. This won't cause the applet – and in particular it's GUI components – to freeze because this *run(...)* method is executing in its own separate thread.

```java
// ** Code taken from jwebdata/portal/PortalApplet.java **
/**
 * Thread run() method to refresh the information regularly.
 */
public void run()
{
    // -- Initialize the WebParser and QueryEngine --
    WebParserWrapper webParser-new WebParserWrapper();
    QueryEngine queryEngine=new QueryEngine();

    // -- Set up the filter --
    Vector filters=new Vector();
    filters.addElement(".table[4].tr[*].td[1].text[0]");
    filters.addElement(".table[4].tr[*].td[3].text[0]");
    filters.addElement(".table[4].tr[*].td[5].text[0]");

    // -- Endless loop to refresh ad infinitum --
    while (true)
    {
      try
      {
        // -- Run the FTSE Query --
        Vector elements=webParser.getElements(
          "http://localhost:8080/JWebData/ShareServlet?exchange=FTSE"
          ,"",WebParserWrapper.GET);

        // -- Get rows that satisfy the filters ---
        Vector ftseRows=queryEngine.getFilteredRows(elements
          ,filters);

        // -- Run the NASDAQ Query --
        elements-webParser.getElements(
          "http://localhost:8080/JWebData/ShareServlet?exchange=NASDAQ"
          ,"",WebParserWrapper.GET);

        // -- Get rows that satisfy the filters ---
        Vector nasdaqRows=queryEngine.getFilteredRows(elements
          ,filters);

        // -- Set the JList models --
        ftseList.setListData(ftseRows);
        nasdaqList.setListData(nasdaqRows);
```

```
    // -- This delay is in addition to the web latency --
    Thread.sleep(1000);
  }
  catch (Exception ex)
  {
    ex.printStackTrace();
  }
 }
}
```

The thread was instructed to sleep in each iteration for 1000 ms. It doesn't mean that the data will refresh every second on the dot because the latency in fetching the data itself is much longer than this; on my Internet connection at least. You could remove this call to *sleep(...)* unless you wish to specify a much longer delay.

Each time the *setListData(...)* method is called (see above code) on one of the lists, that list will be refreshed with its cells rendered via the *getListCellRendererComponent(...)* method shown next.

getListCellRendererComponent(...)

Much of the following code we've seen already in the servlet version, except that this time we're setting the colour or the entire list element to green or red according to the *buy* or *sell* recommendation.

```
// ** Code taken from jwebdata/portal/PortalApplet.java **

/**
 * Swing method to display the information in our own style.
 */
public Component getListCellRendererComponent(JList list, Object value
 , int index, boolean isSelected, boolean cellHasFocus)
{
    SourceElement thisRow=(SourceElement) value;

    // -- Get the share, price and change for this row --
    String share=thisRow[0].getContent();
    String price=thisRow[1].getContent();
    String change=thisRow[2].getContent();

    String listEntry=share+" "+price+" "+change;

    if (change.endsWith("%"))
    {
      change=change.substring(0,change.length()-1);
    }

    float changeFloat=Float.parseFloat(change);

    // -- Set the color and add BUY or SELL according to 'change' --
```

```
Color listEntryColor=Color.black;
if (changeFloat>=upperLimit)
{
  listEntryColor=Color.red;
  listEntry=listEntry+" SELL!";
}
else if (changeFloat<=-lowerLimit)
{
  listEntryColor=Color.green;
  listEntry=listEntry+" BUY!";
}

JLabel listEntryLabel=new JLabel(listEntry);
listEntryLabel.setForeground(listEntryColor);

return listEntryLabel;
}
```

When we run it, the data will refresh at regular intervals until we close the applet. At each refresh the recommendations will be based on the current values for the upper and lower limits. The user may change these values by making new entries in the text boxes and pressing the Set Limits button. Upon pressing the button, the following *actionPerformed(...)* method will be triggered.

actionPerformed(...)

```
// ** Code taken from jwebdata/portal/PortalApplet.java **
/**
  * Set new limits in response to the button press.
  */
public void actionPerformed(ActionEvent event)
{
    if (event.getSource()==limitsButton)
    {
    // -- Get new values for limits if possible --
    try
    {
      lowerLimit=Float.parseFloat(lowerLimitText.getText());
      upperLimit=Float.parseFloat(upperLimitText.getText());
    }
    catch (Exception ex)
    {
      lowerLimit=10;
      upperLimit=10;
    }
    }
}
```

5.4.3   Compiling the PortalApplet

To run the applet we need a HTML file with an appropriate applet tag. Since this is a Java 2 applet that will run via the Java Plug-in, the applet tag takes a different form from that which I showed you in Chapter 2. The Plug-in is launched from Internet Explorer via an *<object>* tag and from Netscape Navigator via and *<embed>* tag. The *PortalApplet.html* file shown here will work with either browser. It should be easy enough to spot the important lines that specify the name of our applet, but it looks a lot more convoluted than the old *<applet>* tag doesn't it?

// ** Code taken from jwebdata/portal/PortalApplet.html **

```
<!doctype html public "-//w3c//dtd html 4.0 transitional//en">
<html>
<body>

<object
  classid="clsid:8AD9C840-044E-11D1-B3E9-00805F499D93"
  width="500" height="500"
  codebase="http://java.sun.com/products/plugin/1.2.2/jinstall-
1-2-2win.cab#Version=1,2,2,0">
  <param NAME="code" VALUE="jwebdata.portal.PortalApplet">
  <param NAME="type" VALUE="application/x-java-applet;version=1.2.2">
  <param NAME="scriptable" VALUE="true">
</object>

<embed
  type="application/x-java-applet;version=1.2.2"
  width="500"
  height="500" align="baseline"
  code="jwebdata.portal.PortalApplet"
  pluginspage="http://java.sun.com/products/plugin/1.2/plugin-
install.html">
</embed>
</body>
</html>
```

The applet can be executed by double-clicking the HTML file, but due to applet security restrictions it might not work first time. Any applet launched from our own web server or local disk will be prevented from accessing data from third-party sites unless we give the appropriate permission. We need a *policy* file like this one for applets executed from the local disk:

// ** Code taken from jwebdata.policy **

```
    grant codeBase "file:/-" {
      permission java.security.AllPermission;
    };
```

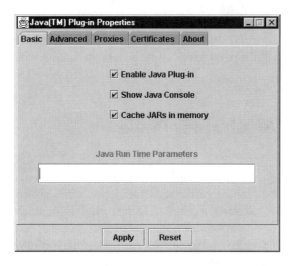

Figure 5.7   Plug-in properties

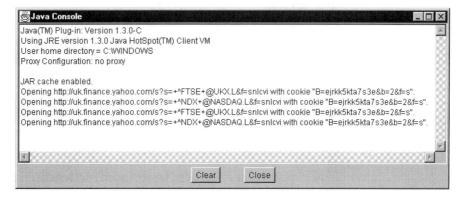

Figure 5.8   Plug-in console

For applets that are launched from a web server, even a locally installed server, you will need to replace the text 'file:/-' with the appropriate URL.

The Java Plug-in has to be made aware of the policy file by launching the Java Plug-in Properties Dialog, which Windows users will find within the Control Panel. You will need to enter the following text – with *Installation-Path* replaced with a valid path to the policy file – into the Java Runtime Parameters box shown in Figure 5.7.

```
-Djava.security.manager -Djava.security.policy
 =file:C://InstallationPath/jwebdata.policy
```

You might be interested to know that if you click the Show Java Console tick-box you'll be able to follow the progress of the applet as it contacts the data sources at each refresh. To see what I mean, take a look at Figure 5.8.

5.5 Chapter Review

In this chapter we've taken the ideas of filtering and querying from Chapter 4 and I've demonstrated the applicability of those techniques to a real-world example, that of a Share Price Information Portal, which we implemented both as a servlet and as a applet. As a Java 2 applet, the latter implementation was dependent on the run-time environment provided by the Java Plug-in, so we looked at some of the issues of running via the plug-in including the new applet tag and the security policy file.

You now have a technical foundation on which to build your own portals that take information from multiple data sources for presentation in new ways with added value. We've addressed the technicality of how to reuse existing data that is provided on-line, but there is a morality aspect to using someone else's data which I'll leave you to ponder.

In order to use data from existing web pages as the basis of you own portal, you first need to find the sites containing the kind of data you want. This is where a search engine comes in handy and we'll look at implementing one in the next chapter.

5.5.1 API classes and interfaces introduced in this chapter

The following Java API classes and interfaces have been introduced for the first time in this chapter's code examples.

- **java.lang.Runnable** interface allows any implementing class to be executed in a separate thread via its *run(. . .)* method.

- **java.lang.Thread** represents a thread of execution within the Java Virtual Machine.

- **javax.swing.JApplet** is the Swing replacement for a *java.awt.Applet*.

Building a Search Engine with Java

You will no doubt have heard the terms *Web Crawler* and *Spider* in the context of the Internet, and that's what I'll be talking about here. The World Wide Web really is like a spider's web, and from any given point there may be many separate threads – hyperlinks – leading us to many new and (we hope) exciting places. In this chapter we'll look at how we can crawl across the web just as a spider does.

We'll use the crawling mechanism as the basis of our own search engine. It will follow the threads of the web from any given starting point, report back what it finds, and tell us whether what it finds matches our search criteria. Whereas our engine will crawl around the web at the time that you submit the search, keep in mind the fact that – for improved performance – many commercial search engines interrogate a pre-compiled summarized directory of the known web pages rather than the web itself. Though, to compile the directory in the first place, a web crawler will most probably have been employed.

The design of our search engine will allow custom behaviour to be plugged-in to the basic crawler, thus providing for a much richer set of search behaviours than at first appears.

6.1 The Design

Our engine, unsurprisingly called *SearchEngine*, will allow a search to be initiated with any given web page as the starting point. It will look at this root page and tell us what it finds there, after which it will continue searching by drilling down through the links and frames that lead to other pages. To limit the extent of the search, any outgoing links will be followed only if the originating page contains data that is of interest to us.

The search will be breadth-first as shown in Figure 6.1. The # numbers show the order in which the search will progress through the links. Note that the search will not actually progress through links #5 and #6 if the originating page (linked Page 2) contains no interesting data.

The breadth-first approach will cause the search to radiate outwards from the root page. My assumption here is that the root page will have been chosen as a reliable *hub* for the kind of data we're looking for, so the further away we move the less likely we are to find what we're looking for. It's a very simplistic assumption, not guaranteed to produce the best results, but it feels better than a depth-first search in which we would go as far as possible down each potential dead-end before backtracking.

There will be a fully customizable mechanism outside the core search engine (the crawler) for determining whether a page contains interesting data and for taking appropriate actions according to the data that has been found. We'll devise a *SearchHandler* interface and we'll provide our an implementation of this interface as a call back object that operates on data items as they are encountered. You should be quite familiar with the call back approach by now, from the work we did in Chapter 3.

The relationships between the classes for this chapter are shown in Figure

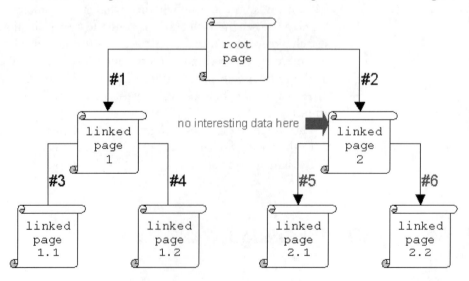

Figure 6.1   Breadth-first search strategy

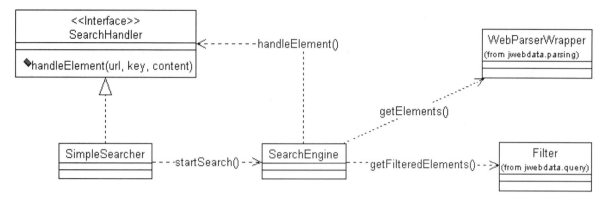

Figure 6.2   UML class diagram for package 'jwebdata.search'

6.2. Notice how the *SimpleSearcher* class invokes the *SearchEngine* and subsequently receives call backs from the *SearchEngine*, through the *SearchHandler* interface.

Impact of Web site Changes

Some of the examples in this chapter are based around data taken directly from the web, rather than from sample data sources that I have provided as home-grown servlets or static HTML/XML files. While this is good for realism, content and format of web sites may change such that these examples will no longer run exactly as presented. There is an implicit exercise and an opportunity for you to test your understanding by bringing any such examples up-to-date with the help of the *FilterViewer* from Chapter 4.

6.2   Core Search Engine/Web Crawler

First we'll look at the core class, the *SearchEngine*, which will implement the basic web crawling mechanism. Everything else will be built on top.

6.2.1   SearchEngine

The search engine will run inside a thread so as not to block the calling program, therefore we'll make it *runnable*, and we'll need some member variables to store the following information:

- A list of pages (links) that we have visited or are due to visit.

- The current link.

- The URL of the starting (root) page.

- A custom handler for (interesting) data.

- Flags for the engine's status.

The basic class definition will be:

```java
// ** Code taken from jwebdata/search/SearchEngine.java **

package jwebdata.search;

import jwebdata.parsing.*;
import jwebdata.query.*;
import java.util.*;

/**
 * Search Engine / Crawler class.
 */
public class SearchEngine implements Runnable
{
    private Vector linkHistory=new Vector(); // -- URLs to be searched --
    private int currentLink; // -- Current position in linkHistory --
    private String beginAt=null; // -- URL where the search began --
    private SearchHandler searchHandler=null; // -- Event handler --
    private boolean searchInProgress=false; // -- Still searching--
    private boolean stopPending=false; // -- Engine asked to stop --

    public boolean searchInProgress()
    { return searchInProgress; }

    public boolean stopPending()
    { return stopPending; }
}
```

Following links

Most of the search engine's functionality can be found within a single method called *followLinks(...)*, which will be recursive. This method fetches the links from a given URL, initially the root page, and adds them to the list of links to be followed. It then picks the next link from the pending list and makes a recursive call back into *followLinks(...)*; a process that will continue until the list contains no more links or until the engine is instructed to stop.

It's worth taking some time to think about that algorithm. Each time we encounter a link we will not follow it immediately with a recursive call to *followLinks(...)*, because that would be a depth-first search. Instead we'll add all of the links found on the current page to the list of pending links, and then follow the next link from the list. In Figure 6.3 I've listed a typical search sequence (based on the example in Figure 6.1 to show what should happen as we visit each page; that is, which new pages are added to the list and which page we should visit next. Notice that when we visit Page 1 we add two new pages, Page 1.1 and Page 1.2, neither of which is visited next because we pull Page 2 as the next page from the list.

For illustration I've included the pages leading from Page 2, denoted as *Page 2.x* in italics in Figure 6.3, to show at what point in the sequence they would be visited. These pages will not actually be visited if the originating Page 2 contains no interesting data. Prior to handling any of the links, the *follow-Links(...)* method fetches the content elements from the current page and passes them on to the custom handler for processing. Links originating at this page are only added to the list – as described above – if the handler reports at least one good 'hit'.

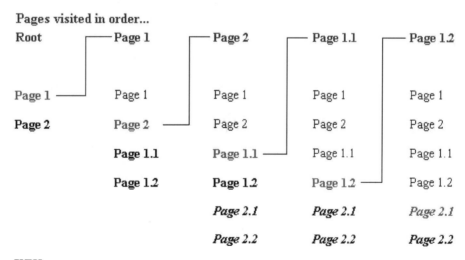

Pages visited in order...

Root	Page 1	Page 2	Page 1.1	Page 1.2
Page 1	Page 1	Page 1	Page 1	Page 1
Page 2	Page 2	Page 2	Page 2	Page 2
	Page 1.1	Page 1.1	Page 1.1	Page 1.1
	Page 1.2	**Page 1.2**	Page 1.2	Page 1.2
		Page 2.1	***Page 2.1***	*Page 2.1*
		Page 2.2	***Page 2.2***	*Page 2.2*

KEY:
normal - pages in the list that have been visited.
bold - pages in list yet to be visited.
italic - pages that would be added to the list if Page 2 contained hits.

Figure 6.3   Search sequence

followLinks(...)

If you've digested the description given above you'll now be ready so see what it looks like in code. Here is the *followLinks(...)* method:

```java
// ** Code taken from jwebdata/search/SearchEngine.java **

/**
 * Adds links (including frames) found at "url" to the list of
 * URLs waiting to be searched. It also passes each element at
 * "url" to the user-supplied handler.
 */
public void followLinks(String url)
{
    // -- Asked to stop, so do no more work. --
    if (stopPending) return;

    try
    {
      boolean drillDown=false;

      // -- Parse the data at this page --
      WebParserWrapper webParser=new WebParserWrapper();
      Vector sortedElements=webParser.getElements(url, "", "WITHGET");

      // -- Get the content for the handler --
      Vector contentElements=Filter.getFilteredElements(
        sortedElements,Filter.CONTENT,"matches","*");

      for (int i=0; i<contentElements.size(); i++)
      {
          SourceElement thisElement=(SourceElement)
            contentElements.elementAt(i);
          String thisKey=(String) thisElement.getKey();
          String thisContent=(String) thisElement.getContent();
          // -- Call the handler, and find out if it was good hit --
          boolean goodHit=searchHandler.handleElement(url,thisKey
            ,thisContent);
          if (goodHit) drillDown=true;
      }

      // -- If at least one good hit on this page, drill down --
      if (drillDown)
      {
          // -- Get the links --
          Vector linkElements=Filter.getFilteredElements(sortedElements
            ,Filter.KEY,"matches","*.a[*].@href[*]");

          for (int i=0; i<linkElements.size(); i++)
          {
              SourceElement thisElement=(SourceElement)
```

```
            linkElements.elementAt(i);

        String thisKey=(String) thisElement.getKey();
        String thisContent=(String)thisElement.getContent();

        // -- Add this link to the pending queue if it is new --
        if (!linkHistory.contains(thisContent))
            linkHistory.addElement(thisContent);
    }

    // -- Get the frames, which are like links --
    Vector frameElements=Filter.getFilteredElements(sortedElements
      ,Filter.KEY,"matches","*.frame[*].@src[*]");

    for (int i=0; i<frameElements.size(); i++)
    {

        SourceElement thisElement=(SourceElement)
          frameElements.elementAt(i);

        String thisKey=(String) thisElement.getKey();
        String thisContent=(String)thisElement.getContent();

        // -- Add link to the pending queue if it is new --
        if (!linkHistory.contains(thisContent))
            linkHistory.addElement(thisContent);
    }
  }
}
catch (Exception ex) {}

// -- Follow the next link from the pending queue --
if (currentLink<linkHistory.size())
{
  String nextLink=(String) linkHistory.elementAt(currentLink++);
  if (nextLink!=null) followLinks(nextLink);
}
}
```

Did you notice that the *getElements(...)* invocation is hard-coded to use the *get* submission method, with no option to use *post*? Here's that line again:

```
Vector sortedElements=webParser.getElements(url, "", "WITHGET");
```

It keeps the code simple, and for all pages beyond the root page this approach is sensible because we'll be following links. Simple HTML links, unlike form actions, are restricted to *get* submissions with no *post* option. You may wish to modify the code – not too difficult, I hope – to allow the initial submission to be posted, which might be appropriate when using an existing search engine as the starting point: more about that later.

You will also have noticed in that code that we're treating embedded frames in the current page in exactly the same way as outgoing hyperlinks; which they are really, it's just that they're normally displayed in the same browser window. It's crucial that we do traverse those frames because many of the home pages that we visit will contain a list of embedded frames and nothing else.

Searching in a separate thread

So as not to block the program that initiates the search, the *SearchEngine* will run in its own separate thread. This might be important if we wish to front the search process with a GUI that includes a Stop Search button, to be pressed at any time by the user before the search completes.

The methods that follow will be used to manage the search thread.

startSearch(...) and run(...)

In order to set the engine in motion we'll add a *startSearch(...)* method which takes a URL (of the root page) and our custom handler for data. After checking that there's not currently a search in progress, it creates a thread for the search engine to run in and starts it.

```
// ** Code taken from jwebdata/search/SearchEngine.java **

/**
 * This method asks the engine to start a search at the given URL, with
 * the user-supplied searchHandler to be called back with events.
 */
public boolean startSearch(String url, SearchHandler searchHandler)
{
    // -- Can't start a search if one is already running --
    if (searchInProgress) return false;

    beginAt=url;
    this.searchHandler=searchHandler;
    this.linkHistory=new Vector();
    this.currentLink=0;

    // -- Start the search in a new thread --
    Thread searchThread=new Thread(this);
    searchThread.start();
    return true;
}
```

Starting the search engine thread triggers the *run(...)* method, which is a requirement of the *Runnable* interface that our search engine implements. In the definition of the *run(...)* method that follows notice that it makes the first call to *followLinks(...)*:

```
// ** Code taken from jwebdata/search/SearchEngine.java **


/**
 * Run the search thread
 */
public void run()
{
    searchInProgress=true;
    followLinks(beginAt);
    searchInProgress=false;
    stopPending=false;
}
```

Besides starting a search we might also want to stop a search, and in fact we have to stop any current search in order to initiate a new one.

stopSearch(...)

The *stopSearch(...)* method is surprisingly simple, with a single statement to set the *stopPending* flag to true:

```
// ** Code taken from jwebdata/search/SearchEngine.java **


public void stopSearch()
{ stopPending=true; }
```

If you look back at the beginning of the *followLinks(...)* method you'll see the effect of setting this flag. The next call to *followLinks(...)* aborts, causing the recursion to unwind until execution is back with the *run(...)* method which then completes. There is no way to stop the current search immediately so we'll need to instigate any new search with code like this:

```
searchEngine.stopSearch();
while (!searchEngine.startSearch("http://someURL",ourHandler))
{
  // -- Loop until the search started. --
}
```

If you're wondering why we need to go to all that trouble when we could just as well call the *stop(...)* method on the thread object, take a look at what the API documentation says . . .

'**Deprecated.** This method is inherently unsafe. Stopping a thread with Thread.stop causes it to unlock all of the monitors that it has locked (as a natural consequence of the unchecked `ThreadDeath` exception propagating up the stack). If any of the objects previously protected by these monitors were in an inconsistent state, the damaged objects become visible to other threads, potentially resulting in arbitrary behavior. Many uses of `stop` should be replaced by code that simply modifies some variable to indicate that the target thread should stop running. The target thread should check this variable regularly, and return from its run method in an orderly fashion if the variable indicates that it is to stop running . . .'

Don't forget that the *startSearch(...)* method is asynchronous, allowing the method that called it to continue while the search progresses in its own thread. If you're calling *startSearch(...)* from within a method (e.g. *main()*) whose completion will cause the virtual machine to exit, you can block until the search completes by adding this line:

```
while (thisEngine.searchInProgress());
```

6.3 Simple Searching Example

That simple search engine, or crawler if you prefer, will be the basis of all our searching applications. Each application will customize the searching behaviour by implementing the *SearchHandler* interface, with no code modifications within the core engine being necessary. Think about that, and when you've seen the following example(s) I hope you'll agree that it's quite ingenious.

As a first example we'll put together a *SimpleSearcher* application, and I'll start by telling you what it will do so that you know what we're aiming for. We'll run the *SimpleSearcher* like this to search from a given starting point (the first argument) for a given keyword (the second argument):

```
java jwebdata.search.SimpleSearcher
http://www.lotontech.btinternet.co.uk/frontpage.html webdatakit
```

The results will be presented as a list of web page URLs leading from the starting point, each having a count of the number of times the keyword has been found at that page. Like this:

```
2 hits at http://www.lotontech.btinternet.co.uk/wdbc/help/help.html
2 hits at http://www.lotontech.btinternet.co.uk/wdbc/index.html
3 hits at http://www.lotontech.btinternet.co.uk/wdbc/help/release.html
7 hits at http://www.lotontech.btinternet.co.uk/wdbc.html#bespoke
```

```
2 hits at http://www.lotontech.btinternet.co.uk/wdbc/index.html#copyright
7 hits at http://www.lotontech.btinternet.co.uk/wdbc.html#SearchEngine
2 hits at http://www.lotontech.btinternet.co.uk/wdbc/help/help.html#Assist
1 hits at http://www.lotontech.btinternet.co.uk/frontpage.html
7 hits at http://www.lotontech.btinternet.co.uk/wdbc.html
2 hits at http://www.lotontech.btinternet.co.uk/wdbc/index.html#examples
```

Notice how the URL http://www.lotontech.btinternet.co.uk/wdbc.html appears three times with the same count, 7, each time. That's because there are three ways into that page, via the unmodified URL and via the *#bespoke* and *#SearchEngine* targets within the page. You can think about whether you would prefer to condense these down to one entry.

The call back approach used by the HTML and XML parsers seems like such a good idea to me that we'll use the same approach here. When we invoke the *SearchEngine* via its *startSearch(...)* method we can pass an instance of type *SearchHandler* as the call back object. Our *SimpleSearcher* will implement the *SearchHandler* interface that has the following definition:

6.3.1   SearchHandler

```java
// ** Code taken from jwebdata/search/SearchHandler.java **
package jwebdata.search;

/**
 * Implement this interface to support custom behaviour.
 */
public interface SearchHandler
{
    public boolean handleElement(String url, String key, String content);
}
```

The search engine will invoke the *handleElement(...)* method each time it wants to tell us the source URL, key, and content of a HTML or XML element that it has found on its travels. Our *SimpleSearcher* will implement *SearchHandler* so as to receive those call backs.

6.3.2   SimpleSearcher

We'll start with a few member variables as shown below. The *keyword* and *startURL* variables are self-explanatory. The *searchEngine* variable will hold a reference to the search engine itself, and the hits *Hashtable* will record the count of hits at each URL visited.

```
// ** Code taken from jwebdata/search/SimpleSearcher.java **

package jwebdata.search;

import java.util.*;

/**
  * Custom SearchHandler implementation for simple searches.
  */
public class SimpleSearcher implements SearchHandler
{
    private SearchEngine searchEngine;
    private String keyword;
    private String startURL;
    private Hashtable hits=new Hashtable();
}
```

Our obligation under the *SearchHandler* interface is to take in a URL, key, and content via the *handleElement(...)* and to return a Boolean value to tell the search engine whether that data represents a valid *hit*. If we report at least one good hit at a particular URL, the search engine will continue the search along the links leading from that page. Otherwise the current page will be considered to be a dead-end.

handleElement(...)

Besides reporting back to the search engine, our *handleElement(...)* method (shown below) will update the hits *Hashtable* entry for the current URL and will instruct the engine to stop once we have collected hits from 10 different URLs.

```
// ** Code taken from jwebdata/search/SimpleSearcher.java **

/**
  * Search Engine / Crawler callback method.
  */
public boolean handleElement(String url, String key, String content)
{
    boolean goodHit=false;

    // -- Count the number of times keyword appears --
    int keywordCount=0;
    int pos=-1;
    while ( ( pos=content.toLowerCase().indexOf(keyword,pos+1) )>=0 )
      keywordCount++;

    if (keywordCount>0)
    {
```

```
      // -- Update the count for this URL --
      Integer count=(Integer) hits.get(url);
      if (count==null)
        hits.put(url,new Integer(1));
      else
      {
        hits.remove(url);
        hits.put(url,new Integer(count.intValue()+keywordCount));
      }

      // -- Tell the engine it was a good hit --
      goodHit=true;
    }

    // -- On 10 hits tell the engine to stop --
    if (hits.size()>=10) searchEngine.stopSearch();

    return goodHit;
  }
```

The *handleElement(...)* method will never be called unless we actually start
the search engine running, which we'll do via a new method called *search(...)*.

search(...)

This method will invoke the engine, give it 1000 ms to start, and then go into
an endless loop while the search is in progress. Control will be returned to this
method when the engine runs out of links to follow or, as specified in our
handleElement(...) method, when we have collected 10 URLs.

```
// ** Code taken from jwebdata/search/SimpleSearcher.java **

/**
 * Method to invoke the search for keyword starting at startURL.
 */
public Hashtable search(String startURL, String keyword)
{
    searchEngine=new SearchEngine();

    this.startURL=startURL;
    this.keyword=keyword;
    this.searchEngine=searchEngine;

    searchEngine.startSearch(startURL,this);
    try {Thread.sleep(1000);} catch (Exception ex) {}

    while (searchEngine.searchInProgress());

    return this.hits;
}
```

Compiling and running the SimpleSearcher

So that we can test it we'll give our *SimpleSearcher* a *main(...)* method that calls the *search(...)* method with arguments taken from the command line, and which prints out the results (as shown earlier) when the search ends.

```java
// ** Code taken from jwebdata/search/SimpleSearcher.java **

/**
 * A main() method to test it.
 */
public static void main(String args)
{
    SimpleSearcher searcher=new SimpleSearcher();
    Hashtable hits=searcher.search(args[0],args[1]);

    System.out.println("URLs="+hits.size());

    for (Enumeration keys=hits.keys(); keys.hasMoreElements(); )
    {
      String thisKey=(String) keys.nextElement();
      int thisCount=((Integer)hits.get(thisKey)).intValue();

      System.out.println(thisCount+" hits at "+thisKey);
    }
}
```

In preparation for compilation you have the following files:

```
jwebdata/search/SearchEngine.java
jwebdata/search/SearchHandler.java
jwebdata/search/SimpleSearcher.java
```

To compile these classes, and to run the *SimpleSearcher* via its *main(...)* method above you should issue the following commands:

```
javac jwebdata/search/*.java

java jwebdata.search.SimpleSearcher
http://www.lotontech.btinternet.co.uk/frontpage.html webdatakit
```

Just in case you've forgotten, I'll remind you that the output will look something like this:

```
2 hits at http://www.lotontech.btinternet.co.uk/wdbc/help/help.html
2 hits at http://www.lotontech.btinternet.co.uk/wdbc/index.html
3 hits at http://www.lotontech.btinternet.co.uk/wdbc/help/release.html
```

```
7 hits at http://www.lotontech.btinternet.co.uk/wdbc.html#bespoke
2 hits at http://www.lotontech.btinternet.co.uk/wdbc/index.html#copyright
7 hits at http://www.lotontech.btinternet.co.uk/wdbc.html#SearchEngine
2 hits at http://www.lotontech.btinternet.co.uk/wdbc/help/help.html#Assist
1 hits at http://www.lotontech.btinternet.co.uk/frontpage.html
7 hits at http://www.lotontech.btinternet.co.uk/wdbc.html
2 hits at http://www.lotontech.btinternet.co.uk/wdbc/index.html#examples
```

It will work well enough for limited single-site searches, and in fact you might want to limit the search to a single domain – e.g. http://www.loton-tech.btinternet.co.uk – which you can do easily within the *handleElement(...)* method. This is good for single site, but users won't wait around while we search the entire web like this, so we need to give our engine a head start for more general searches.

6.4   A Search Engine Search Engine

Before we start I ought to point out that there's no typographical error in this header, as will soon become clear. It's not at all feasible to search the whole World Wide Web on demand. As I see it we have two options here:

- We could set the *SimpleSearcher* to run as a crawler 24 hours per day, seven days per week, to examine web content and summarize what it finds in some sort of directory or index. On demand from the user we'll search the index, not the web.

- We can take advantage of the fact that someone else has already done the hard work in compiling an index or directory of web content, and they've been kind enough to give us a web-based interface to their directory!

What I'm proposing is that we choose one or more existing search engines with an on-line interface and take a ride on the back of them. Rather than searching the web, we'll search the search engines, thus making ours a search engine search engine: a meta-search engine.

The good news is that we have all the tools we need. We know how to drive an existing web-based interface because we covered that in Chapter 2. We know how to parse the results (Chapter 3) and how to apply a filter to find links in the results (Chapter 4). In addition we've now wrapped all that up in a search engine that can follow the links to find yet more interesting stuff. So all we need to do now is provide an existing on-line search engine as the starting point for our *SimpleSearcher*.

To demonstrate the technique I'll use the search engine at http://www.wiley.com, which searches the Wiley book catalog. I know it's a single-site searcher, but bear in mind that it could just as well be Lycos, AltaVista, Google or your favourite search engine. We can submit a search at Wiley by forming a URL as shown in Figure 6.4.

We could submit the same search, for keyword *ejb*, via our *SimpleSearcher* with the following command:

```
java jwebdata.search.SimpleSearcher http://www.wiley.com/search?NS-search-page=results&NS-collection=comp-docs&NS-query=ejb ejb
```

The first time I ran this, the results weren't quite what I'd hoped for as you can see here:

```
URLs=10
2 hits at http://www.wiley.com/search?NS-search-page=document&NS-rel-doc-name=/compbooks/catalog/31717-9.htm&NS-query=ejb&NS-search-type=NS-boolean-query&NS-collection=comp-docs&NS-docs-found=8&NS-doc-number=5
9 hits at http://www.wiley.com/compbooks/catalog/38940-4.htm
2 hits at http://www.wiley.com/search?NS-search-page=document&NS-rel-doc-name=/compbooks/catalog/31972-4.htm&NS-query=ejb&NS-search-type=NS-boolean-query&NS-collection=comp-docs&NS-docs-found=8&NS-doc-number=3
8 hits at http://www.wiley.com/search?NS-search-page=document&NS-rel-doc-name=/compbooks/catalog/40131-5.htm&NS-query=ejb&NS-search-type=NS-boolean-query&NS-collection=comp-docs&NS-docs-found=8&NS-doc-number=4
12 hits at http://www.wiley.com/search?NS-search-page=document&NS-rel-doc-name=/compbooks/catalog/38940-4.htm&NS-query=ejb&NS-search-type=NS-boolean-query&NS-collection=comp-docs&NS-docs-found=8&NS-doc-number=2
12 hits at http://www.wiley.com/search?NS-search-page=results&NS-collection=comp-docs&NS-query=ejb
5 hits at http://www.wiley.com/compbooks/catalog/40131-5.htm
2 hits at http://www.wiley.com/compbooks/catalog/33229-1.htm
3 hits at http://www.wiley.com/search?NS-search-page=document&NS-rel-doc-name=/compbooks/catalog/33229-1.htm&NS-query=ejb&NS-search-type=NS-boolean-query&NS-collection=comp-docs&NS-docs-found=8&NS-doc-number=1
1 hits at http://www.wiley.com/compbooks/catalog/31972-4.htm
```

For a more sensible set of results we need to make a few minor modifications. We'll leave the original application intact by taking a copy of the code for *SimpleSearcher* and calling it *WileySearcher*. That's quite a good name for a searcher, isn't it?

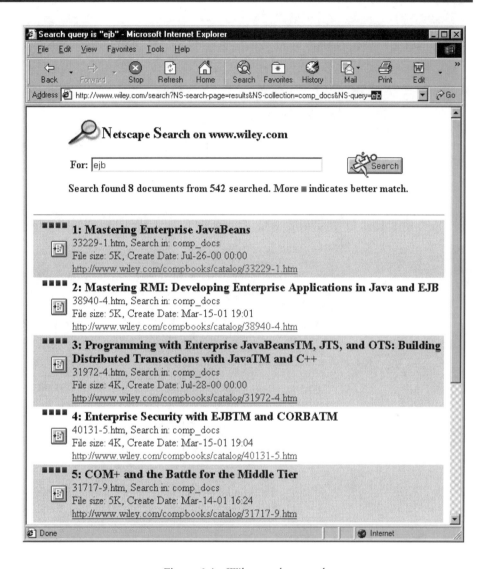

Figure 6.4   Wiley catalog search

6.4.1   WileySearcher

As with the *SimpleSearcher*, the action will take place within a *handleEle-ment(...)* method through which we'll receive some call backs. There are two changes to the *handleElement(...)* method which I've highlighted for you in the code that follows. We're reporting a good hit if the keyword appears at least once in the current page, but we're only adding a new URL to our hit list if that URL represents a Wiley catalogue entry beginning with http://www.wiley.com/compbooks/catalog/. Oh, and we're now collecting just five URLs before asking the engine to stop.

handleElement(...)

```
// ** Code taken from jwebdata/search/WileySearcher.java **

/**
 * Search Engine / Crawler callback method.
 */
public boolean handleElement(String url, String key, String content)
{
    boolean goodHit=false;

    // -- Count the number of times keyword appears --
    int keywordCount=0;
    int pos=-1;
    while ( ( pos=content.toLowerCase().indexOf(keyword,pos+1) )>=0 )
        keywordCount++;

    if ( (keywordCount>0)
      && url.startsWith("http://www.wiley.com/compbooks/catalog/") )
    {
        // -- Update the count for this URL --
        Integer count=(Integer) hits.get(url);
        if (count==null)
          hits.put(url,new Integer(1));
        else
        {
          hits.remove(url);
          hits.put(url,new Integer(count.intValue()+keywordCount));
        }

        // -- Tell the engine it was a good hit --
        goodHit=true;
    }
    else if ( keywordCount>=0 )
    {
        goodHit=true;
    }

    // -- On 5 hits tell the engine to stop --
    if (hits.size()>=5) searchEngine.stopSearch();

    return goodHit;
}
```

Compiling and running the WileySearcher

You can now compile and run the *WileySearcher* with these commands:

```
javac jwebdata/search/WileySearcher.java
```

```
java jwebdata.search.WileySearcher http://www.wiley.com/search?NS-search-
page=results&NS-collection=comp_docs&NS-query=ejb ejb
```

The results that follow are exactly what I was hoping to see the first time round, when using the *SimpleSearcher*. We have established the number of hits at each URL by counting the number of keyword occurrences ourselves in code:

```
URLs=5
7 hits at http://www.wiley.com/compbooks/catalog/31972-4.htm
15 hits at http://www.wiley.com/compbooks/catalog/33229-1.htm
5 hits at http://www.wiley.com/compbooks/catalog/40131-5.htm
9 hits at http://www.wiley.com/compbooks/catalog/38940-4.htm
3 hits at http://www.wiley.com/compbooks/catalog/31717-9.htm
```

Isn't it reassuring that if we arrange these results according to the number of hits (descending), the resulting order is exactly the same as that in Figure 6.4. In other words our hit counting corresponds with that of the original Wiley catalogue search function, which might leave you thinking we've not actually achieved anything.

I know you could get that information simply by submitting the query directly through your browser as in Figure 6.4, but you would not have captured the results into a Java program. Besides which, you wouldn't be able to perform my next trick, which is to search for '*ejb*' books but rank them according to how many times they also mention '*com*'. Here's the command for that slight of hand:

```
java jwebdata.search.WileySearcher http://www.wiley.com/search?NS-search-
page=results&NS-collection=comp_docs&NS-query=ejb com
```

And here are the results of that command:

```
URLs=5
18 hits at http://www.wiley.com/compbooks/catalog/31972-4.htm
29 hits at http://www.wiley.com/compbooks/catalog/33229-1.htm
20 hits at http://www.wiley.com/compbooks/catalog/40131-5.htm
17 hits at http://www.wiley.com/compbooks/catalog/38940-4.htm
52 hits at http://www.wiley.com/compbooks/catalog/31717-9.htm
```

If you think we're limited to searching web pages using the *SearchEngine* and *SimpleSearcher* that we've implemented here, think again. We can search any information source as long as there is a web-based interface that we can drive, and which presents its results as HTML.

For example, there's lots of information to be found in news groups, which we can search via the on-line interface provided by Google. Just use http://groups.google.com/groups?q=mykeyword&site=groups as the starting point for the search, like this:

```
java jwebdata.search.SimpleSearcher
http://groups.google.com/groups?q=mykeywordsite=groupsmykeyword
```

I've listed some sample output from that command below. As with the *WileySearcher* we might need to filter out the results that make sense, and to that end I've highlighted what I think to be the most useful results.

```
URLs=10

131 hits at
http://groups.google.com/groups?q=java&lr=&safe=off&rnum=1&ic=1&selm=99v15
f%24an2%241%40news.netmar.com

50 hits at http://groups.google.com/groups?q=java&lr=&safe=off&scoring=d
```

21 hits at
http://groups.google.com/groups?lr=&safe=off&group=comp.lang.java.developer

```
78 hits at http://groups.google.com/groups?q=java&site=groups

128 hits at
http://groups.google.com/groups?lr=&safe=off&ic=1&th=1da975571aa95681,1&se
ekm=99v15f%24an2%241%40news.netmar.com#p

1 hits at
http://groups.google.com/advanced_group_search?q=java&lr=&safe=off
```

13 hits at
http://groups.google.com/groups?lr=&safe=off&group=comp.lang.java.help

13 hits at
http://groups.google.com/groups?lr=&safe=off&group=comp.lang.java.programmer

16 hits at
http://groups.google.com/groups?lr=&safe=off&group=comp.lang.java.corba

15 hits at
http://groups.google.com/groups?lr=&safe=off&group=comp.lang.java.databases

It should be quite easy for you to spot what the usable results have in common, thus the *WileySearcher* could be transformed into the *GoogleSear-cher*. I leave that as an exercise.

6.5   Chapter Review

In this chapter we've implemented a core search engine in the form of a web crawler, which allows a breadth-first search to be initiated from any given starting point.

The details of determining what exactly we're looking for, and what to do with it once we've found it, have been factored out into a separate plug-in (a *SearchHandler*) that allows for a wide range of searching behaviour. Perhaps wider than you think. It's possible to conceive more advanced implementations of the *SearchHandler* interface, for example to search for combinations of keywords and maybe to do something much more interesting than simply counting the number of occurrences.

As it stands, this search engine implementation is suitable for traversing a web of HTML files that are connected via the standard hyper-linking mechanism. If your interests are biased towards XML you might like to think about adapting this to traverse a web of XML files that are connected via the XPointer mechanism. You can find more information about XPointer at http://www.w3.org/TR/xptr/. As a final exercise, why not combine the searching techniques from this chapter with your knowledge of servlets and applets from Chapters 2 and 5 in order to implement an on-line searching portal?

In the next chapter we'll look at how to take in data from email messages, rather than from the web, and how to transform the structure of those messages to make them susceptible to the same filtering and querying mechanisms as those for web data.

6.5.1   API classes and interfaces introduced in this chapter

No new classes or interfaces have been introduced in this chapter.

Mail Mining with Java

From the work we've done so far it would be tempting to consider the HTTP protocol as our only gateway to HTML and XML content. It may be true to say that the majority of the information available on the Internet, our local intranet, or local file system will be accessible via a URL – beginning *http:* or *file:* – which provides an address from which to *pull* the data. However, there is another source of data that may be suitable for mining, which works on the *push* principle. I'm referring to email.

Think about the volume of information you receive personally via this medium, most as plain text and an ever-increasing amount as HTML. Every day I receive a few eZines (not through choice) and an investment news bulletin that I am genuinely interested in. The latter is in HTML format that may be filtered – as any other HTML page – using the techniques I've described earlier, perhaps with a view to picking out only those news stories relating to the stocks I hold. I'm sure that in the near future I'll be receiving more XML content via email too.

There may be some value in mining email content from a personal perspective, but this value is dwarfed when you take a company wide perspective. Think about the volume of information that flows into any organization via email- in the form of product information requests, technical support queries, job applications to name a few.

7.1 The Design

In this chapter we'll implement a *MailParserWrapper* class that does for email what the *WebParserWrapper* does for web sites. It will collect incoming email messages and parse the content as plain text or, using the *HTMLParserWrap-*

per, as HTML. Once we've implemented that workhorse class I'll take you through an example of what you might want to do with those incoming messages, with the help of an additional class called *SMSRelay*.

The two classes for this chapter and their dependencies on existing classes from previous chapters are shown in Figure 7.1.

The existing *getElements(...)* method on *HTMLParserWrapper* takes a *UrlConnection* as the parameter, and uses this to obtain an *InputStream* containing the data. In the case of email there will be no URL, hence no *UrlConnection*, so we'll be getting hold of an *InputStream* directly and passing this into a redefined version of the *getElements(...)* method on *HTMLParserWrapper*. Therefore we'll be making a minor modification to the *HTMLParserWrapper* class that was introduced in Chapter 3.

I have limited the content types to plain text and HTML, to keep it simple and to give you some scope for enhancement. How about making it work with XML too?

7.1.1 Brief introduction to JavaMail

JavaMail is a standard Java extension, hence the required classes may be found within the *javax.** package structure. It was originally provided as a separate distribution for use with the J2SE SDK, and now comes bundled with the J2EE SDK version 1.3.

In the same way that JDBC separates the protocol specific database drivers from the data access API, so *JavaMail* separates the protocol specific mail drivers from the mail API. Thus it is possible to plug-in support for various mail systems: past, present, and future. In this chapter we'll be using the POP3 provider (or *driver*, if you prefer) that comes with the standard distribution.

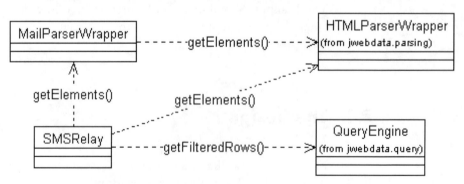

Figure 7.1 UML class diagram for package jwebdata.mail

Post Office Protocol (POP) is the most popular mechanism for retrieval of email messages. It's not the only option provided by the *JavaMail* distribution, you have the choice of IMAP too, but I've chosen what I think is the lowest common denominator to be of interest to the largest number of readers. Since the emphasis of this chapter is on mail *mining*, i.e. collecting information, we won't be looking at the additional protocols – notably Simple Mail Transfer Protocol (SMTP) – for sending messages.

7.2   Parsing Email Messages

As I said earlier, a new *MailParserWrapper* class will do for email messages what the *MailParserWrapper* does for web sites. It will collect incoming email messages and parse the content as plain text or as HTML.

7.2.1   MailParserWrapper

The basic shell of the *MailParserWrapper* will be as shown here:

```
// ** Code taken from jwebdata/mail/MailParserWrapper.java **

package jwebdata.mail;

import java.io.*;
import java.util.*;

import javax.mail.*;
import javax.activation.*;
import javax.mail.internet.*;

import jwebdata.parsing.*;

/**
  * Email equivalent of WebParserWrapper
  */
public class MailParserWrapper
{
}
```

Collecting and processing messages

All the hard work will be done within the *getElements(...)* and *processMess-*

age(...) methods. I'll start with *getElements(...)*.

getElements(...)

This method will have exactly the same purpose as the *getElements(...)* method
on *WebParserWrapper*. We won't be addressing the mail server via a URL so
the signature will be altered to allow specification of a mail server, mail port
(specify -1 as default), POP mailbox user name and POP mailbox password.
After setting up a mail session (*javax.mail.Session*) we'll use these details to
connect to the POP mailbox (*javax.mail.Store*).

From the mail store we'll get hold of the default folder (*javax.mail.Folder*), if
we can, and from it the *inbox* folder for incoming messages. Finally we'll get an
array of messages (*javax.mail.Message*) from the folder by invoking the *get-
Messages(...)* method.

On that final point it's worth noting that the messages might not actually be
fetched straightaway because *JavaMail* takes a lazy approach to collecting
message data. More about that when we look at the *processMessage(...)*
method. For now, take a look at the code for *getElements(...)*:

```
// ** Code taken from jwebdata/mail/MailParserWrapper.java **

/**
 * Method to get a key/value list of HTML or plain text elements
 * of messages originating at a POP mail server.
 */
public Vector getElements(String popServer, int port, String popUser
  , String popPassword) throws Exception
{
    Store store=null;
    Folder folder=null;

    Vector elements=new Vector();

    try
    {
      // -- Set up a mail Session --
      Properties props = System.getProperties();
      Session session = Session.getDefaultInstance(props, null);

      // -- Get a mail Store and connect to it --
      store = session.getStore("pop3");
      store.connect(popServer, -1, popUser, popPassword);

      // -- Get the default folder and its INBOX --

      folder = store.getDefaultFolder();
      if (folder == null)
        throw new Exception("No default folder");
```

```
      folder = folder.getFolder("INBOX");
      if (folder == null)
        throw new Exception("No POP3 INBOX");

      // -- Open the folder for read only --
      folder.open(Folder.READ_ONLY);

      // -- Prepare to fetch the messages --
      Message msgs = folder.getMessages();

      // -- Add elements of each message to cumulative elements --
      for (int msgNum = 0; msgNum < msgs.length; msgNum++)
      {
        Vector msgElements=processMessage(msgs[msgNum],msgNum);
        elements.addAll(msgElements);
      }

      return elements;
    }
    catch (Exception e)
    {
      e.printStackTrace();
      throw new Exception(e.toString());
    }
    finally
    {
      // -- Close down nicely --
      try
      {
        if (folder!=null) folder.close(false);
        if (store!=null) store.close();
      }
      catch (Exception e) {}
    }
}
```

You will have seen that, as we iterate through the list of messages, we invoke a *processMessage(...)* method for each one.

processMessage(...)

Remember what I told you about lazy collection of message data? In this code we'll be calling various *getXXX(...)* methods to retrieve the subject, sender(s) and content of the incoming message and chances are that each piece of information will be fetched *on demand* when we make the call. In most cases this lazy approach will make perfect sense because we wouldn't want to fetch a huge attachment relating to an uninteresting subject.

For each message our aim will be to represent the structure of the message in the same way as we represented the structure of HTML and XML content in web pages, as a vector of *SourceElement* items each having a key and content. Thus the headers of the collection of messages in our mailbox might be represented like this.

```
.msg[0].subject[0] How are you?
.msg[0].from[0] A Friend (afriend+somemail.com)
.msg[1].subject[0] Chasing my invoice.
.msg[1].from[0] Accountant (accountant@acompany.com)
```

You will see already that this representation opens up our email messages to the kind of filtering and querying that I described in Chapter 4. Think about all the other fields that we have to filter on; date, recipient(s), priority, and so on.

In addition to the header information, there will be content for each message. This content may be susceptible to further subdivision, by which I mean parsing. It is possible to establish the type of mail content, just as it was for web content, and we can parse it accordingly. In the following code you will see that we're testing the content type and running our existing *HTMLParser-Wrapper* if the message contains HTML data, otherwise we employ some simple plain text parsing.

```java
// ** Code taken from jwebdata/mail/MailParserWrapper.java **

/**
 * Method to process an individual mail message.
 */
private Vector processMessage(javax.mail.Message message, int msgNum)
  throws Exception
{
    Vector elements=new Vector();

    try
    {
      // -- Get the subject and add as an element --
      String subject=message.getSubject();
      SourceElement sourceElement
        =new SourceElement(".msg["+msgNum+"].subject[0]",subject);
      elements.addElement(sourceElement);

      // -- Get one or more senders and add as elements --
      Address senders=message.getFrom();
      for (int r=0; r<senders.length; r++)
      {
          String thisSender=senders[r].toString();
          sourceElement=new SourceElement(".msg["+msgNum+"].from["+r+"]"
            ,thisSender);
```

```
                    elements.addElement(sourceElement);
            }

            // -- Get the content InputStream --
            InputStream is = message.getInputStream();

            // -- Get the content type and decide how to parse it --
            String contentType=message.getContentType();
            sourceElement=new SourceElement(".contentType["+msgNum+"]"
              ,contentType);
            elements.addElement(sourceElement);

            if (contentType.equals("text/html"))
            {
                // -- Parse content as HTML --
                HTMLParserWrapper htmlParser=new HTMLParserWrapper();
                Vector htmlElements=htmlParser.getElements("file:",is);
                for (int i=0; i<htmlElements.size();i++)
                {
                  sourceElement=(SourceElement) htmlElements.elementAt(i);
                  sourceElement=new SourceElement(".msg["+msgNum+"]"
                    +sourceElement.getKey(),sourceElement.getContent());
                  elements.addElement(sourceElement);
                }
            }
            else
            {
                // -- Parse content as text --
                BufferedReader reader
                  =new BufferedReader(new InputStreamReader(is));
                int lineNum=0;
                String thisLine=reader.readLine();
                while (thisLine!=null)
                {
                    sourceElement=new SourceElement(".msg["+msgNum
                      +"].body["+lineNum+"]",thisLine);
                    elements.addElement(sourceElement);
                    lineNum++;
                    thisLine=reader.readLine();
                }
            }
        }
        catch (Exception e)
        {
            throw new Exception(e.toString());
        }
        return elements;
    }
```

To keep it simple I've assumed that all incoming messages will be single-part

```
.msg[0].subject[0] Better Security Through Biometrics?
.msg[0].from[0] Junk Mail Sender <junk@junkmail.junk.com>
.contentType[0] text/html
.msg[0].title[0].text[0] Better Security Through Biometrics?

...
.msg[0].table[0].tr[0].td[0].table[0].tr[0].td[2].text[0] MON APR 16, 2001
.msg[0].table[0].tr[0].td[0].table[0].tr[2].td[1].text[0] To unsubscribe click
.msg[0].table[0].tr[0].td[0].table[0].tr[2].td[1].a[0].@href[0] http://redir.iz.com/r.pl?rd=35:4:201:::7923431
.msg[0].table[0].tr[0].td[0].table[0].tr[2].td[1].a[0].text[0] here

...
.msg[0].table[0].tr[1].td[0].table[0].tr[1].td[0].table[0].tr[0].td[0].text[0] Better Security Through Biometrics?
.msg[0].table[0].tr[1].td[0].table[0].tr[1].td[0].table[0].tr[1].td[0].text[0] Biometrics promises to make online security easier and more complete.
.msg[0].table[0].tr[1].td[0].table[0].tr[1].td[0].table[0].tr[1].td[0].a[0].@href[0] http://redir.iz.com/r.pl?rd=35:1:201:1135::7923431
.msg[0].table[0].tr[1].td[0].table[0].tr[1].td[0].table[0].tr[1].td[0].a[0].text[0] Click here for more|
```

Figure 7.2   HTML email content

messages comprising only one body of HTML or plain text. The *JavaMail* API also supports reception of multipart messages that may have several content bodies of various types: plain text, HTML, XML, or GIF files to name a few. It's beyond my scope to go into too much detail on that, but I'll help you out by saying that to handle multipart messages you'll need some code like this:

```
Part messagePart=message;
Object content=messagePart.getContent ();

// -- Get the first body part if it is a multipart message --
if (content instanceof Multipart)
  messagePart=((Multipart)content).getBodyPart(0);

// --Get the content type --
String contentType=messagePart.getContentType();
```

As I told you earlier, this implementation will handle (I mean *parse*) HTML or plain text content. I'll now show you the treatment of each kind of data.

Handling HTML content

If we determine the content to be HTML we delegate the parsing task to the *HTMLParserWrapper* from Chapter 3. When I ran the *MailParserWrapper* for the first time I was lucky (if that's the right word) to have some junk mail containing HTML content waiting in my *inbox*. I've presented the result in Figure 7.2 with some of the names changed to protect the guilty.

The structure of the HTML content should be very familiar to you except that each element key is pre-fixed with a message indicator of the form *.msg[X]*. This is necessary because we'll be processing several incoming messages in a single sweep so we need to distinguish the content belonging to each one. The *HTMLParserWrapper* has no concept of message numbers so we're pre-pending that information back in the *MailParserWrapper* as shown again here:

```
// -- Parse content as HTML --
HTMLParserWrapper htmlParser=new HTMLParserWrapper();
Vector htmlElements=htmlParser.getElements("file:",is);
for (int i=0; i<htmlElements.size();i++)
{
  sourceElement=(SourceElement) htmlElements.elementAt(i);
  sourceElement=new SourceElement(".msg["+msgNum+"]"
    +sourceElement.getKey(),sourceElement.getContent());
  elements.addElement(sourceElement);
}
```

If you look closely at the call to *htmlParser.getElements(...)* you'll see that we're passing argument *'is'* (which is an *InputStream*) in the space that you would expect to see a *UrlConnection*. We don't have a *UrlConnection* because we have no URL, but we do have an *InputStream* from which the content may be read. So I've added a new *getElements(...)* method to *HTMLParserWrapper*, which is almost identical to the original one except that it has a different signature. The new method is an addition to the original, not a replacement and is shown below.

```
// ** Code taken from jwebdata/parsing/HTMLParserWrapper.java **

/**
  * Method to get a key/value list of HTML or XML elements from baseURL.
  */
public Vector getElements(String baseURL, InputStream inputStream)
  throws Exception
{
    // -- Initialise the member variables --
    tagHistory=new Vector();
    countHistory=new Vector();
    countHistory.addElement(new Hashtable());
    elements=new Vector();
    currentURL=new URL(baseURL);

    // -- Run the parser on the HTML content --
    InputStreamReader urlReader=new InputStreamReader(inputStream);
    new ParserDelegator().parse(urlReader,this,true);
    urlReader.close();

    return elements;
}
```

Handling plain text content

An ever larger proportion of email is being sent as HTML these days, but it's probably still true to say that plain text accounts for the majority of the email content flying around the globe. The *getElements(...)* method on *MailParser-Wrapper* contains a few lines of code to parse any non-HTML content as plain text. As a reminder it's listed again here:

```
// -- Parse content as text --
BufferedReader reader
  =new BufferedReader(new InputStreamReader(is));
int lineNum=0;
String thisLine=reader.readLine();
while (thisLine!=null)
{
  sourceElement=new SourceElement(".msg["+msgNum
    +"].body["+lineNum+"]",thisLine);
  elements.addElement(sourceElement);
  lineNum++;
  thisLine=reader.readLine();
}
```

For each line of text that we read from the input stream, we're creating a new *SourceElement* with the line of text as its content and with a key in the form *.msg[msgNum].body[lineNum]*. To test it I sent a message to myself, which was parsed as follows:

```
.msg[0].subject[0] Web Mining with Java
.msg[0].from[0] "Tony Loton @ LOTONtech" <tony@lotontech.com>
.contentType[0] text/plain;
    charset="iso-8859-1"
.msg[0].body[0] Hi Tony,
.msg[0].body[1]
.msg[0].body[2] Just a short message to congratulate myself on writing the
new book, Web
.msg[0].body[3] Mining with Java.
.msg[0].body[4]
.msg[0].body[5] Kind regards,
.msg[0].body[6]
.msg[0].body[7] Tony.
```

You can take a look at Figure 7.3 to see how that parsed content relates to my original message, as it would appear in Microsoft Outlook. Notice how the text 'Web Mining with Java' is split across a line.

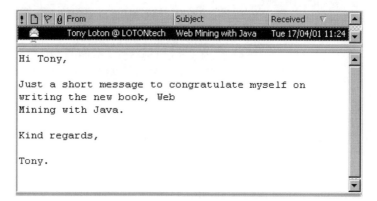

Figure 7.3   Example text email

Compiling and running the MailParserWrapper

For convenience we'll add a *main(...)* method to *MailParserWrapper*, allowing us to test it with a command line like this:

```
java jwebdata.mail.MailParserWrappermyMailServer myPopUserName myPassword
```

You should be able to take suitable values for those arguments from your mail program, e.g. Microsoft Outlook, or by looking through the information provided by your ISP. Unfortunately I can't make it less cryptic by telling you my own account details.

The code for the *main(...)* method, which collects messages from the specified server and prints the parsed content of each message, is shown here:

```java
// ** Code taken from jwebdata/mail/MailParserWrapper.java **
/**
 * A main() method to test it.
 */
public static void main(String args)
{
    try
    {
        // -- Initialise a MailParserWrapper --
        MailParserWrapper mailParser=new MailParserWrapper();

        // -- Get elements from this POP3 server --
        Vector elements
          =mailParser.getElements(args[0],-1,args[1],args[2]);

        // -- Print them out --
```

```
for (int i=0; i<elements.size(); i++)
{
    SourceElement thisElement
      =(SourceElement) elements.elementAt(i);
    System.out.println(thisElement.getKey()+"="
      +thisElement.getContent());
}
}
}
catch (Exception ex) {ex.printStackTrace();}
}
```

In order to compile the *MailParserWrapper* you'll need to make sure that you have the *JavaMail* classes included as part of your SDK, as described in Appendix A. You can now compile and run the *Mail ParserWrapper* by issuing these commands:

```
javac jwebdata\mail\MailParserWrapper.java
java jwebdata.mail.MailParserWrapper myMailServer myPopUserName myPassword
```

Now that you know how to capture email messages into your Java program, what will you do with them? This book is not just about collecting data, but also about re-presenting that data in new ways and novel combinations, so a novel way to re-present those email messages follows.

7.3 Email to SMS Example

My ISP provides a really useful service that sends a Short Message Service (SMS) notification to my mobile phone each time I receive an email message. A typical message as it would appear on my phone is:

```
To: "Tony @ LOTONtech <tony@lotontech.com>" From "Wiley Publishing
<someone@wiley.co.uk>" Subject: Your New Book.
```

It means I can go out and about safe in the knowledge that I won't miss any important messages, and I don't need to periodically dial my ISP just to see if new mail has arrived. On a personal note, as I write this I'm sitting by the coast in Scotland overlooking the Isle of Arran. No telephone socket, no network connection, but I do have my trusty SMS notifications. It's so useful that I thought we'd implement something similar here.

Fortunately there are quite a few web sites offering free SMS services. They

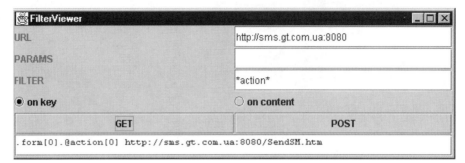

Figure 7.4   SMS form action

Figure 7.5   SMS form method

allow you to type your message and destination phone number into a simple HTML form, press send, and off it goes. This is great news for us because we have the technology to drive such web-based interfaces by simulating form submissions from within Java programs.

Impact of Web Site Changes

Some of the examples in this chapter are based around data taken directly from the web, rather than from sample data sources that I have provided as home-grown servlets or static HTML/XML files. Whilst this is good for realism, the content and format of web sites may change such that these examples will no longer run exactly as presented. There is an implicit exercise and an opportunity for you to test your understanding by bringing any such examples up-to-date with the help of the *FilterViewer* from Chapter 4.

I found a free SMS service provider at http://sms.gt.com.ua:8080, and with the help of the *FilterViewer* from Chapter 4 I worked out how to drive the online interface. Figures 7.4 to 7.7 show how I determined the appropriate form action,

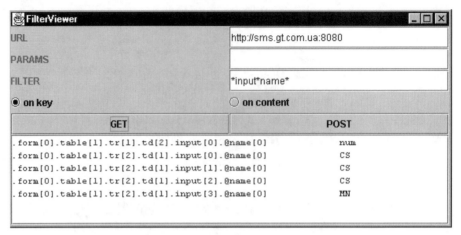

Figure 7.6   SMS form input names

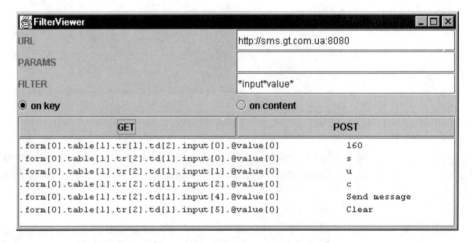

Figure 7.7   SMS form input values

submission method, and input parameters. As you look at these figures try to match up the default values (Figure 7.7) with the input parameter names (Figure 7.6), and note that input parameter *MN* has no default value. In case you're wondering, that parameter will take the number of the destination mobile phone.

There's one extra parameter, to take the message text itself, that may be determined by running the *FilterViewer* again with the filter text '*textarea*' applied (not shown).

I'm not recommending this particular service to you, particularly as there is a restriction of two free messages per day. However, if you're interested you can see in Figure 7.8 how I ran a test submission, again using the *FilterViewer*. I'd like to

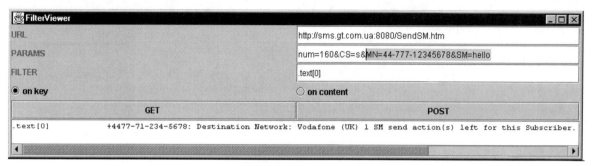

Figure 7.8   SMS submission

draw your attention to the submission parameters for the destination phone number and the message content, highlighted, and the filter text that I have applied in order to extract the confirmation message.

In theory we now have the all the tools we need to capture incoming email messages and send them on as SMS notifications automatically. Let's turn that theory into practice.

7.3.1 SMSRelay

The *SMSRelay* class will have a just one method, *main(...)*, based on the *main(...)* method of the *MailParserViewer*. Whereas the original version simply prints out the incoming messages, this revised version will send them on as SMS notifications – comprising sender and subject – through the free web based SMS interface.

```java
// ** Code taken from jwebdata/mail/SMSRelay.java **
package jwebdata.mail;

import java.util.*;

import jwebdata.query.*;
import jwebdata.parsing.*;

/**
  * Class to relay email messages to a mobile phone as SMS notifications.
  */
public class SMSRelay
{
    /**
      * Everything happens within the main() method.
      */
    public static void main(String args)
```

```
{
  try
  {
    // -- Initialisation --
    MailParserWrapper mailParser=new MailParserWrapper();
    WebParserWrapper webParser=new WebParserWrapper();
    QueryEngine queryEngine=new QueryEngine();

    // -- Get elements from the POP3 server --
    Vector elements
      =mailParser.getElements(args[0],-1,args[1],args[2]);

    // -- Filter messages for sender and subject --
    Vector filters=new Vector();
    filters.addElement(".msg[*].from[*]");
    filters.addElement(".msg[*].subject[*]");
    Vector messageHeaders
      =queryEngine.getFilteredRows(elements,filters);

    // -- Set up a new filter for SMS confirmation --
    filters=new Vector();
    filters.addElement(".text[0]");

    // -- Loop through the email message headers --
    for (int msgNum=0; msgNum<messageHeaders.size(); msgNum++)
    {
      // -- Get filtered elements for 'from' and 'subject' --
      SourceElement thisHeader
        =(SourceElement) messageHeaders.elementAt(msgNum);
      String from=thisHeader[0].getContent();
      String subject=thisHeader[1].getContent();

      // -- Output progress message --
      String phone=args[3];
      System.out.println("Sent message: "+subject);
      System.out.println("from: "+from);
      System.out.println("to phone: "+phone);

      // -- Peform the SMS submission --
      String params="num=160&CS=s&MN="+phone
        +"&SM="+from+" / "+subject;
      Vector smsElements=webParser.getElements(
        "http://sms.gt.com.ua:8080/SendSM.htm",params
        ,WebParserWrapper.POST);

      // -- Get the SMS confirmation result and output it --
      String result="";
      Vector resultVector
        =queryEngine.getFilteredRows(smsElements,filters);

      if (resultVector.size()>0)
```

```
         {
             SourceElement resultRow
               =(SourceElement) resultVector.elementAt(0);
             result=resultRow[0].getContent();
         }
         else
         {
             result="UNKNOWN!";
         }
         System.out.println("with result: "+result);
         System.out.println();
       }
     }
   }
   catch (Exception ex) ·ex.printStackTrace();}
 }
}
```

I sent myself a couple of email messages as a test and ran the *SMSRelay* program with a command like the one shown here:

```
java jwebdata.mail.SMSRelay myMailServer myPopUserName myPassword 44-777-
1234567
```

I've listed the output from the *SMSRelay* program below with an obfuscated telephone number and, although I can't show you, the messages really did arrive at my phone a few seconds later. Take my word for it.

Sent message: Seasons Greetings
from: "Tony Loton @LOTONtech" <tony@lotontech.com>
to phone: 44-777-1234567
with result: +447-77-123-4567: Destination Network: Vodafone
(UK) 1 SM send action(s) left for this Subscriber. Message sent.
Your Web ID:
08341856 Click

Sent message: I hope you are well.
from: "Tony Loton @ LOTONtech" <tony@lotontech.com>
to phone: 44-777-1234567
with result: +447-77-123-4567: Destination Network: Vodafone
(UK) 0 SM send action(s) left for this Subscriber. Message sent.
Your Web ID:
08341857 Click

I couldn't believe my luck so I tried it again straightaway, and that's how I discovered the two free messages per day limitation. Look at the result messages this time.

Sent message: `Seasons Greetings`
from: `"Tony Loton @ LOTONtech" <tony@lotontech.com>`
to phone: `44-777-1234567`
with result: `+447-77-123-4567: Destination Network: Vodafone`
`(UK) Daily SM limit for this Subscriber is reached. Message`
`canceled.`

Sent message: `I hope you are well.`
from: `"Tony Loton @ LOTONtech" <tony@ lotontech.com>`
to phone: `44-777-1234567`
with result: `+447-77-123-4567: Destination Network: Vodafone`
`(UK) Daily SM limit for this Subscriber is reached. Message`
`canceled.`

Compiling and running the SMSRelay

There's not much to tell you really. You can compile the *SMSRelay*, and the *MailParserWrapper* if you haven't already, by issuing the following command. And to run it, take another look at my example given immediately above.

```
javac jwebdata/mail/*.java
```

Of course, since putting the example together that particular web site might no longer exist or its format might have changed. So in trying out this example you'll need to be prepared to find your own free SMS service to jump on the back of, and you'll need to use the *FilterViewer* to figure out how to drive it. It's a good opportunity to really get familiar with the tools and techniques that I've introduced.

7.4 XML in Email

I've demonstrated the mail mining principle in terms of HTML and plain text content. As an exercise you might wish to support, as a third alternative, the parsing of XML content in email. You could do this by extending the *MailPar-*

serWrapper to make use of the *XMLParserWrapper* in the same way that the *WebParserWrapper* did. As a reminder you might want to look back at Chapter 3.

What I have in mind for XML in email is a kind of e-commerce application that allows books to be ordered by sending an XML email message to the bookstore or direct to the publisher. Here is an example XML order – with an inline DTD – that could be transmitted via email:

```
<?xml version="1.0" encoding="ISO-8859-1" standalone="yes"?>

<!DOCTYPE Order [
  <!ELEMENT Order (Customer,Address,Item*)>

  <!ELEMENT Customer (#PCDATA)>
  <!ELEMENT Address (#PCDATA)>

  <!ELEMENT Item (Title,Author,Quantity)>
  <!ELEMENT Title (#PCDATA)>
  <!ELEMENT Author (#PCDATA)>
  <!ELEMENT Quantity (#PCDATA)>
]>

<Order>
  <Customer>Mickey Mouse</Customer>
  <Address>Disneyland, Paris.</Address>
  <Item>
    <Title>Web Mining with Java</Title>
    <Author>Tony Loton</Author>
    <Quantity>5</Quantity>
  </Item>
  <Item>
      <Title>Document Warehousing and Text Mining</Title>
      <Author>Dan Sullivan</Author>
      Quantity>1</Quantity>
    </Item>
</Order>
```

Our *MailParserWrapper* could be used to automate the collection of such orders, the *XMLParserWrapper* could parse them, and the *QueryEngine* could be used flatten the hierarchic structures into a form suitable for loading straight into the order-processing database, i.e:

```
Mickey Mouse|Disneyland, Paris.|Web Mining with Java|Tony Loton|
Mickey Mouse|Disneyland, Paris.|Document Warehousing and Text Mining|Dan
Sullivan|
```

For your information, that was achieved using the *QueryEngine* to apply a few filters to the parsed XML content, with code like this:

```
String url="file:data/book-order.xml";
Vector filters=new Vector();
filters.addElement(".Order[0].Customer[0].#pcdata[0]");
filters.addElement(".Order[0].Address[0].#pcdata[0]");
filters.addElement(".Order[0].Item[*].Title[0].#pcdata[0]");
filters.addElement(".Order[0].Item[*].Author[0].#pcdata[0]");

// -- Parse the elements (at URL) --
WebParserWrapper webParser=new WebParserWrapper();
Vector elements=webParser.getElements(url,"",WebParserWrapper.GET);

// -- Get rows that satisfy the filters ---
QueryEngine queryEngine=new QueryEngine();
Vector rows=queryEngine.getFilteredRows(elements,filters);
```

You might have noticed that I put the words *(at URL)* in brackets because that's what I've done as a demonstration. What I'm suggesting you'd really like to do is parse the elements direct from the email *inbox*.

7.5 More Ideas

While writing this chapter I've had some more ideas for combining the techniques that we've learnt so far, and for adding some useful functionality on top. These ideas are not entirely related to (or should I say *limited* to) email but each one has its origins in what we've covered in this chapter.

7.5.1 Web to SMS

As we have relayed the content of email messages in the form of SMS notifications, so we could transmit any web content in this way. As an example, think back to the share price information service that we implemented in Chapter 5 in the form of the *PortalServlet* and the *PortalApplet*. Now what do you think about the idea of an SMS portal?

Not a portal in the same sense, you understand, since it would be strictly one-way. However, each user could set up a profile on the server – which is possible via a web interface – that determines his or her upper and lower limits for *buy* and *sell* notifications. We could create a Java-based daemon process that checks the share prices exactly as shown in Chapter 5, and when a percentage rise or fall of a particular share matches a particular user's profile he or she could be sent an SMS notification like this:

```
BUY <ARM HOLDINGS> 256.00p -11.72%
```

You may well be familiar with this concept and you're probably already receiving notifications like this quite regularly to keep you up to date with the latest share prices, weather forecasts, lottery numbers, and sports results. However, as you now have the tools to become a provider of such services why not set up a portal that allows users to sign up for a wide range of information services? You could extract the relevant information from the best web sites, using the web parser(s) and filter(s), and broadcast it in SMS form to the mobile phones of your registered users. And they won't need a WAP-enabled phone. You can see a good example of what I mean at the FTMarketWatch site via URL http://www.ft.com/mobile/sms_overview.html.

When you plug it all together, with the original *SMSRelay*, the complete schematic for what I have in mind is shown in Figure 7.9.

7.5.2 Email as a search source

I'm not thinking about searching email messages themselves, though of course

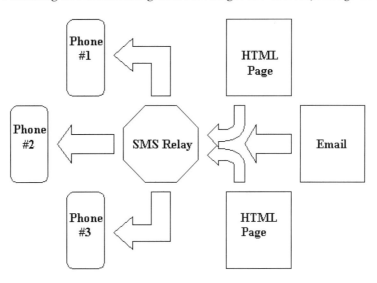

Figure 7.9 SMS relay complete schematic

that's possible. I have another idea, which builds on Chapter 6.

HTML content within email messages will invariably contain links to additional web-based -- that is URL-based -- content. If you're interested in a particular email message, chances are you'll be interested in the additional pages that it references. Think of the original message as a recommendation to visit a particular web site.

Now why not take up that recommendation by supplying one or more of the linked pages as a starting point for the search engine that we implemented in Chapter 6?

7.5.3   Speaking email

Suppose you receive an SMS notification relating to a message that you definitely don't want to miss. You won't have access to email for some time and there's not enough information in the SMS notification for you to guess the content of the message. So what do you do?

Well I suspect it's no accident that my ISP provides minimal information in the form of SMS notifications, despite the fact that SMS allows messages long enough to provide quite a bit more context for each message. A bit of a loss-leader I think, to encourage use of another handy service called *Speech-Mail*. Just call the *SpeechMail* number to have your messages read to you electronically.

I'm quite interested in this idea because I've been toying with a 100 per cent Java text-to-speech idea, which uses the *JavaSound* API. Through a process of concatenating allophones (atomic speech sound segments) to form whole words I managed to come up with something electronic-sounding but just about understandable. By listening carefully to my ISPs implementation I've concluded that they use the same approach, at least in part, but I doubt they've used Java.

By its very nature there's no way to present this ideas in words and pictures; you have to hear it to believe it. And you can. Take a look at my *JavaWorld* article http://www.javaworld.com/javaworld/jw-10-2001/jw-1026-javamail-html for a fuller coverage of the *JavaMail* API and a practical demonstration of the email-to-speech idea.

If I've not yet whetted your appetite, think about all of those situations in which its impractical to take in information through the visual sense. Like when you're driving. How about an in-car email reader, or even an in-car web page reader? Not to mention the scope for extending the accessibility of information for people with visual disabilities.

7.6   Chapter Review

In this chapter we've considered how HTML content, plain text content, and even XML content included in email messages may be parsed (and filtered) in exactly the same way as if it had originated at a web page. In that context we've covered the basics of the *JavaMail* API for fetching incoming messages from a server-based message store.

As collecting the information is only half the story of this book, we've also looked at an interesting way to re-present the email content to mobile users in the form of SMS notifications. We've also highlighted the prospect of transmitting other content, and not just email, in this way too.

Finally, I've introduced some other ideas that sprung into my mind as I was writing this chapter, like talking email and the use of email messages as the starting point for web searches. Food for thought.

7.6.1   API classes and interfaces introduced in this chapter

The following Java API classes and interfaces have been introduced for the first time in this chapter's code examples:

- *java.util.Properties* represents a persistent set of properties that can be saved to, or loaded from, a stream.

- *javax.mail.Address* is an abstract class that models the addresses within an email message.

- *javax.mail.Folder* is an abstract class that represents a folder for mail messages, which may contain subfolders.

- *javax.mail.Message* represents an email message having content and a set of attributes along with a message state.

- *javax.mail.Session* represents a mail session that may be unshared or shared between multiple applications.

- *javax.mail.Store* is an abstract class that models a message store for holding and retrieving messages via an access protocol.

8

Introduction to Text Mining

The subject of this chapter is text mining, and so that we all agree on what we mean by that I'll start with a couple of definitions pulled from other works:

'. . . the art and science of extracting information and knowledge from text'
Document Warehousing and Text Mining (Dan Sullivan, 2001).

'. . . looking for patterns in text . . . to extract information that is useful for particular purposes'
Data Mining (Witten and Frank, 1999).

In this chapter we'll look at how some simple Java could be used as the basis for extracting information from text. To extract information from text we first need to understand the structure of the text. I don't mean the explicit structure of marked-up text that is delimited with HTML and XML tags, but the implicit structure of the text resulting from its conformance to the rules of grammar.

8.1 The Design

Figure 8.1 shows you how individual (English) words may be classified – as *determiners*, *nouns*, *verbs* and so on – and then combined into larger language

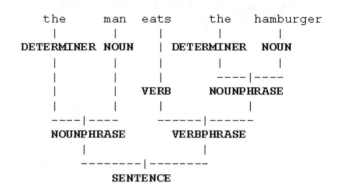

Figure 8.1   Sample phrase structure

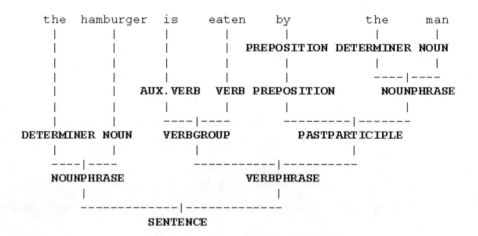

Figure 8.2   Passive phrase structure

units, such as *verb phrases* and *noun phrases*, to form complete sentences. Determining the phrase structure of a sentence in this way is the first step towards understanding the syntax and semantics of the sentence.

An understanding of the syntax is the basis for some simple structural tricks like turning an active sentence (Figure 8.1) into a passive sentence (Figure 8.2). To perform that trick we need to know the phrase structure of the original sentence. We also need a dictionary, or lexicon, of word forms, and some transformation rules.

Such tricks may be fully automated (see notes on Noam Chomsky in Section 8.6) providing we have a big enough lexicon and a good enough set of rules for each language, not limited to English, that we wish to use. At no point do we actually need to know what the sentence really means, i.e. its semantics.

Though it's not a trivial task, we could begin to understand the sentence semantics by using the phrase structure to determine a set of real-world objects (nouns), their interactions (verbs) and their properties (adjectives). By analysing a large number of sentences we could begin to build a knowledge base containing information about which objects typically interact with which other objects, under what circumstances, and in what ways: a *semantic network*.

We won't be transforming sentences here, and certainly not building a real-world knowledge base. In fact we won't even be attempting to determine the complete phrase structure of a sentence, but we'll take the first important step. What we'll implement here is a parser, called *TextParserWrapper*, that will determine the possible types (noun, verb and so on) for each word within a given sentence.

So that we can perform some text mining operations without fully understanding the phrase structure of input sentences, we'll also implement a simpler *FeatureExtractor* class to demonstrate a more straightforward approach.

Figure 8.3 shows the classes that we'll implement in this chapter. Although the *TextParserWrapper* is not itself dependent on any of our other classes, you will see that we're coupling it up with our *WebParserWrapper* (from Chapter 3) and the *QueryEngine* (from Chapter 4) just for testing. The *FeatureExtractor* is necessarily coupled with the *Operator* class from Chapter 4.

While the *TextParserWrapper* and the *FeatureExtractor* will both take input sentences in the form of simple text strings, the idea would be that such

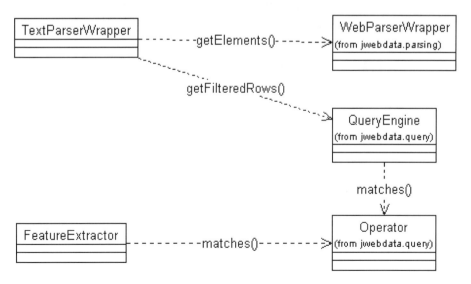

Figure 8.3   UML class diagram for package 'jwebdata.text'

text strings would have their origin in parsed data taken from web pages and/or email messages. Thus I envisage a higher level UML diagram that shows a text mining application class coupled with the *WebParserWrapper* (from Chapter 3), the *MailParserWrapper* (from Chapter 7) and the *TextParser-Wrapper* (from this chapter).

Impact of Web Site Changes

Some of the examples in this chapter are based around data taken directly from the web, rather than from sample data sources that I have provided as home-grown servlets or static HTML/XML files. Whilst this is good for realism, content and format of web sites may change such that these examples will no longer run exactly as presented. There is an implicit exercise and an opportunity for you to test your understanding by bringing any such examples up to date with the help of the FilterViewer from Chapter 4.

8.2 Basic Text Parsing

We need to determine the type (noun, verb, determiner etc.) of each word within the sentence, and for that job we need a lexicon. Such a lexicon would be far to big to list in this book and I don't think for one minute that you would want to type it all in. So we'll take a smarter approach and make use of a lexicon compiled by someone else.

8.2.1 WordNet

The *WordNet* lexicon has been put together by Princeton University , and the great news is that you can use it for free! You can do what you like with the program(s), the database, and the documentation, without fear of copyright infringement as long as you label your usage with the original License State-ment that I have listed in Appendix D. If that news wasn't good enough, I can also tell you that there is a live web-based on-line interface to the *WordNet* database. We can drive that interface, and filter the results, using the tech-niques that should by now be very familiar to you. Take a look at Figures 8.4 and 8.5 to see how the on-line interface works.

I used the *FilterViewer* that we implemented in Chapter 4 to run a test submission for the word 'customers', and to filter the results for the essential text. If you look at Figure 8.6 you will see that we have now gained access to

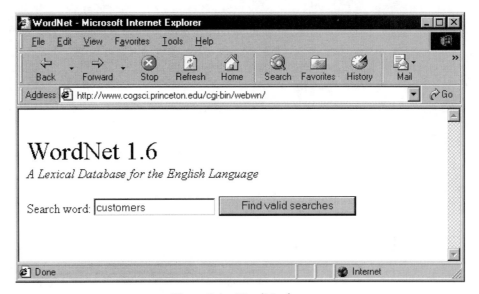

Figure 8.4   WordNet form

the vital information that the word *customers*, listed in canonical form as *customer*, is a *noun*.

Upon issuing a similar submission for the word 'knowing' I was rewarded with three possible interpretations, as you can see in Figure 8.7:

- . . . The noun 'knowing' . . .

- The verb 'knowing' . . .

- The adjective 'knowing'.

Thus the word 'knowing' has three possible (or candidate) types. As a general rule we'll need to handle several candidate types for each word.

We'll implement a new class, the *TextParserWrapper*, that will take plain text as input and produce a list of the constituent words (with their candidate types) as output.

8.2.2   TextParserWrapper

The basic class definition will be:

```
// ** Code taken from jwebdata/mail/TextParserWrapper.java **
package jwebdata.text;
```

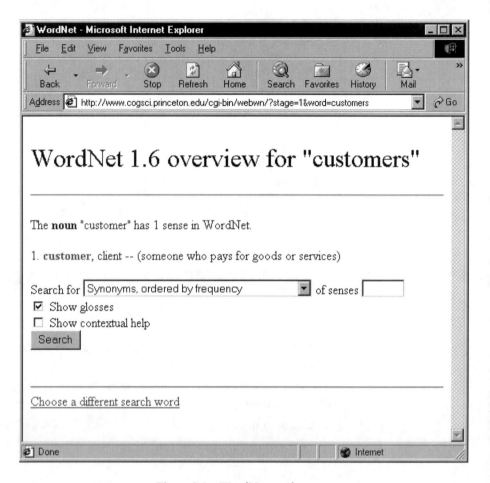

Figure 8.5   WordNet results page

```
import java.util.*;

import jwebdata.query.*;
import jwebdata.parsing.*;

/**
 * Class to establish candidate types for each word in a test string.
 */
public class TextParserWrapper
{
}
```

As with our other *ParserWrapper* classes there will be a *getElements(...)* method that returns a vector of parsed elements.

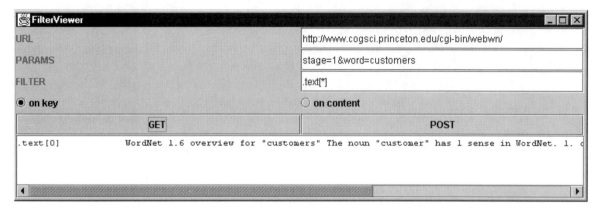

Figure 8.6 WordNet submission and filter for 'customers'

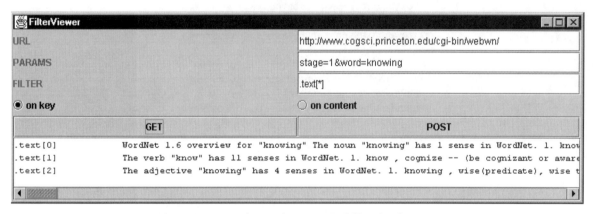

Figure 8.7 WordNet submission and filter for 'knowing'

getElements(...)

For each word in the input string we'll add an entry in the output vector with the key value *.word[n].text[0]*, and followed by a list of candidate types with key values *.word[n].type[m]*. You'll see what I mean in the sample output listing below:

```
.word[0].text[0] Customers
.word[0].type[0] noun
.word[1].text[0] feel
.word[1].type[0] noun
.word[1].type[1] verb
.word[2].text[0] particularly
.word[2].type[0] adverb
.word[3].text[0] vulnerable
.word[3].type[0] adjective
```

In case you've not figured it out, the input text in that case was 'Customers feel particularly vulnerable'.

The following code for the *getElements(...)* method is quite well commented so it should be easy enough to see what's going on. Notice the use of a *StringTokenizer* to split the input text into separate words, and don't forget we're using the *WordNet* on-line interface to look up the candidate types for each word.

```
// ** Code taken from jwebdata/mail/TextParserWrapper.java**

/**
 * Return a set of elements comprising input words with their
 * candidate types.
 */
public Vector getElements(String text)
{
    Vector phraseStructureElements=new Vector();
    try
    {
        // -- Initialize a web parser and query engine --
        WebParserWrapper webParser=new WebParserWrapper();
        QueryEngine queryEngine=new QueryEngine();

        int wordNum=0;

        // -- Split the text into separate words --
        StringTokenizer st=new StringTokenizer(text
          ," ,.<>?/;:!\"£$%^&*()[]{}+=#~");

        while (st.hasMoreTokens())
        {
            String thisWord=st.nextToken();

            // -- Add this word as a new element --
            String thisKey=".word["+wordNum+"].text[0]";
            String thisContent=thisWord;
            SourceElement newElement=new SourceElement(thisKey
              ,thisContent);
            phraseStructureElements.addElement(newElement);

            // -- Look up the word on WordNet --
            String url="http://www.cogsci.princeton.edu/cgi-bin/webwn/";
            String params="stage=1&word="+thisWord.toLowerCase();
            Vector elements=webParser.getElements(url,params
              ,WebParserWrapper.GET);

            // -- Apply the word type filter --
            Vector filters=new Vector();
            filters.addElement(".text[*]");
```

```
            Vector types
              =queryEngine.getFilteredRows(elements,filters);

            // -- Loop through the possible types for this word --
            int typeNum=0;
            for (int i=0; i<types.size(); i++)
            {
                SourceElement row=(SourceElement) types.elementAt(i);
                String typeString=row[0].getContent();

                int startPos=typeString.indexOf("The")+4;
                int endPos=typeString.indexOf("\"",startPos)-1;

                if ( (endPos>startPos) && (startPos>=0))
                {
                  String thisType=typeString.substring(startPos
                    ,endPos);

                  // -- Any spaces indicate not a real word type --
                  if (thisType.trim().indexOf(" ")>=0)
                      thisContent="UNKNOWN";
                  else
                      thisContent=thisType;

                  // -- Add the word type as an element --
                  thisKey=".word["+wordNum+"].type["+typeNum+"]";
                  newElement=new SourceElement(thisKey,thisContent);
                  phraseStructureElements.addElement(newElement);
                }
                typeNum++;
            }
            wordNum++;
        }
      }
    catch (Exception ex) {ex.printStackTrace();}

    return phraseStructureElements;
  }
```

Compiling and running the TextParserWrapper

We'll add a *main(...)* method to the *TextParserWrapper* as a convenient entry
point for our testing. After making a call to *getElements(...)*, this method will
use the *QueryEngine* from Chapter 4 to turn the results into a handy table that
looks like this:

```
Customers | noun |
feel | noun |
feel | verb |
```

```
particularly | adverb |
vulnerable | adjective |
```

You might remember that earlier in this chapter I said that we'd be coupling the TextParserWrapper up with the *QueryEngine* purely for testing purposes.

main(...)

Here's the code for the *main(...)* method.

```java
// ** Code taken from jwebdata/mail/TextParserWrapper.java **

/**
 * A main() method to test it.
 */
public static void main(String args)
{
    try
    {
      String inputText="Customers feel particularly vulnerable"
      +" knowing that no matter how careful they are, they nonetheless"
      +" become identity theft victims.";

      // String inputText="The second way the Act addresses the problem"
      // +" of identity theft is by focusing on customers as victims.";

      // -- Parse the elements at URL --
      TextParserWrapper textParser=new TextParserWrapper();
      Vector elements=textParser.getElements(inputText);

      // -- Get rows that satisfy the filters ---
      Vector filters=new Vector();
      filters.addElement(".word[*].text[0]");
      filters.addElement(".word[*].type[?]");
      QueryEngine queryEngine=new QueryEngine();
      Vector rows=queryEngine.getFilteredRows(elements,filters);

      // -- Print them out --
      for (int r=0; r<rows.size(); r++)
      {
        SourceElement thisRow=(SourceElement) rows.elementAt(r);
        for (int c=0; c<thisRow.length; c++)
        {
          SourceElement thisElement=thisRow[c];
          System.out.print(thisElement.getContent()+"| ");
        }
        System.out.println();
      }
    }
    catch (Exception ex) {ex.printStackTrace();}
}
```

You can compile and run the *TextParserWrapper* by issuing the following commands:

```
javac jwebdata/text/TextParserWrapper.java
java jwebdata.text.TextParserWrapper
```

TextParserWrapper test drive

We'll take the text parser for a test-drive using the two sentences that follow, borrowed from Dan Sullivan's *Text Mining* book. If you look back at the *main(...)* method listed earlier you'll see the same sentences; one commented in, and one commented out.

Customers feel particularly vulnerable knowing that no matter how careful they are, they nonetheless become identity theft victims.

The second way the Act addresses the problem of identity theft is by focusing on customers as victims.

Here's the first test sentence along with the resulting output:

```
Customers feel particularly vulnerable knowing that no matter how
careful they are, they nonetheless become identity theft victims.

Customers | noun |
feel | noun |
feel | verb |
particularly | adverb |
vulnerable | adjective |
knowing | noun |
knowing | verb |
knowing | adjective |
that | UNKNOWN |
no | noun |
no | adjective |
no | adverb |
matter | noun |
matter | verb |
how | adverb |
careful | adjective |
they | UNKNOWN |
are | noun |
are | verb |
they | UNKNOWN |
nonetheless | adverb |
```

```
become | verb |
identity | noun |
theft | noun |
victims | noun |
```

And here's the second test sentence along with the resulting output:

```
The second way the Act addresses the problem of identity theft is by
focusing on customers as victims.

The | UNKNOWN |
second | noun |
second | verb |
second | adjective |
second | adverb |
way | noun |
way | adverb |
the | UNKNOWN |
Act | noun |
Act | verb |
addresses | noun |
addresses | verb |
the | UNKNOWN |
problem | noun |
of | UNKNOWN |
identity | noun |
theft | noun |
is | verb |
by | adjective |
by | adverb |
focusing | noun |
focusing | verb |
on | adjective |
on | adverb |
customers | noun |
as | noun |
as | adverb |
victims | noun |
```

You will notice in both cases that some of the words are marked as UNKNOWN type. As far as I can tell these all appear to be common words like *this*, *that*, *the*, *of* and so on, which have unambiguous types that we could hard-code if we really wanted to.

Performance implications

I've implemented the *TextParserWrapper* in the way that I have, to use the on-line *WordNet* interface, so as to build on the ideas presented in earlier chapters. Not the most efficient way to do it, though, because we have to make a HTTP request for every word that we encounter. So for any real application we need to find a way to speed it up. I have two ideas:

• Download the *WordNet* database.

• Employ a caching mechanism.

Download the WordNet database   It's free to download, and our own local copy would provide significantly quicker access times than anything we can achieve through HTTP communication. It's not an open and shut case and I can think of a few disadvantages:

• Firstly, the storage space required is over 10Mb. This presents no obstacle at all if we host it on a PC, but what if wanted to analyse the textual structure of email content or web data received into our Java-enabled Palmtop computer? Like my Nokia 9210.

• Secondly, we need some additional techniques (which we've not yet developed) to query the information in the database's downloadable format, as well as needing to understand the database schema.

• Finally, the on-line interface not only provides data but also *functionality*. There are many additional functions that I've not told you about, such as the ability to look up *similar* words as you would with a thesaurus. I'll present you with an example of the additional functionality later in this chapter, in the form of a hyponym search.

These three points are not really meant to dissuade you. In the majority of cases a local version of the database, perhaps hosted on our own server, will be the preferred option. However, if you think any of those points are relevant to your situation it's worth giving some thought to the next option.

Employ a caching mechanism   For our first test sentence, eighteen HTTP requests were required to establish the type of each word that appears in the sentence. I mean eighteen requests in total, not per word.

We've discovered that certain common words are not included in the

WordNet database, and in the case of our first test sentence these words are *that* and *they*. Lets assume we'll hardcode the types of those words, italicized below, in our program.

```
Customers feel particularly vulnerable knowing that no
matter how careful they are, they nonetheless become
identity theft victims.
```

That gives a saving of three HTTP requests out of eighteen, which is a 16.7 per cent performance improvement achieved by pre-determining the types of some words. Not quite true, because I'm assuming local retrieval time to be negligible compared with HTTP access time, but there will be some notable improvement.

Now we can take this idea of pre-determining word types a bit further. By retaining the results from the first test sentence we can save on some HTTP requests when processing the second test sentence. Here I've italicized the words that the second sentence has in common with the first, as well as those that we will have hard-coded to give:

```
The second way the Act addresses the problem of identity
theft is by focusing on customers as victims.
```

It gives a saving of seven HTTP requests out of a possible eighteen for that sentence, which is a 38.9 per cent performance improvement. Thus our average performance improvement over the two sentences is 27.8 per cent. Again, assuming negligible local retrieval time.

Over a large body of text we can expect very significant performance improvements by caching previous results without having to download the entire database, store it, and figure out how to access it.

8.3 Phrase Structure Analysis

We've implemented a simple text parser that determines the candidate types of each word in the input sentence, which is an important first step on the road to developing any serious text mining application. As I said in the introduction, we won't be going as far as to determine the complete phrase structure of an input sentence based on the candidate word types. No additional Java techniques would be required, and we'd be straying further away from the *web* aspect of web mining, hence it's not my priority for this book.

What would be required is a really good algorithm, which I think is best left to the experts, but – having now made my excuses – I'll share a few of my thoughts with you anyway. It will give you something to think about as well as providing an incentive for further reading.

8.3.1 Top-down and bottom-up parsing

Natural language analysis is not dissimilar from artificial (e.g. computer) language analysis, and many useful techniques may be borrowed from the art – or science – of compiler writing. For any computer language there will be a set of grammar rules, determined by the creators of the language, which describe that language completely. This grammar may be expressed in the form of a set of production rules which for SQL, might look something like this:

```
[SELECTSTATEMENT] = SELECT [SELECTSPEC] FROM [FROMSPEC] WHERE [WHERESPEC]
[SELECTSPEC] = column | [FUNCTION](column) AS alias {, SELECTSPEC}
[FROMSPEC] = table AS alias {, FROMSPEC}
[WHERESPEC] = alias [OPERATOR] literal
[FUNCTION] = MAX | MIN | UPPER
[OPERATOR] = > | < | =
```

Thanks to the work that Noam Chomsky did in the 1950s we could devise a similar set of production rules for the English language. A limited subset, and I mean a very limited subset, of the rules for English grammar might include:

```
[SENTENCE] = [NOUNPHRASE] [VERBPHRASE]
[NOUNPHRASE] = determiner noun
[VERBPHRASE] = verb [NOUNPHRASE]
[VERBPHRASE] = verb
```

Hopefully you will see from that set of production rules how we might go about combining the candidate word types (nouns, verbs and so on) from our *TextParserWrapper* into larger structures incorporating noun phrases, verb phrases, and ultimately complete sentences. That would be the bottom-up approach. Alternatively we could begin with the root element, [SENTENCE], and follow the production rules to decompose it into smaller structures that would hopefully, at the lowest level, match the candidate types of the words in our input sentence. That would be the top-down approach.

The ultimate aim of determining the phrase structure of input sentences would be to add mark-up to the sentence, perhaps as XML (shown next), thus making the filtering and querying techniques from Chapter 4 applicable.

```
<SENTENCE>
  <NOUNPHRASE>
    <DETERMINER > the</DETERMINER>
    <NOUN > man</NOUN >
  <NOUNPHRASE>
  <VERBPHRASE>
    <VERB > eats</VERB>
    <NOUNPHRASE>
      <DETERMINER > the</DETERMINER>
      <NOUN > hamburger</NOUN>
    </NOUNPHRASE>
  </VERBPHRASE>
<SENTENCE>
```

Whatever our approach, the route we take from the bottom of the grammar to the top, or from the top to the bottom, will determine the phrase structure of the input sentence. Chances are we'll end up with not just one, but several possible candidate phrase structures for any given sentence. In part this will be due to our uncertainty regarding the type of each individual word, but even if we know the type of each word unambiguously it is still possible to fit those words into more than one structure. Dan Sullivan (Sullivan, 2000) presents a good example in terms of the following sentence: 'I saw the technician with the instrument'.

There are (at least) two phrase structures into which this sentence fits. Maybe the subject of the sentence is the technician, who has an instrument. Maybe the subject of the sentence is me, and I use an instrument – presumably a telescope – to see the technician. Figure 8.8 shows both possible phrase structures, and you will notice that in both cases the types of the individual words are the same.

For multiple candidate phrase structures arising in these circumstances the problem is one of semantics rather than syntax. Both structures are syntactically valid, but they mean quite different things. It's impossible for us to determine which is correct without an understanding of the meaning and the context.

For multiple candidate phrase structures arising because of our uncertainty regarding the individual word types there might be something we can do to improve the situation. We could apply some rules of thumb, some heuristics.

Heuristics   Before applying the production rules to a given sentence we could make some educated guesses about the correct – or at least the most likely –

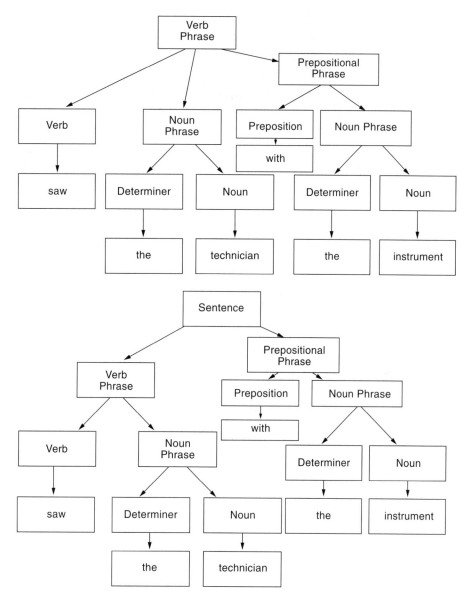

Figure 8.8 Candidate phrase structures. Reproduced from *Document Warehousing and Data Mining*, (Sullivan 2001), by permission of John Wiley & Sons Inc.

type for each of the words. Here are two of the rules of thumb that I have in mind:

Any set of contiguous nouns may be regarded as a single noun
Any word that starts with a capital letter, unless the first word in a sentence, is a (proper) noun

To show how these informal rules can reduce the number of candidate types for each word, and hence help with the bottom-up or top-down parsing process, consider our two original input sentences again:

```
Customers feel particularly vulnerable knowing that no
matter how careful they are, they nonetheless become
identity theft victims.

The second way the Act addresses the problem of identity
theft is by focusing on customers as victims.
```

For the first sentence, our *TextParserWrapper* concluded that the words *indentity*, *theft*, and *victims* were all nouns. By application of my first rule we may regard these three words as representing a single concept, a compound noun *identity theft victims*. For our second sentence, the *TextParserWrapper* concluded that the word *Act* was either a noun or a verb. By application of my second rule we can be confident that it is actually a (proper) noun.

Now I'll confess that I'm not really interested in applying those kinds of rules as an aid to full parsing, but to support certain text mining applications without the need for any understanding of the complete phrase structure. Feature extraction is such an application, which builds on the simple rules that I've just described.

8.4 Feature Extraction

In feature extraction the names of entities, i.e. nouns, within the input text are identified and put into context according to surrounding text that matches a particular pattern. Here's an example:

Whenever I send an email message or a letter to someone I've never met I will usually begin by introducing myself, and I suspect that you do the same. I hope so. My introductions will typically be in one of these forms:

```
I am Tony Loton of LOTONtech Limited.
```

My name is **Tony Loton** and I represent **LOTONtech Limited**.

You will see that I've highlighted the proper nouns that would be identified using the *initial capital letter* and the *compound noun* rules that I introduced in the previous section. Now by applying the these rules in conjunction with a content filter (Chapter 4) we could identify any introductions within a message and pick out the proper nouns reflecting the name of the individual and the company. Using the following patterns:

```
I am [PROPERNOUN] *of [PROPERNOUN]
My name is [PROPERNOUN] *I represent*[PROPERNOUN]
```

The reason I've included the wildcard *s in those patterns is so that the following kinds of introductions will also match correctly. Notice the italicized text representing wildcard replacement:

My name is **Tony Loton** *and I am Principal Consultant* of **LOTONtech Limited**.

My name is **Tony Loton** *and you might like to know that* I represent *a company called* **LOTONtech Limited**.

8.4.1   FeatureExtractor

Here is the basic definition of the *FeatureExtractor* class that will put the theory into practice by picking out the introductory sentences from the input text:

```
// ** Code taken from jwebdata/mail/FeatureExtractor.java **

package jwebdata.text;

import java.util.*;

import jwebdata.query.*;

/**
 * Class to extract feature sentences based on proper nouns
 * and sentence templates.
 */
public class FeatureExtractor
{
}
```

Our entry point will be a *getFeatureSentences(...)* method that returns those input sentences which have the specified features.

getFeatureSentences(...)

You will see that this method contains a loop within a loop. In the outer loop we step through a set of input sentences and for each one we call another method – *tagProperNouns(...)* – to mark the proper nouns within that sentence. In the inner loop we compare each newly marked-up sentence against a set of feature templates.

```
// ** Code taken from jwebdata/mail/FeatureExtractor.java **

/**
 * Return those input sentences that have the features determined
 * by the given templates.
 */
public Vector getFeatureSentences(Vector sentences, Vector templates)
{
    Vector featureSentences=new Vector();

    // -- Step through the input sentences --
    for (int s=0; s<sentences.size(); s++)
    {
        // -- Identify and tag the proper nouns in this sentence --
        String thisSentence=(String) sentences.elementAt(s);
        String newSentence=tagProperNouns(thisSentence);

        // -- Step through the feature templates --
        for (int t=0; t<templates.size(); t++)
        {
            String thisTemplate=(String) templates.elementAt(t);

            // -- Does this sentence match this template? --
            if (Operator.matches(newSentence,thisTemplate))
                featureSentences.addElement(newSentence);
        }
    }
    return featureSentences;
}
```

This feature templates will be supplied in the format that follows, with embedded <*propernoun*> tags to match with the proper nouns within sentences.

```
My name is <propernoun>*</propernoun> *of
<propernoun>*</propernoun>*
```

The comparison between feature templates and input sentences is performed by the *Operator* class from Chapter 4, and for the comparisons to be effective we must mark-up the input sentences with the *<propernoun>* tags where appropriate. That was the purpose of the *tagProperNouns(...)* method which I'll now describe.

tagProperNouns(...)

In this method we are picking out each word from an input sentence, and we're determining whether or not it is a proper noun by using the *initial capital letter* rule. As we go along we're building a new version of the input sentence by concatenating each word as-is, or surrounded by a *<propernoun>* tag, as appropriate. That's not the whole story as we're also collecting contiguous proper nouns as a *compoundName* that is concatenated only upon hitting the next ordinary word.

```java
// ** Code taken from jwebdata/mail/FeatureExtractor.java**

/**
  * Method to identify an tag the proper nouns in an input sentence.
  */
private String tagProperNouns(String sentence)
{
    String newSentence="";
    String compoundNoun="";
    StringTokenizer st=new StringTokenizer(sentence,",-;.",false);
    boolean firstWord=true;

    // -- Step through the words in the sentence --
    while (st.hasMoreTokens())
    {
      String thisWord=st.nextToken();

      char oneChar=new char[1];
      thisWord.getChars(0,1,oneChar,0);

      // -- If the current word begins with an uppercase letter --
      // -- add the word to the current compound proper noun. --
      if (Character.isUpperCase(oneChar[0])&& !firstWord
        && !thisWord.equals("I"))
          compoundNoun=compoundNoun+" "+thisWord;
      else
      {
          // -- This word is not a proper noun so it terminates --
          // -- the current compound proper noun, which we now --
          // -- write out. --
          if (compoundNoun.length()>0)
          {
            newSentence=newSentence+"<propernoun>"
```

```
          +compoundNoun.trim()+"</propernoun>";
        compoundNoun="";
      }
      newSentence=newSentence+" "+thisWord;
    }

    firstWord=false;
  }

  // -- Pick up any outstanding compound proper noun --
  if (compoundNoun.length()>0)
  {
    newSentence=newSentence+" <propernoun>"+compoundNoun.trim()
      +"</propernoun>";
  }

  newSentence=newSentence.trim();
  return newSentence;
}
```

That completes the inner workings of the *FeatureExtractor* which you'll no doubt be keen to test.

Compiling and running the FeatureExtractor

To test it we'll add a *main(...)* method that sets up two test sentences and two feature templates, and which runs them through the *FeatureExtractor*. Towards the end of this code you'll see that we're writing the final output as XML, the reason for which will soon become clear.

```
// ** Code taken from jwebdata/mail/FeatureExtractor.java **

/**
 * A main() method to test it.
 */
public static void main(String args)
{
    // -- Variables to hold the sentences and templates --
    Vector sentences=new Vector();
    Vector templates=new Vector();

    // -- First test sentence --
    sentences.addElement("Dear Sir,");
    sentences.addElement(
      "My name is Tony Loton and I represent LOTONtech Limited.");
    sentences.addElement(
      "I would like to tell you about our products.");
```

```
// -- Second test sentence --
sentences.addElement("Hi,");
sentences.addElement("Allow me to introduce myself.");
sentences.addElement("My name is Tony Loton and I am "
  +"Principal Consultant of LOTONtech Limited.");

// -- Two templates for introductions --
templates.addElement("My name is <propernoun>*</propernoun> "
  +"and I represent <propernoun>*</propernoun>*");
templates.addElement("My name is <propernoun>*</propernoun> *of "
  +"<propernoun>*</propernoun>*");

// -- Initialize a FeatureExtractor and get matching sentences --
FeatureExtractor featureExtractor=new FeatureExtractor();
Vector featureSentences=featureExtractor.getFeatureSentences(
  sentences, templates);

// -- Write out the results as XML --
System.out.println(
  "<?xml version=\"1.0\" encoding"
  +"=\"ISO-8859-1\" standalone=\"yes\"?>");
System.out.println("<!DOCTYPE sentences [");
System.out.println(" <!ELEMENT sentences (sentence*)>");
System.out.println(
  " <!ELEMENT sentence (#PCDATA|propernoun)*>");
System.out.println(" <!ELEMENT propernoun (#PCDATA)>");
System.out.println("]>");

System.out.println("<sentences>");
for (int fs=0; fs<featureSentences.size(); fs++)
{
    String featureSentence=
      (String) featureSentences.elementAt(fs);
    System.out.println("<sentence>"+featureSentence+"</sentence>");
}
System.out.println("</sentences>");
}
```

To compile and run the *FeatureExtractor* you can now issue the following commands:

```
javac jwebdata\text\FeatureExtractor.java
java jwebdata.text.FeatureExtractor > data\features.xml
```

If you typed the second command exactly as shown there you'll see no output on the screen, but a file *features.xml* will have been created with the following content:

```
<?xml version="1.0" encoding="ISO-8859-1" standalone="yes"?>
```

```
<!DOCTYPE sentences [
  <!ELEMENT sentences (sentence*)>
  <!ELEMENT sentence (#PCDATA|propernoun)*>
  <!ELEMENT propernoun (#PCDATA)>
]>

<sentences>

<sentence>My name is <propernoun>Tony Loton</propernoun> and I represent
<propernoun>LOTONtech Limited</propernoun></sentence>

<sentence>My name is <propernoun>Tony Loton</propernoun> and I am
<propernoun>Principal Consultant</propernoun> of <propernoun>LOTONtech
Limited</propernoun></sentence>

</sentences>
```

You should be able to see that we have successfully extracted only those sentences matching our templates, with the others ignored, and within each retained sentence the proper nouns have been marked-up correctly. To make it clearer, we can run the XML content through our *FilterViewer* from Chapter 4 to give Figure 8.9. It's much easier to see the result, isn't it, and suitable for further processing thanks to writing the output as XML.

So we now have the basis of an application to pick out key features from input sentences originating from various sources. It's the latter part of that sentence that's important, and the various sources that I have in mind for input

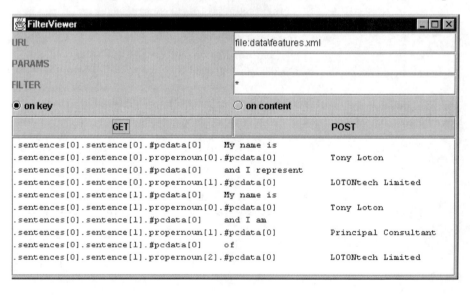

Figure 8.9   Viewing sentence features

sentences are web pages and email messages. Thus the next logical step would be to link the *FeatureExtractor* in some way with the *WebParserWrapper* from Chapter 3 and the *MailParserWrapper* from Chapter 7. I've necessarily kept them separate so as to reduce the inter-dependencies within the book, but I encourage you to now take up the challenge.

8.5   Other Text Mining Applications

Given a set of techniques for text mining, what use would those techniques be to us? What problems could we solve that we couldn't solve before? What follows is not meant to be an exhaustive coverage of the possible applications for text mining techniques, and not necessarily consistent with the accepted wisdom on the subject. I'll offer a couple more ideas for the kinds of applications that I'd like to implement in the near future, and I'll try to put these in the context of the techniques we've covered.

For a better coverage of the full range of possibilities I'll once again point you in the direction of *Document Warehousing and Text Mining* by Dan Sullivan (Wiley, 2001).

8.5.1   Indexing

When complete, this book will need an index that allows you to quickly track down information on particular key terms. You might want to look at every page where I mention 'searching', 'Java Mail' or even 'identity theft victims'. I assume that such an index is in place as you read this.

Compiling an index is a big job, and I'd like to make it a semi-automatic process. First I need to decide on the key terms to be indexed, then I need to record the page numbers on which they occur. For the first part I'll define key terms as being common nouns (e.g. searching), proper nouns (e.g. Java Mail) or compound nouns (e.g. identity theft victims).

Rather than re-reading the whole text to decide on my key terms, I've decided to write a Java program that will pick out all the common, proper, and compound nouns and present them to me as candidate terms for my index. The program will make use of our *WordNet* supported *TextParserWrapper*, enhanced with my heuristic rules for identifying the nouns of various kinds.

Unfortunately I'll be so busy compiling my index manually that I won't have time to write a program to do it, but it was a nice idea while it lasted and I hope it's given you something to think about. If you think I've strayed from the main theme of this book, which is *web mining*, bear in mind the fact that indexing is an important aid to web searching. As I pointed out in Chapter 7, at the time you submit your request, commercial search engines typically search a pre-compiled, *indexed*, directory of web sites rather than the web itself.

8.5.2 Increasing the search scope

In Chapter 6 we implemented a simple crawler-based search engine that looks for web documents that contain a user-supplied keyword.

Suppose the user provided the keyword *customers*. I imagine that what he or she actually wants to find is all web pages referring to the *concept* of a customer, rather than (or at least in addition too) the literal word *customers*. So what about pages referring to *clients, buyers, shoppers, patrons* and so on? To improve the scope of our searching we would want to look for words that are similar to – that is, synonyms of – the original keyword.

Look back at Figure 8.5 and you will see that the *WordNet* results page for the word *customers* includes a further HTML form that may be used to look for related words. In Figure 8.10 you will see that I am selecting the *hyponyms (is a kind of)* option, and in Figure 8.11 you will see a web page containing a list of those words that are similar in concept to the word *customers*.

By applying the techniques that we've covered throughout this book we could now automate the following steps for any keyword supplied as input:

- Issue a hyponym search on *WordNet*.

- Applet a filter to the results.

- Perform a search, using the search engine from Chapter 6, that includes the original word and it's hyponyms.

As an extension of that, I have an idea for a search similar documents feature to be included in the on-line interface to our search engine. You can think of this as an exercise.

Search similar documents

For each document (i.e. a web page) returned by a search submission, how about providing the user with a 'Search Similar Documents' button that triggers the following functionality:

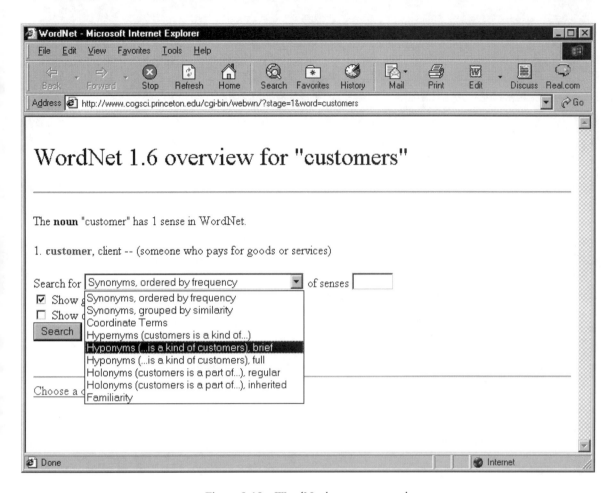

Figure 8.10   WordNet hyponyms search

- Use the *TextParserWrapper* to pick out the nouns in the document.

- Choose the nouns reflecting the key concepts in the document, for example by frequency of occurrence or by the fact that they are proper nouns beginning with a capital letter.

- Obtain the hyponyms of those words from *WordNet*.

- Search for documents containing the words, and the hyponyms, from the original document.

- Use statistical techniques to rate the documents with a percentage similarity.

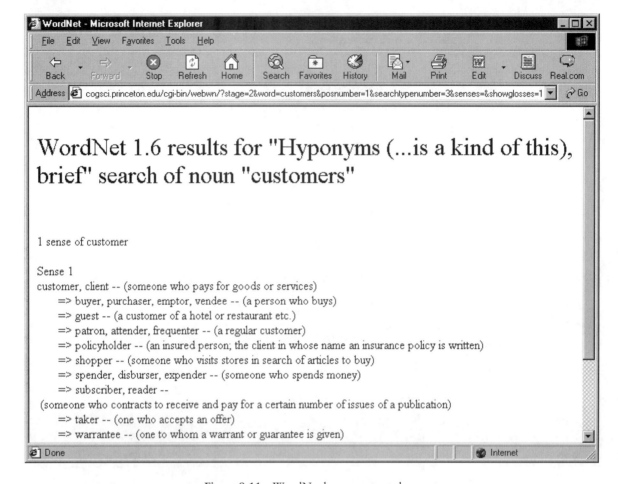

Figure 8.11   WordNet hyponyms results

You might have seen something very similar to this implemented by the commercial search engines that you have used.

8.6 Chapter Review

In this chapter we've looked at how apparently unstructured text does in fact posses implicit structure based on the rules of grammar. Understanding these grammar rules allows us to mark-up the text and hence make it susceptible to filtering and querying.

Determining the phrase structure of a sentence also allows us to apply transformation techniques, e.g. *passivation* of an active sentence, and this idea has its roots in the work of Noam Chomsky. In the 1950s Chomsky first presented a view that all languages have a *deep structure* that lends itself to the transformation of sentences by the application of simple rules. If you want to read more about Chomsky's revolutionary (at that time) ideas a good starting point would be the introductory biographies provided at these URLs:

http://www.factmonster.com/ce6/people/A0812034.html

http://www.britannica.com/seo/n/noam-chomsky/

The starting point for any serious text parsing is to identify the type (i.e. part-of-speech) of each of word within a sentence. For that we need a lexicon and so we took advantage of the on-line *WordNet* lexicon, which we gained access to by drawing on techniques from Chapters 2 to 4.

As an alternative to fully parsing text into a phrase structure, or maybe in addition, I offered some simpler rules for identifying the key concepts within a sentence. As a demonstration we implemented a *FeatureExtractor* class that put some of that simpler theory into practice.

8.6.1   API classes and interfaces introduced in this chapter

The following class was introduced for the first time in this chapter:

* *java.lang.Character* is an object wrapper for a value of primitive type *char*.

Introduction to Data Mining

The subject of this chapter is data mining, and so that we all agree on what we mean by that I'll start with a couple of definitions pulled from other works:

the process of exploration and analysis . . . of large quantities of data in order to discover meaningful patterns and rules.

Mastering Data Mining (Berry and Linoff, 2000)

the extraction of implicit, previously unknown, and potentially useful information from data

Data Mining (Witten and Frank, 2000)

It sounds similar to text mining, doesn't it? However, data mining is concerned with structured data, neatly arranged in database rows and columns, whereas text mining is concerned with (apparently) unstructured data.

The two disciplines are not mutually exclusive though. If we impose a grammar based superstructure onto the source text, as described in Chapter 8, that text may itself become suitable for the data mining techniques described in this chapter. Particularly if the text benefits from also being marked-up as HTML or XML.

9.1 The Design

In the second half of this chapter we'll take a more theoretical standpoint and I'll introduce some data mining ideas without going down to the level of Java programming. Rest assured that the ideas can be implemented in Java, and have been by other practitioners.

As preparation for the second half we'll implement a couple of Java classes, the first of which – *CensusDataFetcher* – will be used to fetch some data from the web to be used in one of the examples. That class is coupled up with the *WebParserWrapper* from Chapter 3 and the *QueryEngine* from Chapter 4, as you can see in Figure 9.1.

The second class, *Function*, will be a utility class comprising static methods for applying some common functions to data. In use it will be much like the *Operator* class from Chapter 4 and, in fact, is coupled up with it. You will notice from Figure 9.1 that the *Function* class is also coupled up with itself. In normal operation it won't be, but for testing I've added a *main(...)* method that calls the *max(...)* function on the same class.

The *CensusDataFetcher* won't be used to perform any data mining operations, its sole purpose being simply to fetch some test data for my examples. In order to demonstrate a few data mining operations I'll make use of the *QueryEngine* and *SqlGui* classes that we implemented in Chapter 4. For convenience, and because it's beyond the scope of this book to develop such a complete tool here, I'll get a little extra help from the commercial WebDataKit SQL Engine.

In this chapter we'll take UK Census information from a live web site, transform the HTML representation of the data to an XML representation

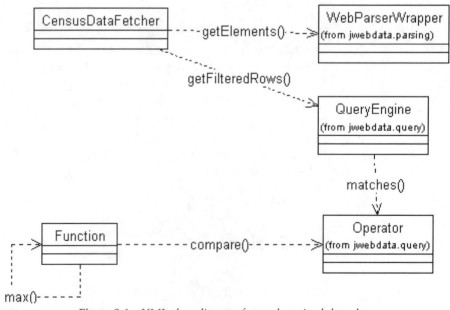

Figure 9.1   UML class diagram for package jwebdata.data

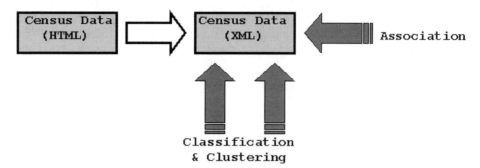

Figure 9.2   Data mining operations

that facilities mining, and explore a few of the data mining operations that may be applied, as shown in Figure 9.2.

Impact of Web Site Changes

Some of the examples in this chapter are based around data taken directly from the web, rather than from sample data sources that I have provided as home-grown servlets or static HTML/XML files. Whilst this is good for realism the content and format of web sites may change such that these examples will no longer run exactly as presented. There is an implicit exercise and an opportunity for you to test your understanding by bringing any such examples up-to-date with the help of the *FilterViewer* from Chapter 4.

9.2 Fetching Data

As I said earlier, the *CensusDataFetcher* will take UK census information, marked-up as HTML, from a live web site and write it out again with more meaningful XML tags.

The web site used was that of the UK Public Records Office found at http://www. pro.gov.uk and, cautious as I am not to encourage copyright infringement, I've listed their copyright notice in Appendix D. It seems you're safe enough using and transcribing the information as long as you acknowledge the source and steer clear of the actual document images and other chargeable items. At the time of writing this is a pilot site for the 1891 census, limited to the county of Norwich; so it's not useful for any practical purpose, but is certainly interesting as a source of test data.

9.2.1   CensusDataFetcher

The complete code for the *CensusDataFetcher* is shown next. We're driving an on-line search form in the style to which we've become accustomed, using the *post* method, and we're then extracting the required data with the help of a few filters and the *QueryEngine*; also in the style to which we've become accustomed. The four field values that we'll be collecting for each person instance returned are:

- *Name*; the name of the individual, as recorded on the census questionnaire.
- *Age*; the age of the individual, as recorded.
- *Head*; the name of the head of the household, as recorded.
- *Relationship*; the relationship between this individual and the head.

Finally, we're writing out each result row as XML in the following format.

```
<instance>
  <name>A Brown</name><age>10</age>
  <head>George Brown</head><relation>Son</relation<
</instance>
```

Here's the code

```java
// ** Code taken from jwebdata/data/CensusDataFetcher.java **

package jwebdata.data;

import jwebdata.parsing.*;
import jwebdata.query.*;

import java.util.*;

/**
 * Class to fetch some data mining test data.
 */
public class CensusDataFetcher
{
    /**
     * Everything happens in the main() method.
     */
```

```java
public static void main(String args)
{
    try
    {
        // -- Capture command-line parameters --
        String searchName=args[0];
        String listSize=args[1];

        // -- Initialise the web parser and query engine --
        WebParserWrapper webParser=new WebParserWrapper();
        QueryEngine queryEngine=new QueryEngine();

        // -- URL and parameters for census data --
        String url="http://census.pro.gov.uk/SearchServlet";
        String params
="rType=BAS&button=submit&minNumSearchChars=2&charsBeforeWildcard=2&exactM
atch=true&listSize="+listSize+"&lastName="+searchName;

        // -- Filters for name, age, head, and relation --
        Vector filters=new Vector();

filters.addElement(".form[0].table[0].tr[0].td[0].table[0].tr[3].td[0].tab
le[0].tr[0].td[0].table[0].tr[*].td[0].a[0].text[0]");

filters.addElement(".form[0].table[0].tr[0].td[0].table[0].tr[3].td[0].tab
le[0].tr[0].td[0].table[0].tr[*].td[1].text[0]");

filters.addElement(".form[0].table[0].tr[0].td[0].table[0].tr[3].td[0].tab
le[0].tr[0].td[0].table[0].tr[*].td[3].text[0]");

filters.addElement(".form[0].table[0].tr[0].td[0].table[0].tr[3].td[0].tab
le[0].tr[0].td[0].table[0].tr[*].td[4].text[0]");

        // -- Run the census query and apply the filters --
        Vector elements=webParser.getElements(url,params
          ,WebParserWrapper.POST);
        Vector rows=queryEngine.getFilteredRows(elements,filters);

        // -- Loop through the rows --
        for (int r=0; r<rows.size(); r++)
        {
            SourceElement thisRow
              =(SourceElement) rows.elementAt(r);
            String name=thisRow[0].getContent();
            String ageString=thisRow[1].getContent();
            String head=thisRow[2].getContent();
            String relation=thisRow[3].getContent();

            // -- Write XML record for row if there is valid age --
            try
            {
                int age=new Integer(ageString).intValue();
```

```
                        age=(age/10)*10;

                        System.out.println("<instance>");
                        System.out.println(" <name>"+name+"</name><age>"+age

                          +"</age><head>"+head+"</head><relation>"+relation
                          +"</relation>");
                        System.out.println("</instance>");
                    }
                catch (Exception e) {}
            }
        }
        catch (Exception ex) { ex.printStackTrace(); }
    }
}
```

Compiling and running the CensusDataFetcher

The *main(...)* method of that class takes a *searchName* and a *listSize* as command line arguments, to be posted as part of the form submission. To accumulate some test data, I ran it three times with these commands:

```
java jwebdata.data.CensusDataFetcher brown 30 > brown.xml
java jwebdata.data.CensusDataFetcher jones 30 > jones.xml
java jwebdata.data.CensusDataFetcher smith 30 > smith.xml
```

I then concatenated the three sets of results and pre-pended an appropriate XML DTD that described my census record structure. The end result, *census.xml*, starts like this:

```
<?xml version="1.0" encoding="ISO-8859-1" standalone="yes"?>

<!DOCTYPE data [
    <!ELEMENT data (instance*)>
    <!ELEMENT instance (name,age,head,relation)>
    <!ELEMENT name (#PCDATA)>
    <!ELEMENT age (#PCDATA)>
    <!ELEMENT head (#PCDATA)>
    <!ELEMENT relation (#PCDATA)>
]>

<data>
<instance>
  <name>... Brown</name><age>0</age>
  <head>William Brown</head><relation>Grand Daughter</relation>
```

```
</instance>
<instance>
  <name>. . . Brown</name><age>90</age>
  <head>George Larner</head><relation>Mother In Law</relation>
</instance>
<instance>
  <name>A Brown</name><age>10</age>
  <head>George Brown</head><relation>Son</relation>
</instance>
<instance>
  <name>Aaron Brown</name><age>60</age>
  <head>Aaron Brown</head><relation>Head</relation>
</instance>
```

I've included the complete content of the *census.xml* test file in Appendix E.

The simplest way to create the XML-tagged results was by explicitly printing the field contents and surrounding tags with a series of *System.out.println(...)* statements. Look back at the code to see what I mean. For the record I could have used the DOM APIs to construct a valid XML *document* as an internal representation instead then written it out as a file. It's not worth the effort in this case, I think, but you might like to think about that for your own applications.

The idea behind using the *CensusDataFetcher* is to take the data and store it locally for further processing. There are many things we might want do with the data, and it would be somewhat inefficient to re-read it each time via HTTP. In addition, it's a safeguard against the source web site having change by the time you read this.

As we're going to the trouble of writing a local version we might as well put it in a form that lends itself to subsequent processing, hence the XML representation. Now that we have a handy XML file full of data, I'll use it as a vehicle for introducing a last Java class called *Function*.

9.2.2   The Function class

The *Function* class that we'll implement here will be a useful addition to our repertoire, and now seems the best time to introduce it. You might be pleased to hear that it's the last piece of Java code you'll see in this book, outside of the appendices.

The basic class definition is:

```
// ** Code taken from jwebdata/data/Function.java **
package jwebdata.data;
```

```
import jwebdata.parsing.*;
import jwebdata.query.*;

import java.util.*;

/**
 * Class to perform some data functions.
 */
public class Function
{
}
```

There are some common functions that you might want to apply to the values within a set of data rows. I'm talking about the *max(...)*, *min(...)*, and *avg(...)* functions (plus many more) that will be familiar to you if you're a regular user of SQL.

The functions

All of those functions will be provided as static methods on the *Function* utility class, callable whenever and from wherever you like. Each function will take as parameters a set of rows, obtained from the *QueryEngine* (Chapter 4), and a column number on which to apply the function.

I'll implement only the *max(...)* function here, as a demonstration, and you'll be able to use it as the basis of your own full set of useful functions.

max(...)

This function will simply work through the values in the given column of the given row set in order to establish the maximum value. In the code that follows you'll see that we're making good use of the *Operator* class from Chapter 4 in order to compare textual or numeric values.

```
// ** Code taken from jwebdata/data/Function.java **

public static String max(Vector rows, int columnNum)
{
  String maxValue="";

  for (int r=0; r<rows.size(); r++)
  {
    SourceElement thisRow
        =(SourceElement) rows.elementAt(r);
    String thisValue=thisRow[columnNum].getContent();

    if (Operator.compare(thisValue,">",maxValue))
```

```
            maxValue=thisValue;
    }

    return maxValue;
}
```

You should be aware that because we're using the *compare(...)* method of our *Operator* class, this function will work equally well for finding a lexical – i.e. character string – maximum value or a numeric maximum value.

Compiling and running the function class

Purely for testing, a *main(...)* method will be added to the *Function* class. In the code that follows we take data from the output of the *CensusDataFetcher*, in the form of an XML file, we build a set of rows from it, and we apply the *max(...)* function to the age and relation fields.

```
// ** Code taken from jwebdata/data/Function.java **

/**
 * A main() method to test it.
 */
public static void main(String args)
{
    try
    {
        // -- Initialise the web parser and query engine --
        WebParserWrapper webParser=new WebParserWrapper();
        QueryEngine queryEngine=new QueryEngine();

        // -- URL local copy of census data --
        String url="file:data/census.xml";

        // -- Filters for name, age, head, and relation --
        Vector filters=new Vector();
        filters.addElement(".data[0].instance[*].name[0].#pcdata[0]");
        filters.addElement(".data[0].instance[*].age[0].#pcdata[0]");
        filters.addElement(".data[0].instance[*].head[0].#pcdata[0]");
        filters.addElement(".data[0].instance[*].relation[0].#pcdata[0]");

        // -- Run the query and apply the filters --
        Vector elements=webParser.getElements(url,""
          ,WebParserWrapper.GET);
        Vector rows=queryEngine.getFilteredRows(elements,filters);

        // -- Apply the MAX functions --
        String maxAge=Function.max(rows,1);
        String maxRelation=Function.max(rows,3);
```

```
    // -- Print the results --
    System.out.println("maxAge="+maxAge+", maxRelation="+maxRelation);
    }
    catch (Exception ex) { ex.printStackTrace(); }
}
```

The lines that follow show the commands to compile and run the *Function* class along with the resulting output, which I hope is what you were expecting to see:

```
> javac jwebdata\data\Function.java
> java jwebdata.data.Function

maxAge=90, maxRelation=Wife
```

So there we have possibly the simplest of data mining techniques, finding a maximum value within a data table. There's more to data mining than that, of course, so we'll now turn our attention to data mining techniques in a wider sense.

9.3 Data Mining Techniques

From this point on I'll take a more theoretical standpoint as I give you my interpretation of three common data mining techniques. The first two, *classification* and *association*, I'll demonstrate via a Java-based SQL Engine that is a logical extension of the work we did in Chapter 4. The last one *clustering* I'll demonstrate using a simple spreadsheet program, with the implication that I could have used Java if I really wanted to. Maybe you will really want to, in which case I'll point you in the right direction.

Remember that this book is not intended to be a comprehensive guide to data mining, so if you want to take the ideas further once I've whetted your appetite I suggest you take a look at Witten and Frank (2000).

9.3.1 Classification

Classification involves separating data instances into named groups according to their properties or values. The key to classification – and its differentiator from clustering, discussed later – is that we have a pre-determined set of groups (classes) and a pre-determined set of rules for assigning instances to classes.

Chapter 5 example

We implemented a very simple classification in Chapter 5. Each share was classified as (to) *sell*, (to) *buy* or (to) *hold*, according to the percentage change in the share price, and we displayed the classification of each share on our portal. Classification may be though of as an '*is a*' relationship of the form:

   BAE SYSTEMS *is a* (to) BUY share.

   BP AMOCO *is a* (to) SELL share.

I hope you don't take those as concrete recommendations for trading!

You might also have noticed that we're performing a very simple classification, in a sense, within the *CensusDataParser* code as we write each instance out as XML. We're quantizing the values of the age field such that the instances fall within age bands of 0 (real age 0–9, *young children*), 10 (real age 10–19, *older children*), 20 (real age 20–29, *young adults*) and so on.

Census data example

The results of the census data may be classified according to the field values of each instance. One possible classification would be based on the *relation* field, with the effect that each instance – representing an individual person – would be classified as a son, daughter, niece, nephew and so on.

We already have the bones of a tool to perform this kind of classification, in the form of the SQL application that we implemented in Chapter 4. SQL lends itself to picking out sets of instances according to specified criteria, so it's just right for the classification job.

In Figure 9.3 you will see that I've constructed a simple SQL query to pick out all instances for which the *relation* field contains the text *son*, that is all instances belonging to the *son* class. It won't be too taxing for you to figure out how this could be adapted to pick out the members of the *daughter* class, the *niece* class, and all the other classes based on this field.

I'll now take this idea further and consider classification based on more than one field value or attribute. The SQL application that we have developed shows what is possible in principle, but the functionality is limited. It's beyond the scope of this book to put together a complete SQL tool for web data, so for

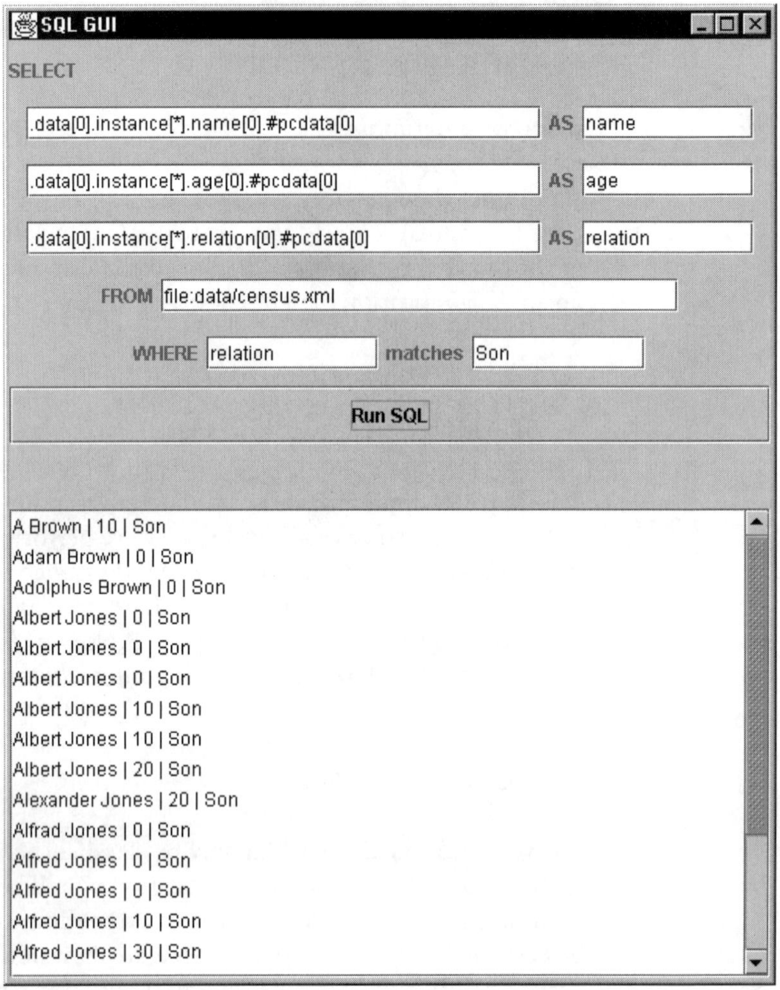

Figure 9.3   SQL for son class instances

my next demonstration I'll resort to using our commercial WebDataKit SQL implementation.

Taking the idea of classifying individuals according to their relation (-ship) to the head of the household further, I'd now like to sub-divide that classification according to age. Rather than picking out all *son* instances, *daughter* instances etc., I'd like to pick out the *young sons*, *old sons*, *young daughters*, and *old daughters*. I'm particularly interested to find out how many men are still living at home with their parents, beyond the age of 20. The SQL statement, and the corresponding results, are given in Figure 9.4. It shows how

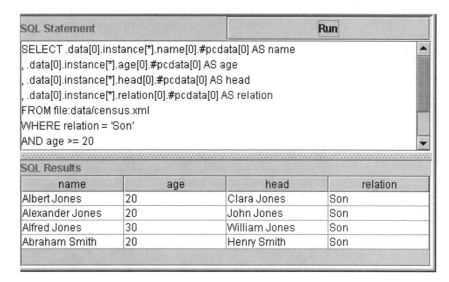

| SQL Statement | | | Run |

SELECT .data[0].instance[*].name[0].#pcdata[0] AS name
, .data[0].instance[*].age[0].#pcdata[0] AS age
, .data[0].instance[*].head[0].#pcdata[0] AS head
, .data[0].instance[*].relation[0].#pcdata[0] AS relation
FROM file:data/census.xml
WHERE relation = 'Son'
AND age >= 20

SQL Results

name	age	head	relation
Albert Jones	20	Clara Jones	Son
Alexander Jones	20	John Jones	Son
Alfred Jones	30	William Jones	Son
Abraham Smith	20	Henry Smith	Son

Figure 9.4   SQL for son living with parents class instances

SQL may be used effectively for classification based on more than one attribute value.

To complete the discussion of classification, I'll show how comparisons between field values could be used as the basis of a classification. Consider a new class (the *Like father, like son* class) whose instances are those sons who share a name with the head of the household, their father. The criteria for this classification should be quite apparent in the SQL query shown in Figure 9.5.

It's no accident that I've presented that example to you, because its related to one of the *association* examples that I'll present in the next section. In effect, these instances will constitute the exceptions to the association rule that I'll offer.

Where does Java fit in?

If you take a look at Frank and Witten (2000) you'll find a Java algorithm for classification. Why not take their tried and tested algorithm and apply it to data sets obtained from the web using the techniques that I've described?

Alternatively, why not take the basic *QueryEngine* from Chapter 5 and adapt it to support an SQL syntax like the one that I propose? You'll then be able to run the kinds of queries shown in Figures 9.4 and 9.5 and, importantly, capture the results into your Java programs. If that sounds too much like hard

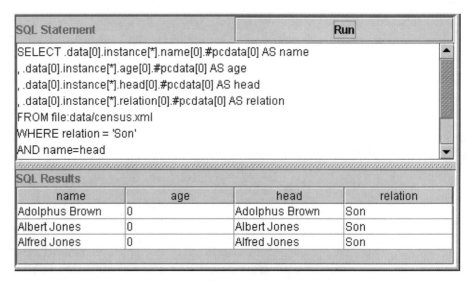

Figure 9.5   SQL for like father, like son class instances

work you could find out about the WebDataKit commercial implementation at http://www.lotontech.com/wdbc.html or I can refer you to the Web Data Toolkit case study in *Professional Java Data* (Wrox Press, 2001).

9.3.2   Association

Associations are linkages between sets of data instances. These linkages may be summarized in the form of *association rules* that determine (according to the attribute values) which instances are related to, or associated with, certain other instances.

Background example

A simple example would be an association rule that links sales of beer to sales of salted peanuts, which I've based loosely on a well used example linking beer sales with diapers. Informally, and with my supermarket manager's hat on, I'll define the rule as *shoppers who buy beer also buy salted peanuts*.

   This might be rephrased more formally as *the set of shoppers who buy beer is a subset of the set of shoppers who buy peanuts*. Thus every member of the beer buying set is a also a member of the peanut buying set. Very useful information for any supermarket manager!

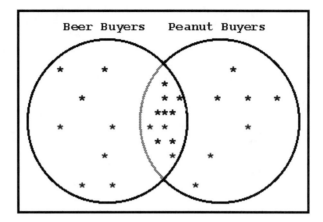

Figure 9.6   Venn diagram for beer buyers and peanut buyers

In reality beer buyers will probably not form a neat subset of peanut buyers. A more likely scenario is that the two sets will overlap, or intersect, as shown in Figure 9.6. You will see that many (but not all) beer buyers are also peanut buyers, so my association rule is not simply *true* or *false*. It is true, *to a certain extent*.

How true my rule, or hypothesis, is may be expressed in terms of the number of common instances (11) as a percentage of the total instances (26) and as a percentage of the beer buyers (19). These figures represent the *coverage* (or *support*) and *accuracy* (or *confidence*), respectively, of my rule.

Thus the rule *shoppers who buy beer also buy salted peanuts* is supported by 42 per cent of instances and is 59 per cent accurate.

I've presented this example, before moving on to our census data, because it will be meaningful to you. I'm sure you'll appreciate how valuable such data about buying habits is.

Census data example

In the context of our census data, I have a new hypothesis. In the absence of any explicit *relation* field, we could determine which instance represents the head of each household by equating the name of the individual with the name of the head. Here's my proposed rule: *any individual having the same name as the head must, in fact, be the head.*

In Figure 9.7 I've executed a SQL statement to select the results for which this rule is true. I know the rule is true for these instances because I'm using the *relation* field itself as a double-check. The count of results for this statement is

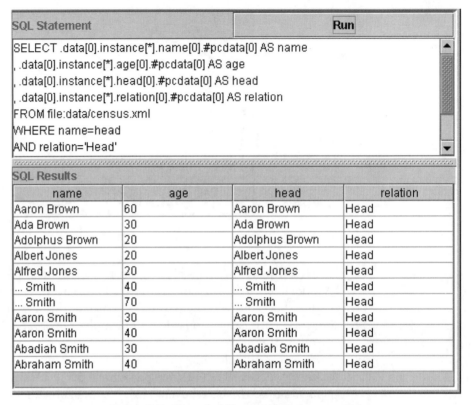

Figure 9.7 Household head association coverage

11, out of 90 total instances, making the coverage (or support) for this rule approximately 12 per cent.

In Figure 9.8 I've executed a SQL statement to select those instances for which the rule is applicable (name = head) regardless of whether the relation field confirms the result. There are 14 instances for which the rule is applicable, and we have already established the number of true results as 11, so the accuracy is 79 per cent.

Take a look at the at the results in Figure 9.8 for which the rule is applicable but not true. As I hinted earlier, these exceptions to the rule correspond with the instances of class *Like father, like son* shown first in Figure 9.5.

You might be wondering why we should bother with this association rule at all. After all, the relation field – which was used for confirmation – tells us exactly what we want to know, doesn't it?

Suppose I tell you that prior to 1891 the census questionnaire was different – with *name*, *age*, and *head* fields but no *relation* field. How would you find out the age of each household head? You'd need to determine which instances

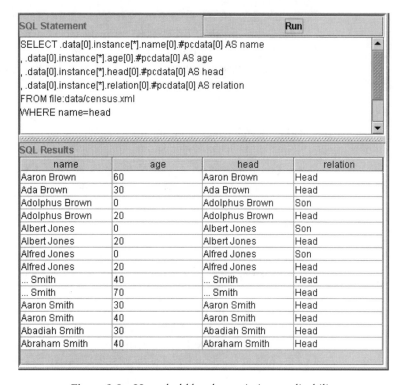

Figure 9.8   Household head association applicability

were the head instances, and without an explicit relation field the only option would be to use my rule. According to our training data, this would establish the correct age 79 per cent of the time.

Now suppose there has always been a relation question in the census, but we suspect that many questionnaires before 1891 we completed incorrectly. Our test data coverage tells us to expect 12 per cent of the population to be household heads, so if we found say 24 per cent of instances to have 'Head' in the relation field we'd smell a rat. Therefore, we'd have an opportunity to do some *data cleansing*.

Disclaimer

While I've done enough here to demonstrate the principles, and to show how the kinds of tools we've implemented may be used for these purposes, I should stress that this is all hypothetical. I don't really know what questions were included in the 1891 census or in any of the previous decades. I'm also keen to avoid the implication that a training data sample of 90 instances would be useful for any kind of serious prediction.

So my message is to take the ideas, take the techniques, but take the concrete results with a pinch of salt.

Where does Java fit in?

So where does Java fit in? Well in pretty much the same way as for classification. I encourage you to think more about SQL applied to web data, and also to take a look at the tried and tested association algorithm(s) included in Frank and Witten (2000).

9.3.3   Clustering

As with classification, clustering involves separating data instances into groups according to their properties or values. But this time not into *named* groups, or a least not into predefined groups that have names at the outset. Instances are grouped according to how similar they are to each other.

To start with, I'll take you back to the Share Price Information Portal that we implemented in Chapter 5. I have in my head the picture of an ideal *income* stock. It's one that is stable because it trades at low volumes and has a low percentage change in its share price. So no nasty surprises regarding the share price while we sit and watch the dividends roll in. Again, you should take my investment advice at your own risk.

In Table 9.1 I've listed some stocks along with their last trading volume and their last percentage change. That accounts for the first three columns. In the next two columns I've normalized the data so that the volumes fall within the range 0 to 100, each pro-rata, as do the percentage changes. The final column contains a value reflecting the *distance* of each share away from the ideal share (zero volume, zero change). I've calculated the distance as:

(Normalized Volume + Normalized Change)/2

You will see from that calculation the importance of normalizing the values, so that the volume and percentage change each has an equal effect on the final result. Finally as you look at Table 9.1 bear in mind that I've summarized it, so the normalization will not appear to be correct. You can find the whole table in Appendix F.

Table 9.1   Share volumes and percentages. For the full table please see Appendix F

SHARE	VOLUME	CHANGE %	NORMAL VOLUME	NORMAL CHANGE	DISTANCE
BASS PLC	273 400	0.13%	1.00	−2.00	0.00
BOC GROUP PLC	337 832	−0.29%	1.00	3.00	0.00
PEARSON PLC	661 121	0.21%	2.00	−3.00	0.00
ASTRAZENECA	735 058	−0.15%	3.00	2.00	0.00
AMVESCAP	728 656	−0.81%	3.00	10.00	1.00
LAND SECURITIES	261 700	−0.89%	1.00	11.00	1.00
LATTICE GROUP	1 371 301	0.74%	5.00	−10.00	1.00
STNDRD CHART BK	1 930 231	−0.60%	8.00	8.00	1.00
LOGICA PLC	770 266	−1.53%	3.00	20.00	2.00
CANARY WHARF GRP	382 434	−1.61%	1.00	21.00	2.00
BG GROUP PLC	4 845 641	−0.09%	21.00	1.00	2.00
CENTRICA	2 177 700	−1.58%	9.00	21.00	2.00
DAILY MAIL TST A	55 873	−2.40%	0.00	32.00	3.00
CELLTECH GROUP	152 581	−2.41%	0.00	32.00	3.00
CARLTON COMMS	4 219 807	−2.05%	18.00	27.00	3.00
ELECTROCOMPONENT	234 849	2.40%	1.00	−33.00	3.00
BANK OF SCOTLAND	8 733 069	−1.29%	37.00	17.00	4.00
CMG PLC	1 811 341	−3.14%	7.00	42.00	4.00
HALIFAX GROUP	2 998 345	−3.18%	12.00	42.00	4.00
LLOYDS TSB GRP	9 844 032	−1.35%	42.00	18.00	4.00
ARM HOLDINGS	5 574 605	−3.85%	24.00	51.00	5.00
CABLE & WIRELESS	11 902 399	−2.47%	51.00	33.00	6.00
ENERGIS PLC	6 138 840	−4.59%	26.00	61.00	6.00
SHIRE PHARM GRP	13 765 951	−2.89%	59.00	38.00	7.00
B SKY B	5 143 355	−5.02%	22.00	67.00	7.00
SHELL TRNPT(REG)	15 847 345	1.64%	68.00	−23.00	7.00
MARCONI PLC	8 747 642	−5.41%	37.00	72.00	8.00
GRANADA	15 830 746	−3.98%	68.00	53.00	8.00
TELEWEST COMMUNI	4 711 424	−6.30%	20.00	84.00	8.00
INVENSYS	9 709 980	−6.03%	42.00	80.00	9.00
BP	22 317 632	1.75%	96.00	−24.00	9.00
COLT TELECOM GRP	2 839 768	−7.45%	12.00	100.00	10.00
BRITISH TELECOM	23 064 828	−2.30%	100.00	30.00	10.00

In Figure 9.9 I've plotted the shares by volume (x-axis) and percentage change (y-axis) and shaded and sized them according to how close they are to the ideal. We could draw a circle of arbitrary radius, centred on the point (0,0), and we could say that all instances falling within the circle belong to the *ideal* category and all those falling outside do not. Or we could draw a series of concentric circles, corresponding with the bands, and say that each instance belongs to the ideal category to a greater or lesser extent.

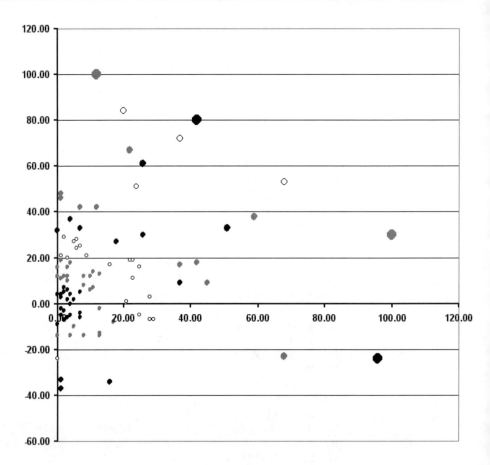

Figure 9.9   Share volumes by percentage change

Now let's replace the concept of an ideal stock with the idea that there are many ideals, depending on your investment strategy and attitude to risk. As a day trader you might be more interested in highly volatile shares whose prices swing wildly throughout a typical trading day. In Figure 9.10 I've drawn a few more circles to encompass stocks belonging to the following categories:

• Low change, low volume.

• Positive change, low volume.

• Low change, high volume.

• Moderate change, moderate volume.

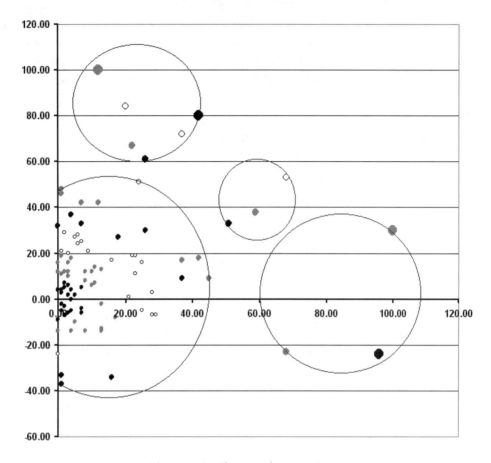

Figure 9.10   Share stock categories

So far this smacks more of *classification* than *clustering*, because I've chosen my own categories. However, an important distinction is how the inclusion (or exclusion) of instances within each category is calculated using a simple, impartial, distance formula applied across all attributes rather than a specific set of rules for each category. When I say 'across all attributes' you can take this in a more general sense to mean three, four, five or *n* attributes for some data sets.

The second point to consider in moving from classification to clustering is how the centres of the circles in Figure 9.10 are chosen. In this case I chose them myself to illustrate the point, but it is possible to choose these local centres of gravity algorithmically using an iterative process. A popular algorithm for this is the *k-means* algorithm described in more detail in Berry and Linoff (2000). The *k* part refers to the number of clusters, and the *means* part refers to the arithmetic mean – what I've called the centre of gravity – of each cluster. To give you a feel for how the algorithm works, here is a short extract:

Records are assigned to clusters through an iterative process that starts with clusters centered at essentially random locations in the record space and moves the cluster centroids (another name for the cluster means) around until each one is actually at the center of some cluster of records.

To complete this topic I should also point out that cluster instances do not necessarily have to fall within circles, ellipses, or any other regular shapes. Any shape will do as long as there is a mean, centroid, or centre of gravity (call it what you will) towards which the instances gravitate.

Where does Java fit in?

Well, Java was used to fetch the data in the first place from the web. Although I've used a spreadsheet application to compile Table 9.1, to normalize the values and calculate their distances from an ideal, and to plot the graphs, I could have used a Java program instead.

In that context, it's no accident that I introduced you to the *max(...)* function earlier in this chapter. The ability to normalize data within a certain range is dependent on our ability to find the maximum value for the specific files within a data set. We can then normalize the values with this calculation:

normalizedValue = (originalValue/maxValue) * 100

Perhaps you won't be surprised to here that if you wish to take the clustering idea further, I can point you again in the direction of Frank and Witten (2000) for a complete clustering algorithm implemented in Java.

9.4 Chapter Review

In common with the rest of the book, this chapter began on a practical footing with a class that fetches a dataset for a limited data-mining demonstration. That demonstration focused on how SQL could be applied to web data in such a way to support two common data mining operations, namely *classification* and *association*. Though we didn't go as far as implementing a complete SQL engine, I've tried to show how that idea follows directly on from the work we did in Chapter 4.

Then followed an utility class whose purpose was to provide a common set of aggregation functions for values in row sets. The particular function that we implemented, to find the maximum of a set of values, could be useful in normalizing data as a precursor to *clustering*.

I concluded by giving you my interpretation of a third data mining operation, *clustering*. I don't yet consider myself to be among the experts on this subject, but I hope to have opened a doorway in your mind that you might like to walk through. Using Java, of course.

If you like the idea of SQL applied to web data, which has underpinned much of this chapter, you can find out more about the commercial Web-DataKit implementation at http://www.lotontech.com/wdbc.html. If you'd like to have a go at implementing something similar yourself, you can find a case study describing the internals of an early version in *Professional Java Data* (Wrox Press, 2001).

Loose Ends and Looking Ahead

In this final chapter I'll tie up one of the loose ends that this book has so far left untied, by giving some attention to metadata. I'll use this as a lead-in to a fairly new technology, Resource Description Framework (RDF), that supports standardized metadata definitions in XML. Then I look further ahead at what additional technologies are worth investigating as you take my ideas forward, in both the short- and long-term.

10.1 Loose Ends: Metadata

In compiling this book I've been surprised that it's not really been necessary for me to resort to metadata in order to explore the various techniques. Maybe that's a function of being slightly ahead of the RDF wave, thus no widely used metadata standard was applicable.

In an nutshell, metadata is data that describes other data. By interpreting the metadata for a resource you can get a feel for the content and the organization of the resource itself.

Notice that I say 'the content and organization of the resource'. In some situations, and according to some definitions, the term metadata implies a description of how the resource data is arranged. In some situations, and according to other definitions, the term metadata implies a description of the resource content. In both cases the metadata helps you in your understanding of the data that it describes.

You should also be aware that the concept is not at all new, and when I say resource you can take it to mean a HTML page, a document, or even a relational database. To complicate things further I'll say that the distinction between data and metadata is often subjective: one man's data is another man's metadata.

10.1.1 Metadata in relational databases

I first encountered the concept of metadata when working with relational databases in the late 1980s and early 1990s. It's quite straightforward to create new relational database tables, to insert data into them, and to select data from them, all using SQL and an advance understanding of the database schema.

Now suppose you wanted to write a graphical application to visualize a database schema. You would want such an application to determine the schema automatically for any database that was presented to it for inspection. Believe it or not, determining the schema of any database can be achieved by issuing an SQL statement – not one that selects data from tables, but one that selects table structure information from other tables.

Typically you can run a statement like this one:

```
SELECT table, column FROM syscolumns
```

and you'll be rewarded with the names of all the tables, and their constituent columns, in the current database. Like this:

Table	Column
employee	lastname
employee	firstname
employee	employee-id
address	employee-id
address	street
address	town
address	postcode
salary	employee-id
salary	hourly-rate

This is metadata of the kind that describes the organization of the resource, since it tells you how the resource (i.e. the database) is subdivided into tables and columns. And if the tables and columns have meaningful names it also provides a summary of the content within the resource, in the sense that you know this database deals with employees, their addresses, and their salaries.

10.1.2   Metadata in HTML pages

Choose the *View Source* option in your browser when visiting any typical web page and you're likely to see something like this at the top of the source text:

```
<head>
<meta http-equiv="Content-Type" content="text/html; charset=iso-8859-1">
<meta name="GENERATOR" content="Mozilla/4.76 [en] (Win98; U) [Netscape]">
<meta name="Author" content="LOTONtech">
<meta name ="KEYWORDS" content="web mining ">
<meta name ="DESCRIPTION" content="Web Mining Techniques">
<title>LOTONtech Web Mining</title>
</head>
```

This shows that HTML supports a *<meta>* tag that allows arbitrary metadata to be recorded in the form of simple name/value pairs that are not rendered as part of the page content. The *<meta>* tags provide summarized information about the key features of a HTML page that may be useful to search engines, document management systems, and other applications.

Note that in this context the meta-elements are used in the main as a summarization mechanism for the key features of the resource content. The organizational metadata is encoded in the form of the HTML tags.

10.1.3   Metadata in this book

In my earlier example for metadata in relational databases I showed how we could determine the subdivision of a table into individual columns. In Chapters 3 and 4, I showed you how we could determine the subdivision of a HTML web page into it's uniquely addressable constituent elements. We're essentially working at the metadata level, and our filters are picking out individual elements according to the structure defined by that metadata.

Do you remember Figure 4.4 from Chapter 4? I thought not, so I've reproduced it again for you here as Figure 10.1.

In the commercial SQL implementation we've taken this further by drawing a distinction between a data selection (in which case we know the keys of the elements we wish to select) and metadata selection (in which case we're asking what keys are available for selection). I've shown the contrast in Figures 10.2 and 10.3, and in the latter you should take note that I'm selecting an element (*._key[]*) that doesn't exist at the data level.

In my example for metadata in HTML pages (shown earlier) I told you that web pages typically contain a set of name/value pairs enclosed in *<meta>*

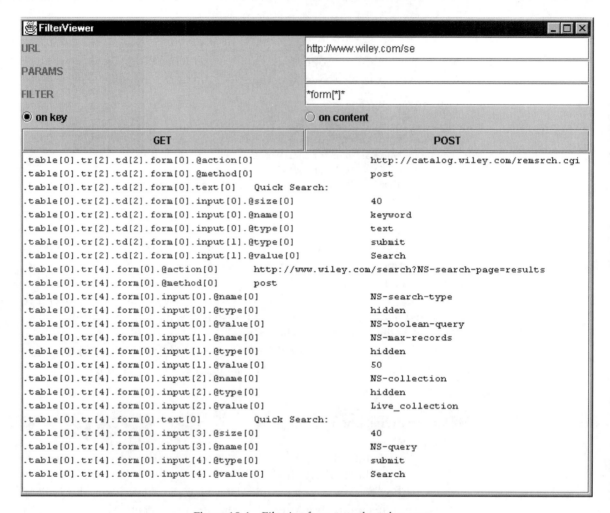

Figure 10.1   Filtering form metadata elements

tags. We can use the filtering techniques from Chapter 5 to just pick out metadata elements from a HTML page, with a filter like this:

```
.meta[*].*
```

However, now we're attaching a slightly different meaning to the term metadata than the one I described previously. Remember what I said about one man's data being another man's metadata?

To add to the confusion I'll say that HTML, in it's XHTML variant, is an instance of a meta model defined using XML. For HTML, read *data* and for XML, read *metadata*. If you are confused, don't worry as you're in good

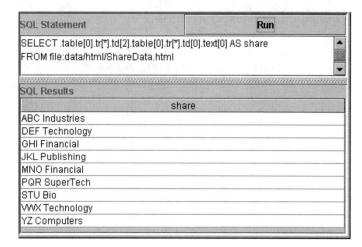

Figure 10.2   Data selection

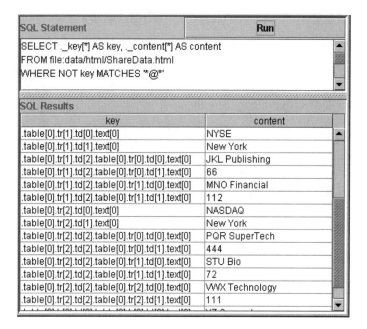

Figure 10.3   Metadata selection

company. The important thing to remember is that whenever someone talks of metadata they're talking about a set of data that you can query to find out about the organization and/or content of some other set of data.

10.2 Looking Ahead

So what's worth looking out for as you move forward with web mining and Java? Straight up ahead I see the RDF as providing a rich set of metadata to be mined on the web, and as a summary mechanism it could well improve the performance of our searching applications. On the subject of searching, you might like to think about searching a web of XML pages – via the XPointer mechanism – in the same way that we searched a web of HTML pages using the standard hyperlinking mechanism.

Also in the immediate future I think it's worth paying a bit more attention to the presentation aspects of our mining applications. The XSLT and Java Server Pages technologies could help out a lot here in decoupling the content from its final presentation.

10.2.1 Resource description framework

RDF is a recent standard for defining metadata associated with web resources. Used with HTML or XHTML documents, RDF could be used to describe the content of the pages – or the data required by certain web sites – in a standardized and summarized form.

In terms of describing the content of web pages, I mean that certain key information (author, title, subject, synopsis) could be recorded along with, yet separate from, the main web page. In terms of data required by certain web sites, I mean that your browser could record your contact details (name, email address and so on) and provide these automatically to sites in response to an RDF request.

Where HTML *<meta>* elements support a simple listing of name/value pairs, RDF provides a more structured metadata description that may be likened to an entity-relationship diagram or an object diagram. RDF *resources* correspond with objects and RDF *properties* correspond with instance variables.

No particular representation is mandatory for RDF, though the XML representation is probably the most natural, and certainly the most popular in the context of the World Wide Web. The following listing shows a snippet of RDF, expressed as XML, and describing the *author*, *publisher* and *title* of an on-line document:

```
<?xml version="1.0"?>
<rdf:RDF
  xmlns:rdf="http://www.w3.org/1999/02/22-rdf-syntax-ns#"
```

```
xmlns:s="http://description.org/schema/">
<rdf:Description about="http://www.w3.org/Home/Lassila">
  <s:Author>Tony Loton </s:Author >
  <s:Publisher>John Wiley & Sons </s:Publisher>
  <s:Title>Web Mining with Java</s:Title>
</rdf:Description>
</rdf:RDF>
```

In its XML form this RDF description is open to the querying techniques we covered in Chapter 5, thus we're RDF ready.

Although I'm not doing much RDF work right now I imagine that I might well be in the near future. So might you be too, in which case you could find out more by referring to the latest version of the RDF syntax available at http://www.w3.org/TR/REC-rdf-syntax.

There are also a few books that you might like to take at look at:

Creating Web Services with RDF, Johan Hjelm, Wiley, 2001.
Creating the Semantic Web with RDF, Johan Hjelm, Wiley, 2001.

10.2.2 XPointer and XPath

As I mentioned in a previous chapter, XML files may be hyperlinked to (locations within) other XML files using the XPointer mechanism. Thus you might like to adapt the search engine in Chapter 6 to traverse linked XML files in the same way that it will currently traverse linked HTML files. You can find XPointer information at: http://www.w3.org/TR/xptr/

To link to a specific location within a target XML file, XPointer make use of the XPath syntax. XPath syntax has some similarities with, and some differences from, the notation I have used to address individual XML elements. At this point in time I think my notation is more intuitive, equally suited to both HTML and XML, and lends itself to querying via SQL. However, the XPath notation does have some handy tricks up its sleeve for addressing elements relative to other elements, and for addressing elements according to their content, so I see it as a logical next step to combine the best parts of XPath with the work we have done here. You can find XPath information at: http://www.w3.org/TR/xpath

10.2.3 Presentation techniques

Besides collecting and manipulating data from web sources, a central theme of this book has been the re-presentation of that data in new ways. On the whole I've limited the *presentation* discussion to the logical dimension, i.e. how to combine previously unrelated information and present it in composite with added value.

There is also a physical dimension to presentation. I've scratched the surface by covering applets and servlets as delivery channels, as well as hinting at some less obvious presentation mechanisms such as human speech and SMS message delivery. For web-based delivery of content there are (at least) two other technologies that you might find indispensible: XSLT and Java Server Pages (JSPs).

XSLT

In Chapter 5 we developed a portal by gathering information from two separate web sources and rendering that information, via a servet, as a composite HTML page. The format of the HTML page, the ordering of the lists and the colours used, was fixed. Now suppose we'd like to allow our users to set preferences for how they'd like to see that data: the same data for all users, but a different presentation style for each.

Rather than modifying our *PortalServlet* to render the HTML in many different ways, we could instead render the combined content as XML to be transformed through XSLT into HTML format according to the individual user's preferences. Thus decoupling the final style presentation from the original content presentation.

That gives you an idea of what we could do with XSLT, but it's beyond the scope of this book to go into the technical details. It's not my speciality anyway, but if you're interested in this technology you could read more about it in *XSLT: Professional Developer's Guide*, Wiley, 2001.

Java server pages

JSPs is a technology layer that sits on top of the servlet layer, and which allows variable (dynamic) content to be embedded into web pages without necessarily going down to the level of servlet programming.

You can encapsulate Java functions in JSP tags and these tags may be embedded in web pages to include some specific content in a specific location on the page. I see a good opportunity here to wrap up our web queries in JSP tags like this one:

```
<bean:stockPrice symbol="ABC"/>
```

I don't have a specific recommendation for a book on JSPs, but if you're interested you'll find plenty of them.

10.3 Looking Further Ahead

RDF, XPointer, Xpath, XSLT, and JSP are available now for you to experiment with. Looking further ahead you might be interested to know that there's a Java Data Mining API on the way; maybe. In addition, did you know that for taking data from the web, via a JDBC like interface, as we have in this book, there's a Java class called *WebRowSet*? It's not very well publicized and I've never seen it used.

10.3.1 Java data mining API

At the time of writing, the Java Data Mining API exists only as a specification (JSR 000073) which you can find out more about at:

http://java.sun.com/aboutJava/communityprocess/jsr/jsr_073_dmapi.html

By the time you read this, the specification may well have been realized in code, and I've reproduced clause 2.1 from the specification here so that you can get a feel for its purpose:

2.1 Please describe the proposed Specification:

> The JDMAPI specification will address the need for a pure
> Java™ API that supports the building of data mining
> models, the scoring of data using models, as well as the
> creation, storage, access and maintenance of data and
> metadata supporting data mining results, and select data
> transformations.

What that paragraph tells me is that this API, when implemented, could provide standardized versions of the kinds of data processing algorithms provided by Frank and Witten (2000). Thus making them obsolete, or maybe increasing their relevance.

In terms of the techniques I've described in this book I'm slightly uneasy that this specification also deals with '. . . access . . . of data . . .', but comforted by a later clause 2.3 that expresses the aim

> '. . . The ultimate goal of JDMAPI is to provide for data
> mining systems what JDBC™ did for relational
> databases.'

Thus I imagine a set of third-party drivers from JDMAPI in the style of JDBC drivers. The techniques that I've described, if taken to their logical conclusion with SQL, effectively constitute a JDBC driver for web data. So it's conceivable that they could be adapted to constitute a JDMAPI for web data in the new scheme.

10.3.2   WebRowSet

Something else that might be worth looking out for is the *WebRowSet* variant of the *CachedRowSet* provided as part of the JDBC 2.0 Optional Package. Although I've seen mentions of this going as far back as 1998, and then more recently in *Professional Java Data* (Wrox Press) to which I contributed, I've not yet seen or heard about it being used generally. It's somewhat conspicuous by its absence.

As you read this it might be conspicuous by its presence so it's worth telling you what to look out for. You can see in Figure 10.4 that the basic idea is quite similar to the one I presented in Chapter 4 (Figure 4.12). A relational database will be queried by a servlet that re-presents the data records as XML content accessible over a HTTP connection. The client side *WebRowSet* will, with the help of an *XMLReader* class, allow you to step through the XML-encoded HTTP-served records as though stepping through the records or the originating database.

Before we leave this topic, I can think of a possible reason for the low profile of the *WebRowSet*. It's just one of a few suggested implementations of the *RowSet* interface(s) that could be offered by independent vendors. Or another explanation is that – at the time of writing – I've just read something about the *XmlReader* that supports the process not actually working properly with the SAX implementation. This may not be true, and I'm just reporting what I've heard.

10.4   Chapter Review

In this final chapter I've tied up a few loose ends, firstly by discussing metadata, which – to my surprise – was not essential to the plot of this book. Though not essential, it is relevant and I hope to have provided an overview of metadata in the context of the relevance to us; as well as encouraging you to look further into the RDF.

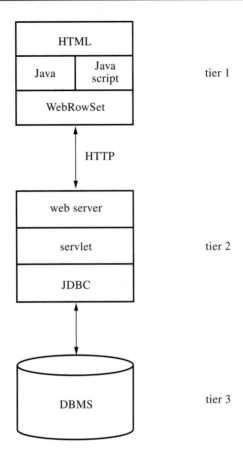

Figure 10.4   WebRowSet schematic.

I see RDF and XPointer as logical next places to set sail for on the web mining voyage, possibly stopping off *en-route* to look at XSLT and JSP. Looking out from my crow's nest I've seen the Java Data Mining API coming up over the horizon, and I've caught a fleeting glimpse of the *WebRowSet*.

Appendix A

Software Installation and Configuration

This appendix describes how the pre-requisite Java software and the accompanying software for this book should be installed and configured.

A.1 Third-Party Software

The pre-requisite third-party software for this book, all of which is available for download from the Sun Microsystems Java web site at http://www.java.sun.com or the Apache Software Foundation web site at http://www.apache.org includes:

- The Java 2 Standard Edition (J2SE) Software Development Kit version 1.3 or later from http://java.sun.com/j2se/ (required for all examples).

- The Java API for XML Processing (JAXP) version 1.1 or later from http://java.sun.com/xml/xml_jaxp.html (required for all examples).

- The 'Tomcat' Servlet Engine Reference Implementation v4.0 or later from http://jakarta.apache.org/site/binindex.html (required for servlet examples).

- JavaMail and JavaBeans Activation Framework (JAF) from
  http://java.sun.com/products/javamail/index.html
  and http://java.sun.com/products/javabeans/glasgow/jaf.html respectively
  (required for chapter 7 only).

Note that the Java 2 Enterprise Edition (J2EE) contains all of the required classes, but I've assumed the separate downloads as the lowest common denominator amongst readers.

A.1.1   J2SE SDK installation

The Java 2 SDK is required for all examples in this book. It is supplied as a self-installing executable file, which on my Windows system is called:

```
j2sdk-1_3_win.exe
```

Run this file and follow the instructions along with any additional instructions provided with the download distribution.

A.1.2   JAXP

The Java API for XML Processing is required for all examples in this book. It is supplied as an archive, which on my Windows system is called:

```
jaxp-1_1.zip
```

There is no installer program to run, so you simply unpack the archive into a convenient location and set your CLASSPATH to include the appropriate jar files, which are:

```
crimson.jar
jaxp.jar
xalan.jar
```

A.1.3   JavaMail and JAF

JavaMail is only required for Chapter 7, and to use it requires two software distributions: the JavaMail download itself and the JavaBeans Activation Framework (for handling of MIME types). Again these are packaged as simple archives, on my Windows system:

```
javamail-1_2.zip
jaf1_0_1.zip
```

And the jar files that you need to include are:

```
mail.jar
activatin.jar
```

A.1.4   Tomcat server

For the servlet examples you will need a servlet engine. As one of the most popular servlet engines – in fact the reference implementation for the servlet v2.3 specification – I recommend Tomcat. Again a simple archive to be unpacked into a convenient place, in my cse:

```
jakarta-tomcat-4.0-b7.zip
```

Several jar files are included, but to compile the examples in this book all you'll need to include in your CLASSPATH is:

```
servlet.jar
```

A.2   This Book's Software

You will find the software for this book on the companion web site at http://www.lotontech.com/wiley. All binary and source code is included in a file called *jwebdata.zip*. You should unpack this archive into a convenient location and you'll see that the directory structure looks like that shown in Figure A.1.

The source code and compiled Java class files are included in nine packages that map to chapters of the book as follows:

jwebdata\applet and jwebdata\servlet (Chapter 2),

jwebdata\parsing (Chapter 3),

jwebdata\query (Chapter 4),

jwebdata\portal (Chapter 5),

jwebdata\search (Chapter 6),

jwebdata\mail (Chapter 7),

jwebdata\text (Chapter 8),

jwebdata\data (Chapter 9).

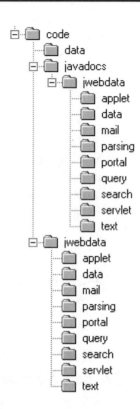

Figure A.1   Code directory structure

If you recompile the code in those packages I assume you'll do so from a command window opened on the directory directly above the `jwebdata` directory. Thus you'll need to add the current directory '.' to your CLASS-PATH, along with the jar files for the pre-requisite Java software that I mentioned earlier. As a comparison you might like to know that my CLASS-PATH looks like this:

```
C:\WINDOWS>echo %CLASSPATH%
.;C:\Apps\Java\jaxp-1.1\crimson.jar;C:\Apps\Java\jaxp-
1.1\jaxp.jar;C:\Apps\Java\jaxp-1.1\xalan.jar;C.:\Apps\Java\javamail-
1.2\mail.jar;C:\Apps\Java\jaf-1.0.1\activation.jar;C:\Apps\Java\jakarta-
tomcat-4.0-b7\common\lib\servlet.jar
```

You will also have noticed in Figure A.1 that the *JavaDoc* generated documentation for the example classes has been provided in the \javadocs directory.

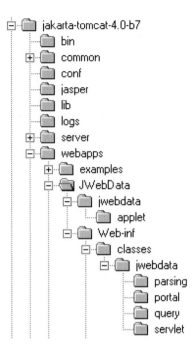

Figure A.2   Tomcat deployment directory structure

A.2.1   Servlet deployment

To work with the servlet examples you'll need to deploy the appropriate example classes into the Tomcat servlet engine or other servlet engine of your choice. The easiest way to do this is to create a new directory (a web application context) called *JWebData* within the \webapps directory, then copy packages into that directory to mirror the structure shown in Figure A.2.

To make the servlet engine aware of the new web context you will also need to add the following lines to the *server.xml* file within the *conf* directory:

```
<!-- Tomcat WebMining Context -->
<Context path="/JWebData" docBase="JWebData" debug="0"/>
```

Finally, you'll need to place the web.xml file listed here, and included in the download, into the \WEB-INF directory:

```
<?xml version="1.0" encoding="ISO-8859-1"?>

<!DOCTYPE web-app
```

```
    PUBLIC "-//Sun Microsystems, Inc.//DTD Web Application 2.3//EN"
    "http://java.sun.com/j2ee/dtds/webapp_2_3.dtd">

<web-app>
  <servlet>
    <servlet-name>
      SimpleServlet
    </servlet-name>
    servlet-class>
      jwebdata.servlet.SimpleServlet
    </servlet-class>
  </servlet>

  <servlet>
    <servlet-name>
      PortalServlet
    </servlet-name>
    <servlet-class>
      jwebdata.portal.PortalServlet
    </servlet-class>
  </servlet>

  <servlet>
    <servlet-name>
      ShareServlet
    </servlet-name>
    <servlet-class>
      jwebdata.portal.ShareServlet
    </servlet-class>
  </servlet>
  <servlet-mapping>
    <servlet-name>
      SimpleServlet
    </servlet-name>
    <url-pattern>
      /SimpleServlet
    </url-pattern>
  </servlet-mapping>

  <servlet-mapping>
    <servlet-name>
      PortalServlet
    </servlet-name>
    <url-pattern>
      /PortalServlet
    </url-pattern>
  </servlet-mapping>

  <servlet-mapping>
    <servlet-name>
```

```
        ShareServlet
      </servlet-name>
      <url-pattern>
        /ShareServlet
      </url-pattern>
    </servlet-mapping>
  </web-app>
```

Testing the deployment

To check that you have deployed the code correctly you can open a browser window and try connecting to the following URLs in turn.

http://localhost:8080/JWebData/SimpleServlet

http://localhost:8080/JWebData/ShareServlet?exchange=FTSE

http://localhost:8080JWebData/ShareServlet?exchange=NASDAQ

http://localhost:8080/JWebData/PortalServlet

Note that where source code is listed, any URLs pointed at resources – servlets and applets – running within the Tomcat installation will be of the form http://localhost:8080/JWebData/xxx. If you deploy against a different servlet engine, or if you configure Tomcat to run on a port other than its default, you'll need to edit and recompile the code to suit.

To help you, I'll tell you now that this affects the following Java classes:

```
jwebdata\applet\HTTPApplet.java
jwebdata\portal\PortalServlet.java
jwebdata\portal\PortalApplet.java
```

Appendix B

JavaDoc Extracts

In this appendix I've reproduced extracts from the JavaDoc generated comments for the classes implemented in each chapter. It will serve as a handy guide to the full set of classes, their relationships, and their methods as you read (or re-read) each chapter.

All of the information in this appendix was produced using the Java SDK *javadoc* tool by issuing the following command:

```
javadoc -d ./javadocs jwebdata.applet jwebdata.data jwebdata.mail
jwebdata.parsing jwebdata.portal jwebdata.query jwebdata.search
jwebdata.servlet jwebdata.text
```

B.1 Overview

This section lists the full set of classes across all chapters, fully qualified with their package names.

B.1.1 Class hierarchy

- class java.lang.Object
  - class java.net.Authenticator
    - class jwebdata.parsing.ProxyAuthenticator
  - class jwebdata.data.CensusDataFetcher
  - class java.awt.Component (implements java.awt.image.ImageObserver, java.awt.MenuContainer, java.io.Serializable)
    - class java.awt.Container

- class java.awt.Panel (implements javax.accessibility.Accessible)
  - class java.applet.Applet
    - class jwebdata.applet.HTTPApplet (implements java.awt.event.ActionListener)
    - class javax.swing.JApplet (implements javax.accessibility.Accessible, javax.swing.RootPaneContainer)
      - class jwebdata.portal.PortalApplet (implements java.awt.event.ActionListener, javax.swing.ListCellRenderer,java.lang.Runnable)
    - class jwebdata.applet.SimpleApplet (implements java.awt.event.ActionListener)
- class java.awt.Window (implements javax.accessibility.Accessible)
  - class java.awt.Frame (implements java.awt.MenuContainer)
    - class javax.swing.JFrame (implements javax.accessibility.Accessible, javax.swing.RootPaneContainer, javax.swing.WindowConstants)
      - class jwebdata.query.FilterViewer (implements java.awt.event.ActionListener, javax.swing.ListCellRenderer, javax.swing.event.ListSelectionListener)
      - class jwebdata.query.SqlGui (implements java.awt.event.ActionListener)
- class org.xml.sax.helpers.DefaultHandler (implements org.xml.sax.ContentHandler, org.xml.sax.DTDHandler, org.xml.sax.EntityResolver, org.xml.sax.ErrorHandler)
  - class jwebdata.parsing.XMLParserWrapper (implements jwebdata.parsing.WebParser)
- class jwebdata.parsing.DOMParserWrapper (implements jwebdata.parsing.WebParser)
- class jwebdata.text.FeatureExtractor
- class jwebdata.query.Filter
- class jwebdata.data.Function
- class javax.servlet.GenericServlet (implements java.io.Serializable, javax.servlet.Servlet, javax.servlet.ServletConfig)
  - class javax.servlet.http.HttpServlet (implements java.io.Serializable)
    - class jwebdata.portal.PortalServlet

- ○ class jwebdata.servlet.SimpleServlet
- ○ class org.xml.sax.HandlerBase (implements
  org.xml.sax.DocumentHandler,
  org.xml.sax.DTDHandler, org.xml.sax.EntityResolver,
  org.xml.sax.ErrorHandler)
  - ○ class jwebdata.parsing.LegacyXMLParserWrapper (implements
    jwebdata.parsing.WebParser)
- ○ class javax.swing.text.html.HTMLEditorKit.ParserCallback
  - ○ class jwebdata.parsing.HTMLParserWrapper (implements
    jwebdata.parsing.WebParser)
- ○ class jwebdata.mail.MailParserWrapper
- ○ class jwebdata.query.Operator
- ○ class jwebdata.query.QueryEngine
- ○ class jwebdata.search.SearchEngine (implements java.lang.Runnable)
- ○ class jwebdata.search.SimpleSearcher (implements
  jwebdata.search.SearchHandler)
- ○ class jwebdata.mail.SMSRelay
- ○ class jwebdata.parsing.SourceElement
- ○ class jwebdata.text.TextParserWrapper
- ○ class jwebdata.parsing.WebParserWrapper
- ○ class jwebdata.search.WileySearcher (implements
  jwebdata.search.SearchHandler)

B.1.2 Interface hierarchy

- ○ interface jwebdata.search.SearchHandler
- ○ interface jwebdata.parsing.WebParser

B.2 Chapter 2 Classes

This section lists the class information, subdivided by package, for Chapter 2.

```
Package jwebdata.applet
```

Class Summary	
HTTPApplet	Applet that drives the SimpleServlet by POSTing a HTTP request.
SimpleApplet	A first applet that presents a simple GUI form.

Package jwebdata.servlet

Class Summary	
SimpleServlet	A first servlet that presents a simple GUI form.

B.2.1 HTTPApplet

public class **HTTPApplet**
extends java.applet.Applet
implements java.awt.event.ActionListener
Applet that drives the SimpleServlet by POSTing a HTTP request.

Constructor Summary
HTTPApplet

Method Summary	
void	actionPerformed(java.awt.event.ActionEvent event) This method POSTs the HTTP request in response to the button click.
void	init() Initialization method.

B.2.2 SimpleApplet

public class **SimpleApplet**
extends java.applet.Applet
implements java.awt.event.ActionListener
A first applet that presents a simple GUI form.

Constructor Summary
SimpleApplet()

Method Summary	
void	actionPerformed(java.awt.event.ActionEvent event)
	Method for responding to the button click.
void	init()
	Initialization method.

B.2.3   SimpleServlet

public class **SimpleServlet**
extends javax.servlet.http.HttpServlet
A first servlet that presents a simple GUI form.

Constructor Summary
SimpleServlet()

Method Summary	
void	doGet(javax.servlet.http.HttpServletRequest req, javax.servlet.http.HttpServletResponse res)
	Servlet method to process a GET submission.
void	doPost(javax.servlet.http.HttpServletRequest req, javax.servlet.http.HttpServletResponse res)
	Servlet method to process a POST submission.

B.3   Chapter 3 Classes

This section lists the class information, subdivided by package, for Chapter 3.

```
Package jwebdata.parsing
```

Interface Summary	
WebParser	Generic Parser interface implemented by HTMLParserWrapper and XMLParserWrapper.

Class Summary	
DOMParserWrapper	This class parses an XML file using DOM.
HTMLParserWrapper	This class parses a HTML file using Java 2's Editor Kit
LegacyXMLParserWrapper	
ProxyAuthenticator	A Java 2 Authenticator to provide the proxy/firewall password.
SourceElement	An instance of this class is created for every HTML or XML element.
WebParserWrapper	Entry point for all web access, delegates to HTMLParserWrapper or XMLParserWrapper according to the content type.
XMLParserWrapper	This class parses an XML file using SAX.

B.3.1   WebParser

public interface **WebParser**
Generic Parser interface implemented by HTMLParserWrapper and XMLParserWrapper.

Method Summary	
java.util.Vector	getElements(java.lang.String baseURL, java.net.URLConnection urlConnection)

B.3.2   DOMParserWrapper

public class **DOMParserWrapper**
extends java.lang.Object
implements WebParser
This class parses an XML file using DOM.

Constructor Summary
DOMParserWrapper()

Method Summary

void	characters(char[]data, int start, int length)
void	endElement(java.lang.String uri, java.lang.String localName, java.lang.String qName)
java.util.Vector	getElements(java.lang.String baseURL, java.net.URLConnection urlConnection)
	Method to get a key/value list of XML elements at baseURL.
static void	main(java.lang.String args)
void	startElement(java.lang.String uri, java.lang.String localName, java.lang.String qName, org.xml.sax.Attributes attributes)

B.3.3   HTMLParserWrapper

public class **HTMLParserWrapper**
extends javax.swing.text.html.HTMLEditorKit.ParserCallback
implements WebParser
This class parses a HTML file using Java 2's Editor Kit

Constructor Summary

HTMLParserWrapper()

Method Summary

java.util.Vector	getElements(java.lang.String baseURL, java.io.InputStream inputStream)
	Method to get a key/value list of HTML elements at baseURL.
java.util.Vector	getElements(java.lang.String baseURL, java.net.URLConnection urlConnection)
	Method to get a key/value list of HTML elements at baseURL.
void	handleEmptyTag(javax.swing.text.html.HTML.Tag tag, int pos)
	Parser call back method.
void	handleEndTag(javax.swing.text.html.HTML.Tag tag, int pos)
	Parser call back method.
void	handleSimpleTag(javax.swing.text.html.HTML.Tag tag, javax.swing.text.MutableAttributeSet attributes, int pos)
	Parser call back method.
void	handleStartTag(javax.swing.text.html.HTML.Tag tag, javax.swing.text.MutableAttributeSet attributes, int pos)
	Parser callback method.
void	handleText(char[]data, int pos)
	Parser call back method.
static void	main(java.lang.String[]args)

B.3.4   ProxyAuthenticator

public class **ProxyAuthenticator**
extends java.net.Authenticator
A Java 2 Authenticator to provide the proxy/firewall password.

Constructor Summary

ProxyAuthenticator(java.lang.String user, java.lang.String password)
   Constructor to take the username and password.

Method Summary

protected java.net.PasswordAuthentication	getPasswordAuthentication() Method to give up the username and password if requested.
java.net.PasswordAuthentication	

B.3.5   SourceElement

public class **SourceElement**
extends java.lang.Object
An instance of this class is created for every HTMLor XML element.

Constructor Summary

SourceElement(java.lang.String key, java.lang.String content)

Method Summary

java.lang.String	getContent() Each element has content.
java.lang.String	getKey() Each element is addressed via a unique key.
void	setKey(java.lang.String key)

B.3.6   WebParserWrapper

public class **WebParserWrapper**
extends java.lang.Object
Entry point for all web access, delegates to HTMLParserWrapper or XMLParserWrapper according to the content type.

Field Summary	
static java.lang.String	GET
Static java.lang.String	POST

Constructor Summary
WebParserWrapper()

Method Summary	
java.util.Vector	getElements(java.lang.String baseURL, java.lang.String params, java.lang.String method) Method to get a key/value list of HTML or XML elements from baseURL.
static void	main(java.lang.String[]args) A main() method for testing.

B.3.7   XMLParserWrapper

public class **XMLParserWrapper**
extends org.xml.sax.helpers.DefaultHandler
implements WebParser
This class parses an XML file using SAX.

Constructor Summary
XMLParserWrapper()

Method Summary	
void	characters(char[]data, int start, int length) Parser call back method.
void	endElement(java.lang.String uri, java.lang.String localName, java.lang.String qName) Parser call back method.

java.util.Vector	getElements(java.lang.String baseURL, java.net.URLConnection urlConnection)
	Method to get a key/value list of XML elements at baseURL.
static void	main(java.lang.String[]args)
void	startElement(java.lang.String uri, java.lang.String localName, java.lang.String qName,org.xml.sax.Attributes attributes)
	Parser call back method.

B.4 Chapter 4 Classes

This section lists the class information, subdivided by package, for Chapter 4.

Package jwebdata.query

Class Summary

Filter	Utility class to filter HTML or XML elements by key or content.
FilterViewer	GUI application for visualizing a filter.
Operator	A class to perform simple numeric and lexical comparisions.
QueryEngine	A class for combining filters into structured queries.
SqlGui	GUI application to demonstrate web access via SQL.

B.4.1 Filter

public class **Filter**
extends java.lang.Object
Utility class to filter HTML or XML elements by key or content.

Field Summary

static java.lang.String	CONTENT
static java.lang.String	KEY

Constructor Summary

Filter()

Method Summary

static java.util.Vector	getFilteredElements(java.util.Vector sortedElements, java.lang.String fieldConstant, java.lang.String operator, java.lang.String compareString)
	Static method for applying a filter to a set of elements.

B.4.2   FilterViewer

public class **FilterViewer**
extends javax.swing.JFrame
implements   java.awt.event.ActionListener,   javax.swing.event.ListSelection-
Listener, javax.swing.ListCellRenderer
GUI application for visualizing a filter.

Constructor Summary

FilterViewer(java.lang.String title)
   Constructor to create the GUI.

Method Summary

void	actionPerformed(java.awt.event.ActionEvent event)
	Method to respond to the button click by applying the filter.
java.awt.Component	getListCellRendererComponent(javax.swing.JList list, java.lang.Object value, int index, boolean isSelected, boolean cellHasFocus)
	Swing method to display each filtered element in our own style.
static void	main(java.lang.String args)
	A main() method to test it.
void	valueChanged(javax.swing.event.ListSelectionEvent event)
	Transfer the clicked element to the filter box, for convenience.

B.4.3   Operator

public class **Operator**
extends java.lang.Object
A class to perform simple numeric and lexical comparisions.

Constructor Summary

Operator()

Method Summary

static boolean	compare(java.lang.String realContent, java.lang.String operator, java.lang.String compareContent)
	Compares two values according to the supplied operator.
static boolean	matches(java.lang.String realString, java.lang.String wildCardString)
	Performs a wildcard comparison of two strings.

B.4.4 QueryEngine

public class **QueryEngine**
extends java.lang.Object
A class for combining filters into structured queries.

Constructor Summary

QueryEngine()

Method Summary

java.util.Vector	getFilteredRows(java.util.Vector elements, java.util.Vector filters)
	Entry point to this class, returns a set of rows comprising elements selected by the
	supplied filters.
static void	main(java.lang.String args)
	A main() method to test it.

B.4.5 SqlGui

public class **SqlGui**
extends javax.swing.JFrame
implements java.awt.event.ActionListener
GUI application to demonstrate web access via SQL.

Constructor Summary

SqlGui(java.lang.String title)
   Constructor to create the GUI.

Method Summary	
void	actionPerformed(java.awt.event.ActionEvent event)
	Method to run the query in response to the button press.
static void	main(java.lang.String[]args)
	A main() method to test it.

B.5   Chapter 5 Classes

This section lists the class information, subdivided by package, for Chapter 5.

```
Package jwebdata.portal
```

Class Summary	
PortalApplet	Portal implementation as an applet.
PortalServlet	Portal implementation as an servlet.

B.5.1   PortalApplet

public class **PortalApplet**
extends javax.swing.JApplet
implements java.awt.event.ActionListener, java.lang.Runnable,
javax.swing.ListCellRenderer
Portal implementation as an applet.

Constructor Summary
PortalApplet()

Method Summary	
void	actionPerformed(java.awt.event.ActionEvent event)
	Set new limits in response to the button press.
java.awt.Component	getListCellRendererComponent(javax.swing.JList list,
	java.lang.Object value, int index,
	boolean isSelected, boolean cellHasFocus)
	Swing method to display the information in our own style.
void	init()
	Initialization method.
void	run()
	Thread run() method to refresh the information regularly.

B.5.2   PortalServlet

public class **PortalServlet**
extends javax.servlet.http.HttpServlet
Portal implementation as a servlet.

Constructor Summary
PortalServlet()

Method Summary	
void	doGet(javax.servlet.http.HttpServletRequest req, javax.servlet.http.HttpServletResponse res) Servlet method to process a GET submission.
void	doPost(javax.servlet.http.HttpServletRequest req, javax.servlet.http.HttpServletResponse res) Servlet method to process a POST submission.

B.6   Chapter 6 Classes

This section lists the class information, subdivided by package, for Chapter 6.

    Package jwebdata.search

Interface Summary	
SearchHandler	Implement this interface to support custom behaviour.

Class Summary	
SearchEngine	Search Engine/Crawler class.
SimpleSearcher	Custom SearchHandler implementation for simple searches.
WileySearcher	

B.6.1   SearchHandler

public interface **SearchHandler**

Implement this interface to support custom behaviour.

Method Summary	
boolean	handleElement(java.lang.String url, java.lang.String key, java.lang.String content)

B.6.2   SearchEngine

public class **SearchEngine**
extends java.lang.Object
implements java.lang.Runnable
Search Engine/Crawler class.

Constructor Summary
SearchEngine()

Method Summary	
void	followLinks(java.lang.String url) Adds links (including frames) found at 'url' to the list of URLs waiting to be searched.
void	run() Run the search thread
boolean	searchInProgress() This method tells you that a search is in progress.
boolean	startSearch(java.lang.String url, SearchHandler searchHandler) This method asks the engine to start a search at the given URL, with the user-supplied searchHandler to be called back with events.
boolean	stopPending() This method tells you that the current search will stop soon.
void	stopSearch() This method asks the engine to stop the current search.

B.6.3   SimpleSearcher

public class **SimpleSearcher**

extends java.lang.Object
implements SearchHandler
Custom SearchHandler implementation for simple searches.

Constructor Summary

SimpleSearcher()

Method Summary

boolean	handleElement(java.lang.String url, java.lang.String key, java.lang.String content) Search Engine/Crawler call back method.
static void	main(java.lang.String[]args) A main() method to test it.
java.util.Hashtable	search(java.lang.String startURL, java.lang.String keyword) Method to invoke the search for keyword starting at startURL.

B.6.4 WileySearcher

public class **WileySearcher**
extends java.lang.Object
implements SearchHandler

Constructor Summary

WileySearcher()

Method Summary

boolean	handleElement(java.lang.String url, java.lang.String key, java.lang.String content) Search Engine/Crawler call back method.
static void	main(java.lang.String[]args)
java.util.Hashtable	search(java.lang.String startURL, java.lang.String keyword)

B.7   Chapter 7 Classes

This section lists the class information, subdivided by package, for Chapter 7.

```
Package jwebdata.mail
```

Class Summary	
MailParserWra pper	Email equivalent of WebParserWrapper
SMSRelay	Class to relay email messages to a mobile phone as SMS notifications.

B.7.1   MailParserWrapper

public class **MailParserWrapper**
extends java.lang.Object
Email equivalent of WebParserWrapper

Constructor Summary
MailParserWrapper()

Method Summary	
java.util.Vector	getElements(java.lang.String popServer, int port, java.lang.String popUser, java.lang.String popPassword) Method to get a key/value list of HTML or plain text elements of messages originating at a POP mail server.
static void	main(java.lang.String[]args) A main() method to test it.

B.7.2   SMSRelay

public class **SMSRelay**
extends java.lang.Object
Class to relay email messages to a mobile phone as SMS notifications.

Constructor Summary
SMSRelay()

Method Summary

static void   main(java.lang.String args)
                      Everything happens within the main() method.

B.8   Chapter 8 Classes

This section lists the class information, subdivided by package, for Chapter 8.

      Package jwebdata.text

Class Summary

FeatureExtractor   Class to extract feature sentences based on proper nouns and sentence
                      templates.
TextParserWrapper   Class to establish candidate types for each word in a test string.

B.8.1   FeatureExtractor

public class **FeatureExtractor**
extends java.lang.Object
Class to extract feature sentences based on proper nouns and sentence templates.

Constructor Summary

FeatureExtractor()

Method Summary

java.util.Vector   getFeatureSentences(java.util.Vector sentences, java.util.Vector templates)
                    Return those input sentences that have the features determined by the
               given templates.
static void   main(java.lang.String[]args)
                    A main() method to test it.

B.8.2   TextParserWrapper

public class **TextParserWrapper**
extends java.lang.Object
Class to establish candidate types for each word in a test string.

Constructor Summary
TextParserWrapper()

Method Summary	
java.util.Vector	getElements(java.lang.String text) Return a set of elements comprising input words with their candidate types.
static void	main(java.lang.String args) A main() method to test it.

B.9   Chapter 9 Classes

This section lists the class information, subdivided by package, for Chapter 9.

Package jwebdata.data

Class Summary	
CensusDataFetcher	Class to fetch some data mining test data.
Function	Class to perform some data functions.

B.9.1   CensusDataFetcher

public class **CensusDataFetcher**
extends java.lang.Object
Class to fetch some data mining test data.

Constructor Summary
CensusDataFetcher()

Method Summary	
static void	main(java.lang.String[]args) Everything happens in the main() method.

B.9.2   Function

public class **Function**
extends java.lang.Object
Class to perform some data functions.

Constructor Summary
Function()

Method Summary	
static void	main(java.lang.String[]args) A main() method to test it.
static java.lang.String	max(java.util.Vector rows, int columnNum)

Appendix C

Earlier Versions of JAXP

In this appendix I'll offer some advice on what to do if you're using an IDE or an application server that's not quite up to the J2EE v1.3 standard in terms of the Java API for XML Processing (JAXP). I'll list two sets of symptoms, for the *XMLParserWrapper* and the *DOMParserWrapper* respectively, and suggest some solutions.

C.1 Symptoms and Solutions

You might experience the following symptoms when you try to compile and run the JAXP-dependent parsing classes.

C.1.1 XMLParserWrapper

When you try to compile the *XMLParserWrapper* you might see:

```
jwebdata\parsing\XMLParserWrapper.java:10: cannot resolve symbol
symbol : class DefaultHandler
location: package helpers
public class XMLParserWrapper extends org.xml.sax.helpers.DefaultHandler
                                                          ^
jwebdataYparsingYXMLParserWrapper.java:38: cannot resolve symbol
symbol : class Attributes
location: class jwebdata.parsing.XMLParserWrapper
    localName, java.lang.String qName, Attributes attributes)
                                       ^
```

or maybe a simple version like this:

```
"XMLParserWrapper.java": Error #: 302 : cannot access class
org.xml.sax.helpers.DefaultHandler; class
org.xml.sax.helpers.DefaultHandler not found in stable package at line 10,
column 59
```

If you see something like that then chances are you have a version of JAXP supporting the SAX1 API rather than the SAX2 API.

I have seen that problem with at least one IDE and I fixed it by adapting the *XMLParserWrapper* to use the SAX 1 APIs. You will need to change the class definition as shown here (notice we're now extending org.xml.sax.Handler-Base):

```
public class XMLParserWrapper extends org.xml.sax.HandlerBase implements
WebParser
```

Also the *startElement(...)* and *endElement(...)* methods will need to be changed to reflect these implementations:

```
public void startElement(java.lang.String localName, AttributeList
attributes)
{
  String tag=localName.toString();

  // -- Update the count of this tag at this level --
  int tagCountInt=-1;
  Hashtable tagCounts=(Hashtable) countHistory
    .elementAt(tagHistory.size());
  Integer tagCountInteger=(Integer) tagCounts.get(tag);
  if (tagCountInteger!=null) tagCountInt=tagCountInteger.intValue();
  tagCountInt=tagCountInt+1;
  tagCounts.remove(tag);
  tagCounts.put(tag,new Integer(tagCountInt));

  // -- Put this tag on the stack and start a new count--
  tagHistory.addElement(tag+"["+tagCountInt+"]");
  countHistory.addElement(new Hashtable());

  int attCount=attributes.getLength();
  for (int i=0; i<attCount; i++)
  {

      String attributeName=attributes.getName(i);
      String attributeValue=attributes.getValue(i);

      // -- Add this attribute --
      String tagKey="";
      for (int ti=0; ti<tagHistory.size(); ti++)
        tagKey=tagKey+"."+tagHistory.elementAt(ti);
```

```
          elements.addElement(new SourceElement(tagKey+".@"
            +attributeName+"[0]",attributeValue));
      }
  }

  public void endElement(java.lang.String localName)
  {
    // -- Pop the tag off the stack --
    if (tagHistory.size()>0)
    {
      tagHistory.remove(tagHistory.size()-1);
      countHistory.remove(countHistory.size()-1);
    }
  }
}
```

Alternatively, if your IDE or application server allows, you could download and install the JAXP distribution recommended in Appendix A.

C.1.2 DOMParserWrapper

When you try to compile the *DOMParserWrapper* you might see:

```
jwebdata\parsing\DOMParserWrapper.java:29: cannot resolve symbol
symbol  : class DocumentBuilderFactory
location: class jwebdata.parsing.DOMParserWrapper
        DocumentBuilderFactory dbf =
        ^
jwebdata\parsing\DOMParserWrapper.java:30: cannot resolve symbol
symbol  : variable DocumentBuilderFactory
location: class jwebdata.parsing.DOMParserWrapper
          DocumentBuilderFactory.newInstance();
          ^
jwebdata\parsing\DOMParserWrapper.java:36: cannot resolve symbol
symbol  : class DocumentBuilder
location: class jwebdata.parsing.DOMParserWrapper
        DocumentBuilder db = null;
        ^
jwebdata\parsing\DOMParserWrapper.java:67: cannot resolve symbol
symbol  : method getNamespaceURI ()
location: interface org.w3c.dom.Node
              this.startElement(n.getNamespaceURI(),n.getLocalName()
                                ^
jwebdata\parsing\DOMParserWrapper.java:67: cannot resolve symbol
symbol  : method getLocalName ()
location: interface org.w3c.dom.Node
              this.startElement(n.getNamespaceURI(),n.getLocalName()
                                                    ^
```

I encountered that problem when compiling against the J2EE v1.2 rather than v1.3, and I can think of three solutions:

- Don't worry about it as the *DOMParserWrapper* was only provided for illustration. As long as you can compile and run the *XMLParserWrapper* you'll be OK with this book.

- Upgrade to J2EE v1.3.

- Download and install the JAXP distribution recommended in Appendix A.

Appendix D

License and Copyright Statements

The license and copyright statements for WordNet, and for the Public Records Office 1891 Census sample data, are reproduced here for your information.

D.1 WordNet License Statement

I have taken the Princeton University WordNet License Statement from this URL: http://www.cogsci.princeton.edu/~wn/license/

In authoring this book, my use and reproduction of any materials (software, documentation, and database) has – to the best of my knowledge – been in accordance with the license.

WordNet – a Lexical Database for English

Cognitive Science Laboratory
Princeton University
221 Nassau St.
Princeton, NJ 08542

Commercial Use of WordNet

WordNet® is unencumbered, and may be used in commercial applications in accordance with the following license agreement. An attorney representing the commercial interest should review this WordNet license with respect to the intended use.

This software and database is being provided to you, the LICENSEE, by Princeton University under the following license. By obtaining, using and̃or copying this software and database, you agree that you have read, understood, and will comply with these terms and conditions.:

Permission to use, copy, modify and distribute this software and database and its documentation for any purpose and without fee or royalty is hereby granted, provided that you agree to comply with the following copyright notice and statements, including the disclaimer, and that the same appear on ALL copies of the software, database and documentation, including modifications that you make for internal use or for distribution.

WordNet 1.6 Copyright © 1997 by Princeton University. All rights reseved.

THIS SOFTWARE AND DATABASE IS PROVIDED "AS IS" AND PRINCETON UNIVERSITY MAKES NO REPRESENTATIONS OR WARRANTIES, EXPRESS OR IMPLIED. BY WAY OF EXAMPLE, BUT NOT LIMITATION, PRINCETON UNIVERSITY MAKES NO REPRESENTATIONS OR WARRANTIES OF MERCHANTABILITY OR FITNESS FOR ANY PARTICULAR PURPOSE OR THAT THE USE OF THE LICENSED SOFTWARE, DATABASE OR DOCUMENTATION WILL NOT INFRINGE ANY THIRD PARTY PATENTS, COPYRIGHTS, TRADEMARKS OR OTHER RIGHTS.

The name of Princeton University or Princeton may not be used in advertising or publicity pertaining to distribution of the software and/or database. Title to copyright in this software, database and any associated documentation shall at all times remain with Princeton University and LICENSEE agrees to preserve same.

D.2 Census 1891 Information Copyright

I have reproduced here the copyright notice relating to the Census data provided at the Public Record Office web site at:
http://census.pro.gov.uk/disclaimer.html#copyright
To the best of my knowledge, my limited use of the demonstration data in

Chapter 9 has been in accordance with this notice.

Disclaimer of Liability

The Public Record Office (PRO) on behalf of HM Government has made available to the public the information on this site. Whilst the PRO endeavours to ensure that the information is correct, in no event shall the PRO nor the publisher of information on this site Defence Evaluation and Research Agency (DERA), be responsible for any loss or damage of whatever kind arising out of access to or use of or reliance on any information posted on this site or any hypertext link to any other website or any information contained on or accessed through such website.

Full Copyright Notice and Limited Reproduction Permissions

The contents of these pages are © Crown copyright 2001 unless otherwise stated. All Rights Reserved. Information on this site has been published by DERA under licence and on behalf of the PRO. **You may transcribe, use and publish the information so long as you acknowledge the PRO as the source and give the appropriate document reference. You may only reproduce the images of documents in hard copy for your personal research, private study or education.**

The images may not otherwise be reproduced, distributed or transmitted to any other person or incorporated in any way into another document or other material without the prior written permission of the Controller of Her Majesty's Stationery Office (Licensing Unit, HMSO, St Clement's House, 2–16 Colegate, Norwich NR3 1BQ).

Any copy of these materials which you make must retain all copyright and other proprietary notices shown on the initial download or printout.

Privacy Statement

This privacy statement applies to the 1891 Census Pilot Website.

Customers may pay for chargeable services using their Credit/Debit cards. These transactions are conducted using Secure Sockets Layer (SSL) which encrypts all information submitted. Requested full address information, although not mandatory, is used to permit the Helpdesk to corroborate a caller's bona fide identity in the event of an account query related to a particular session.

Any data collected is used solely for the delivery of the supplied services and will not be passed to third parties for any other purpose.

Cookies are used in the provision of this service, but only to support chargeable sessions which have a maximum duration of 24 hours. The cookies do not contain personal information and do not persist beyond 1 day.

Appendix E

Census 1891 Data XML

This appendix contains the complete XML representation of the Census data set that I used for demonstration in Chapter 9. Note that the XML tags were inserted by the *CensusDataFetcher* implementation from Chapter 9 and the pre-fixed XML DTD was added manually.

```
<>?xml version="1.0" encoding="ISO-8859-1" standalone="yes"?>

<!DOCTYPE data [
    <!ELEMENT data (instance*)>
    <>!ELEMENT instance (name,age,head,relation)>
    <>!ELEMENT name (#PCDATA)>
    <>!ELEMENT age (#PCDATA)>
    <>!ELEMENT head (#PCDATA)>
    <!ELEMENT relation (#PCDATA)>
]>

<data>
<instance>
  <name>... Brown</name><age>0</age>
  <head>William Brown</head><relation>Grand Daughter</relation>
</instance>
<instance>
  <name>... Brown</name><age>90</age>
  <head>George Larner</head><relation>Mother In Law</relation>
</instance>
<instance>
  <name>A Brown</name><age>10</age>
  <head>George Brown</head><relation>Son</relation>
</instance>
<instance>
  <name>Aaron Brown</name><age>60</age>
  <head>Aaron Brown</head><relation>Head</relation>
</instance>
```

```
<instance>
  <name>Ada Brown</name><age>0</age>
  <head>Charles Wm Brown</head><relation>Daughter</relation>
</instance>
<instance>
  <name>Ada Brown</name><age>0</age>
  <head>Julia B Brown</head><relation>Daughter</relation>
</instance>
<instance>
  <name>Ada Brown</name><age>0</age>
  <head>Fredrick Brown</head><relation>Daughter</relation>
</instance>
<instance>
  <name>Ada Brown</name><age>0</age>
  <head>Walter Brown</head><relation>Daughter</relation>
</instance>
<instance>
  <name>Ada Brown</name><age>10</age>
  <head>William Ths Brown</head><relation>Daughter</relation>
</instance>
<instance>
  <name>Ada Brown</name><age>10</age>
  <head>John Brown</head><relation>Daughter</relation>
</instance>
<instance>
  <name>Ada Brown</name><age>10</age>
  <head>William Batch</head><relation>Daughter</relation>
</instance>
<instance>
  <name>Ada Brown</name><age>20</age>
  <head>Barnabas Brown</head><relation>Daughter</relation>
</instance>
<instance>
  <name>Ada Brown</name><age>20</age>
  <head>Josiah T Poyser</head><relation>Servant</relation>
</instance>
<instance>
  <name>Ada Brown</name><age>20</age>
  <head>William Nichols</head><relation>Assistant</relation>
</instance>
<instance>
  <name>Ada Brown</name><age>30</age>
  <head>Ada Brown</head><relation>Head</relation>
</instance>
<instance>
  <name>Adam Brown</name><age>0</age>
  <head>Adam H Brown</head><relation>Son</relation>
</instance>
```

```xml
<instance>
<name>Adam Brown</name><age>30</age>
  <head>Adam H Brown</head><relation>Head</relation>
</instance>
<instance>
  <name>Adela Brown</name><age>20</age>
  <head>William R Palmer</head><relation>Border</relation>
</instance>
<instance>
  <name>Adelaide Brown</name><age>0</age>
  <head>William Brown</head><relation>Daughter</relation>
</instance>
<instance>
  <name>Adelaide Brown</name><age>0</age>
  <head>Thomas J Brown</head><relation>Daughter</relation>
</instance>
<instance>
  <name>Adelaide Brown</name><age>0</age><head>William Brown</head>
  <relation>Daughter</relation>
</instance>
<instance>
  <name>Adelaide Brown</name><age>30</age>
  <head>John Brown</head><relation>Wife</relation>
</instance>
<instance>
  <name>Adelaide Brown</name><age>40</age>
  <head>William Ths Brown</head><relation>Wife</relation>
</instance>
<instance>
  <name>Adeline Brown</name><age>10</age>
  <head>William S Brown</head><relation>Daughter</relation>
</instance>
<instance>
  <name>Adolphus Brown</name><age>0</age>
  <head>Adolphus Brown</head><relation>Son</relation>
</instance>
<instance>
  <name>Adolphus Brown</name><age>20</age>
  <head>Adolphus Brown</head><relation>Head</relation>
</instance>
<instance>
  <name>Agnes Brown</name><age>0</age>
  <head>Alfred C Brown</head><relation>Daughter</relation>
</instance>
<instance>
  <name>Adelaide Jones</name><age>20</age>
  <head>Edith M W Harrison</head><relation>Governess</relation>
</instance>
```

```xml
<instance>
  <name>Agnes Jones</name><age>10</age>
  <head>George Jones</head><relation>Daughter</relation>
</instance>
<instance>
  <name>Agnes Jones</name><age>30</age>
  <head>Ann Jones</head><relation>Daughter</relation>
</instance>
<instance>
  <name>Agness Jones</name><age>0</age>
  <head>Julia Jones</head><relation>Daughter</relation>
</instance>
<instance>
  <name>Albert Jones</name><age>0</age>
  <head>Dennis Jones</head><relation>Son</relation>
</instance>
<instance>
  <name>Albert Jones</name><age>0</age>
  <head>William Ed Jones</head><relation>Son</relation>
</instance>
<instance>
  <name>Albert Jones</name><age>0</age>
  <head>Albert Jones</head><relation>Son</relation>
</instance>
<instance>
  <name>Albert Jones</name><age>10</age>
  <head>Thomas Jones</head><relation>Son</relation>
</instance>
<instance>
  <name>Albert Jones</name><age>10</age>
  <head>Frederick Jones</head><relation>Son</relation>
</instance>
<instance>
  <name>Albert Jones</name><age>20</age>
  <head>Clara Jones</head><relation>Son</relation>
</instance>
<instance>
  <name>Albert Jones</name><age>20</age>
  <head>Albert Jones</head><relation>Head</relation>
</instance>
<instance>
  <name>Alexander Jones</name><age>20</age>
  <head>John Jones</head><relation>Son</relation>
</instance>
<instance>
  <name>Alfrad Jones</name><age>0</age>
  <head>Arthur Jones</head><relation>Son</relation>
</instance>
```

```xml
<instance>
  <name>Alfred Jones</name><age>0</age>
  <head>Alfred Jones</head><relation>Son</relation>
</instance>
<instance>
  <name>Alfred Jones</name><age>0</age>
  <head>Henry Jones</head><relation>Son</relation>
</instance>
<instance>
  <name>Alfred Jones</name><age>10</age>
  <head>William Jones</head><relation>Son</relation>
</instance>
<instance>
  <name>Alfred Jones</name><age>20</age>
  <head>Alfred Jones</head><relation>Head</relation>
</instance>
<instance>
  <name>Alfred Jones</name><age>30</age>
  <head>William Jones</head><relation>Son</relation>
</instance>
<instance>
  <name>Alfred Jones</name><age>40</age>
  <head>Alfred J Jones</head><relation>Head</relation>
</instance>
<instance>
  <name>Alice Jones</name><age>0</age>
  <head>Edward Jones</head><relation>Daughter</relation>
</instance>
<instance>
  <name>Alice Jones</name><age>0</age>
  <head>William Jones</head><relation>Daughter</relation>
</instance>
<instance>
  <name>Alice Jones</name><age>0</age>
  <head>Mehetabel Jones</head><relation>Daughter</relation>
</instance>
<instance>
  <name>Alice Jones</name><age>0</age>
  <head>Thomas Jones</head><relation>Daughter</relation>
</instance>
<instance>
  <name>Alice Jones</name><age>10</age>
  <head>Robert Jones</head><relation>Daughter</relation>
</instance>
<instance>
  <name>Alice Jones</name><age>10</age>
  <head>George Jones</head><relation>Daughter</relation>
</instance>
```

```xml
<instance>
  <name>Alice Jones</name><age>10</age>
  <head>David Gillings</head><relation>Servant</relation>
</instance>
<instance>
  <name>Alice Jones</name><age>10</age>
  <head>Mary A Moore</head><relation>Grand Daughter</relation>
</instance>
<instance>
  <name>Alice Jones</name><age>20</age>
  <head>George Walker</head><relation>Boarder</relation>
</instance>
<instance>
  <name>* Smith</name><age>0</age>
  <head>William Smith</head><relation>Son</relation>
</instance>
<instance>
  <name>... Smith</name><age>20</age>
  <head>Peter S ...</head><relation>Boarder</relation>
</instance>
<instance>
  <name>... Smith</name><age>40</age>
  <head>... Smith</head><relation>Head</relation>
</instance>
<instance>
  <name>... Smith</name><age>60</age>
  <head>Robert Smith</head><relation>Wife</relation>
</instance>
<instance>
  <name>... Smith</name><age>70</age>
  <head>... Smith</head><relation>Head</relation>
</instance>
<instance>
  <name>Aaron Smith</name><age>0</age>
  <head>William Smith</head><relation>Son</relation>
</instance>
<instance>
  <name>Aaron Smith</name><age>10</age>
  <head>Joseph Smith</head><relation>Son</relation>
</instance>
<instance>
  <name>Aaron Smith</name><age>30</age>
  <head>Aaron Smith</head><relation>Head</relation>
</instance>
<instance>
  <name>Aaron Smith</name><age>40</age>
<head>Aaron   Smith</head><relation>Head</relation>
</instance>
```

```xml
<instance>
  <name>Abadiah Smith</name><age>30</age>
  <head>Abadiah Smith</head><relation>Head</relation>
</instance>
<instance>
  <name>Abel Smith</name><age>0</age>
  <head>Robert Smith</head><relation>Son</relation>
</instance>
<instance>
  <name>Abel Smith</name><age>0</age>
  <head>Blanche S Smith</head><relation>Son</relation>
</instance>
<instance>
  <name>Abgail Smith</name><age>30</age>
  <head>Joshua Smith</head><relation>Wife</relation>
</instance>
<instance>
  <name>Abi Smith</name><age>50</age>
  <head>James Smith</head><relation>Wife</relation>
</instance>
<instance>
  <name>Abraham Smith</name><age>20</age>
  <head>Henry Smith</head><relation>Son</relation>
</instance>
<instance>
  <name>Abraham Smith</name><age>40</age>
  <head>Abraham Smith</head><relation>Head</relation>
</instance>
<instance>
  <name>Ada Smith</name><age>0</age>
  <head>Walter Smith</head><relation>Daughter</relation>
</instance>
<instance>
  <name>Ada Smith</name><age>0</age>
  <head>David Smith</head><relation>Daughter</relation>
</instance>
<instance>
  <name>Ada Smith</name><age>0</age>
  <head>Frederick Smith</head><relation>Daughter</relation>
</instance>
<instance>
  <name>Ada Smith</name><age>0</age>
  <head>Elijah H Smith</head><relation>Daughter</relation>
</instance>
<instance>
  <name>Ada Smith</name><age>0</age>
  <head>Thomas Snelling</head><relation>Niece</relation>
</instance>
```

```
<instance>
  <name>Ada Smith</name><age>0</age>
  <head>John Smith</head><relation>Daughter</relation>
</instance>
<instance>
  <name>Ada Smith</name><age>0</age>
  <head>Miles Smith</head><relation>Grand Daughter</relation>
</instance>
<instance>
  <name>Ada Smith</name><age>10</age>
  <head>Walter Frederick Smith</head><relation>Daughter</relation>
</instance>
<instance>
  <name>Ada Smith</name><age>10</age>
  <head>Robert Smith</head><relation>Daughter</relation>
</instance>
<instance>
  <name>Ada Smith</name><age>10</age>
  <head>Susan Boud</head><relation>Servant</relation>
</instance>
<instance>
  <name>Ada Smith</name><age>10</age>
  <head>Thomas Smith</head><relation>Daughter</relation>
</instance>
<instance>
  <name>Ada Smith</name><age>10</age>
  <head>William C Smith</head><relation>Daughter</relation>
</instance>
</data>
```

Appendix F

Share Price Cluster Data

This appendix contains the complete spreadsheet for the clustering example that I presented in Chapter 10. The *normal volume* entries correspond with the *volume* entries normalized to fall within the range 0–100. The *normal change* entries correspond with the *change* % entries normalized to fall within the range 0–100. The *distance* entries are calculated as the average of the *normal volume* and *normal change* at each row.

SHARE	VOLUME	CHANGE %	NORMAL VOLUME	NORMAL CHANGE	DISTANCE
BASS PLC	273 400	0.13%	1.00	−2.00	0.00
BOC GROUP PLC	337 832	−0.29%	1.00	3.00	0.00
PEARSON PLC	661 121	0.21%	2.00	−3.00	0.00
ASTRAZENECA	735 058	−0.15%	3.00	2.00	0.00
BOOTS CO PLC	803 921	−0.16%	3.00	2.00	0.00
SCHRODERS NV	73 912	−0.31%	0.00	4.00	0.00
KINGFISHER PLC	1 125 386	0.00%	4.00	0.00	0.00
GUS	233 639	−0.37%	1.00	4.00	0.00
SMITHS GROUP	359 275	−0.36%	1.00	4.00	0.00
HILTON GROUP	231 402	0.33%	1.00	−5.00	0.00
SAINSBURY (J)	650 978	−0.38%	2.00	5.00	0.00
BRITISH AIRWAYS	1 235 912	−0.15%	5.00	2.00	0.00
CGNU PLC	1 045 738	−0.37%	4.00	4.00	0.00
GKN PLC	1 060 229	0.32%	4.00	−5.00	0.00
BLUE CIRCLE INDS	723 844	0.41%	3.00	−6.00	0.00
MORRISON SUPMKT	725 434	−0.50%	3.00	6.00	0.00
UNITED UTILITIES	524 252	0.50%	2.00	−7.00	0.00
CADBURY SCHWEPPE	667 875	−0.57%	2.00	7.00	0.00
ALLIED DOMECQ	1 678 473	0.24%	7.00	−4.00	0.00
RIO TINTO PLC	1 804 700	−0.44%	7.00	5.00	0.00
RECKITT BENCKSR	219 636	0.63%	0.00	−9.00	0.00
ROYAL BK OF SCOT	1 630 831	0.44%	7.00	−6.00	0.00

SHARE	VOLUME	CHANGE %	NORMAL VOLUME	NORMAL CHANGE	DISTANCE
HANSON	1 669 300	0.43%	7.00	−6.00	0.00
AMVESCAP	728 656	−0.81%	3.00	10.00	1.00
LAND SECURITIES	261 700	−0.89%	1.00	11.00	1.00
LATTICE GROUP	1 371 301	0.74%	5.00	−10.00	1.00
STNDRD CHART BK	1 930 231	−0.60%	8.00	8.00	1.00
BRIT AM TOBACCO	2 523 147	−0.45%	10.00	6.00	1.00
ALLIANCE & LEICS	153 305	−0.95%	0.00	12.00	1.00
SCOT & NEWCASTLE	544 848	−0.93%	2.00	12.00	1.00
BAA PLC	694 978	−0.90%	3.00	12.00	1.00
SCOT & STH ENRGY	2 604 195	−0.57%	11.00	7.00	1.00
POWERGEN	3 170 388	0.14%	13.00	−2.00	1.00
SCHRODERS	144 986	1.02%	0.00	−14.00	1.00
DIAGEO PLC	2 023 219	−0.93%	8.00	12.00	1.00
OLD MUTUAL	1 075 780	0.99%	4.00	−14.00	1.00
RENTOKIL INITIAL	2 510 249	−0.90%	10.00	12.00	1.00
ASSOC.BR.FOODS	148 001	−1.23%	0.00	16.00	1.00
ROLLS ROYCE	1 916 115	1.03%	8.00	−14.00	1.00
BARCLAYS PLC	736 502	−1.20%	3.00	16.00	1.00
HAYS PLC	801 173	−1.25%	3.00	16.00	1.00
LEGAL & GENERAL	2 626 785	−1.07%	11.00	14.00	1.00
GLAXOSMITHKLINE	3 151 484	−1.04%	13.00	13.00	1.00
ANGLO AMERICAN	3 181 534	0.92%	13.00	−13.00	1.00
ICI PLC	936 860	−1.38%	4.00	18.00	1.00
COMPASS GROUP	4 097 934	0.57%	17.00	−8.00	1.00
EMI GROUP PLC	368 393	−1.47%	1.00	19.00	1.00
NATIONAL GRID	3 157 003	1.03%	13.00	−14.00	1.00
LOGICA PLC	770 266	−1.53%	3.00	20.00	2.00
CANARY WHARF GRP	382 434	−1.61%	1.00	21.00	2.00
BG GROUP PLC	4 845 641	−0.09%	21.00	1.00	2.00
CENTRICA	2 177 700	−1.58%	9.00	21.00	2.00
BAE SYSTEMS	3 876 858	−1.29%	16.00	17.00	2.00
SA BREWERIES	119 189	1.75%	0.00	−24.00	2.00
REUTERS GROUP	1 531 037	−1.81%	6.00	24.00	2.00
UTS BUSINESS MED	5 416 682	−0.83%	23.00	11.00	2.00
MARKS & SPENCER	5 945 822	0.37%	25.00	−5.00	2.00
REED INTL PLC	1 634 118	−1.93%	7.00	25.00	2.00
PRUDENTIAL	1 257 502	−2.02%	5.00	27.00	2.00
BILLITON PLC	6 628 854	−0.29%	28.00	3.00	2.00
WPP GROUP	1 608 486	−2.09%	6.00	28.00	2.00
SAFEWAY	6 635 956	0.46%	28.00	−7.00	2.00
MISYS PLC	590 323	−2.22%	2.00	29.00	2.00
DIXONS GROUP	5 160 908	−1.42%	22.00	19.00	2.00
INTL POWER	5 959 455	−1.20%	25.00	16.00	2.00
UNILEVER PLC	5 433 464	−1.44%	23.00	19.00	2.00
SAGE GROUP	6 725 369	0.46%	29.00	−7.00	2.00

SHARE	VOLUME	CHANGE %	NORMAL VOLUME	NORMAL CHANGE	DISTANCE
DAILY MAIL TST A	55 873	−2.40%	0.00	32.00	3.00
CELLTECH GROUP	152 581	−2.41%	0.00	32.00	3.00
CARLTON COMMS	4 219 807	−2.05%	18.00	27.00	3.00
ELECTROCOMPONENT	234 849	2.40%	1.00	−33.00	3.00
IMPERIAL TOBACCO	1 746 841	−2.48%	7.00	33.00	3.00
RAILTRACK	351 447	2.73%	1.00	−37.00	3.00
NYCOMED AMERSHAM	937 581	−2.81%	4.00	37.00	3.00
SCOTTISH POWER	3 912 702	2.47%	16.00	−34.00	3.00
HSBC HOLDINGS	8 656 324	−0.68%	37.00	9.00	3.00
ABBEY NATIONAL	6 043 945	−2.27%	26.00	30.00	3.00
BANK OF SCOTLAND	8 733 069	−1.29%	37.00	17.00	4.00
CMG PLC	1 811 341	−3.14%	7.00	42.00	4.00
HALIFAX GROUP	2 998 345	−3.18%	12.00	42.00	4.00
LLOYDS TSB GRP	9 844 032	−1.35%	42.00	18.00	4.00
TESCO PLC	10 406 491	−0.71%	45.00	9.00	4.00
DIMENSION DATA	243 811	−3.50%	1.00	46.00	4.00
CAPITA GROUP	311 302	−3.63%	1.00	48.00	4.00
ARM HOLDINGS	5 574 605	−3.85%	24.00	51.00	5.00
CABLE & WIRELESS	11 902 399	−2.47%	51.00	33.00	6.00
ENERGIS PLC	6 138 840	−4.59%	26.00	61.00	6.00
SHIRE PHARM GRP	13 765 951	−2.89%	59.00	38.00	7.00
B SKY B	5 143 355	−5.02%	22.00	67.00	7.00
SHELL TRNPT(REG)	15 847 345	1.64%	68.00	−23.00	7.00
MARCONI PLC	8 747 642	−5.41%	37.00	72.00	8.00
GRANADA	15 830 746	−3.98%	68.00	53.00	8.00
TELEWEST COMMUNI	4 711 424	−6.30%	20.00	84.00	8.00
INVENSYS	9 709 980	−6.03%	42.00	80.00	9.00
BP	22 317 632	1.75%	96.00	−24.00	9.00
COLT TELECOM GRP	2 839 768	−7.45%	12.00	100.00	10.00
BRITISH TELECOM	23 064 828	−2.30%	100.00	30.00	10.00

Appendix G

Glossary of Acronyms

In this appendix I list and define the acronyms (capitalized abbreviations) used throughout this book. The scope of this glossary is limited to the book content and is not intended as a wider dictionary of technical computing terms.

API, Application Programming Interface – a library of functions that programmers can use to build software.

ASP, Active Server Pages – a server-side scripting language for Microsoft Internet Information Server.

CGI, Common Gateway Interface – a legacy programming script for generating HTML pages dynamically in response to form submissions.

DOM, Document Object Model – an API specification for manipulating XML content as an in-memory document.

GUI, Graphical User Interface – a human-computer interaction format based on graphical presentation.

HTML, HyperText Mark-up Language – the text mark-up language used most widely for constructing web pages.

HTTP, HyperText Transfer Protocol – a communication protocol used for transfer of information on the World Wide Web.

IIS, Internet Information Server – a file and application server provided with Microsoft NT operating system.

IMAP, Internet Message Access Protocol – a protocol for accessing email messages stored on a central server.

ISP, Internet Service Provider – a telecommunications company that provides internet access and / or web hosting services.

JAF, JavaBeans Activation Framework – a Java API for manipulating arbitrary data types, particularly MIME types.

J2EE, Java 2 Enterprise Edition – the Java 2 technology standard for enterprise application development.

J2SE, Java 2 Standard Edition – the Java 2 technology standard for non-enterprise application development.

JAR, Java ARchive – a file format for combining multiple Java classes and other resources comprising an application or library, optionally compressed.

JAXP, Java API for XML Processing – a Java API for manipulating XML content, based on SAX and DOM.

JDBC, Java DataBase Connectivity – a Java API for vendor-independent access to relational databases.

JSP, Java Server Pages – a technology layer above the servlet layer that allows server-generated content to be embedded into web pages using simple tags.

MIME, Multipurpose Internet Mail Extensions – a standardized way of representing and encoding a wide variety of media types for transmission via the Internet.

POP, Post Office Protocol – a widely used protocol for accessing incoming email messages stored on a central server.

SAX, Simple API for XML Processing – a lightweight alternative to DOM, suitable for parsing XML content.

SGML, Standard Generalized Mark-up Language – an ISO specification for defining mark-up languages.

SMS, Short Message Service – a globally accepted wireless service that enables the transmission of alphanumeric messages between mobile subscribers.

SDK, Software Development Kit – a collection of tools, including a compiler, used by programmers to build software.

SMTP, Simple Mail Transfer Protocol – a widely used method for sending outgoing email messages.

SQL, Structured Query Language – an ANSI standard command language for accessing and manipulating the content of relational databases.

TCP/IP, Transmission Control Protocol/Internet Protocol – a suite of data communications protocols that underpin the Internet.

UML, Unified Modeling Language – a widely used notation for the design and documentation of object oriented systems.

URI, Uniform Resource Identifier – a more generic term for addressing network resources, incorporating URL (see next).

URL, Uniform Resource Locator – an address that uniquely identifies a resource on the World Wide Web.

WAP, Wireless Application Protocol – a protocol that allows wireless devices to retrieve information from the Internet.

XHTML, eXtensible HyperText Mark-up Language – bridges the gap between non-extensible HTML and XML by providing a definition of HTML in XML.

XML, eXtensible Mark-up Language – a simpler variant of SGML, providing a lowest common denominator for information interchange of the World Wide Web

References

Berry, Michael J. A. and Linoff, Gordon S., 2000. *Mastering Data Mining – The Art and Science of Customer Relationship Management.*

Hjelm, Johan, 2001. *Creating Web Services with RDF.* John Wiley & Sons, Inc., New York.

Sullivan, Dan, 2001. *Document Warehousing and Text Mining – Techniques for Improving Business Operations, Marketing and Sales.* John Wiley & Sons, Inc., New York.

Witten, Ian H. and Eibe, Frank, 2000. *Data Mining – Practical Machine Learning Tools and Techniques with Java Implementations.* Morgan Kaufmann.

Wrox Author Team, 2001. *Professional Java Data,* Wrox Press.

Further Reading

The books and web sites listed here are not directly referenced in this book, but you might like to take a look at them.

Books

Here is a list of some other books that I've read, or which – judging from the titles – will be useful additional reading. There's a mix of (Enterprise) Java programming, XML, RDF, UML, web services, data mining and text mining to pick up on several of the topics introduced in this book.

Ahmed, Kal *et al.* 2001. *Professional Java XML.* Wrox Press.

Aviram, Mariva H, 1998. *XML for DUMMIES.* IDG Books.

Bates, Chris, 2000. *Web Programming – Building Internet Applications.* Wrox Press.

Bigus, Jospeh and Bigus, Jennifer, 2001. *Constructing Intelligent Agents Using Java.* John Wiley and Sons.

Booch, Grady, Rumbaugh, James and Jacobson, Ivar, 1999. *The Unified Modeling Language User Guide.* Addison-Wesley.

Brogden, William and Minnick, Chris, 2001. *Java Developer's Guide to E-Commerce with XML and JSP.* SYBEX.

Chang, George, 2001. *Mining the World Wide Web: An Information Search Approach.* Kluwer International.

Cook, John L., 2000. *WAP Servlets: Developing Dynamic Web Content With Java and WML.* John Wiley and Sons.

Fowler, Martin, 1997. *UML Distilled.* Addison-Wesley.

Hackathorn, Richard D., 1998. *Web Farming for the Data Warehouse.* Morgan Kaufmann.

Hjelm, Johan, 2001. *Creating the Semantic Web with RDF.* John Wiley and Sons.

Hjelm, Johan and Stark, Peter, 2001. *XSLT: Professional Developer's Guide.* John Wiley and Sons.

Horton, Ivor, 1999. *Beginning Java 2.* Wrox Press.

Hunter, David *et al.*, 2000. *Beginning XML.* Wrox Press.

McLaughlin, Brett and Loukides, Michael, 2001. *Java and XML.* O'Reilly.

Michalski, R., 1998. *Machine Learning and Data Mining.* John Wiley & Sons.

Perrone, Paul, 2000. *Building Java Enterprise Systems with J2EE.* SAMS.

Subrahmayam Allaramaju *et al.*, 2000. *Professional Java Server Programming, J2EE Edition.* Wrox Press.

Quin, L., 2000. *XML Database Toolkit*. John Wiley & Sons.
Thomas, Stephen, 2001. *HTTP Essentials*. John Wiley & Sons.
Zukowski, John, 1998. *Mastering Java 1.2*. SYBEX.

Web sites (technology)

There are many web sites devoted to coverage of the Java language. At the sites I've listed
here you will find a wide variety of news, feature articles and other resources that will help
you to master the techniques that I've introduced.

Java Developer's Journal @ http://www.javadevelopersjournal.com
Java Report @ http://www.javareport.com
JavaSoft @ http://www.javasoft.com
JavaWorld @ http://www.javaworld.com
The XML Industry Portal @ http://www.xml.org/
XML Journal @ http://www.sys-con.com/xml/

Web sites (data and text mining)

There are a few good sites dedicated to web mining, data mining, text mining, knowledge
discovery and machine learning. Here are a few that you might be interested in:

KDnuggets (Data Mining, Web Mining and Knowledge Discovery Guide) @
   http://www.kdnuggets.com
'WEKA' Java Data Mining Software (web site of Witten and Frank) @
   http://www.cs.waikato.ac.nz/ml/weka/
Data Miners Inc. (web site of Berry and Linoff) @ http://www.data-miners.com/
Companion Web Site for Sullivan (2001) @
   http://www.wiley.com/compbooks/sullivan/dan/
Knowledge Management World @ http://www.kmworld.com/
Knowledge Management Magazine @
   http://www.destinationcrm.com/km/dcrm_km_index.asp

Index

accuracy, 220
Active Server Pages (ASP), 22, 26, 291
Apache Software Foundation, 243
API *see* Application Programming Interface

applets, a brief history, 14–15
  and HTTP communication, 26–27, 30,
    254
  and performance implications, 29–30
  and search filters, 202
  as a delivery channel, 13–19, 30, 238
  building a portal using, xv, 4, 109,
    119–129, 151, 172, 263
  security restrictions, 128–129
  simple example, 15–18
  vs. servlets, 20, 23–24, 119–120
application delivery, 18–19, 23
application logic, 24
Application Programming Interface (API) –
    see also JAXP, JDMAPI, JavaMail,
    DOM & SAX
  data access, 154
  definition, 291
  documentation, 139–140
  Java classes, xiii–xiv, 9, 31–32, 64–65,
    106–108, 175, 205
  servlet, 19
applications, demonstration, xiv–xvii
  graphical, 40, 67, 73, 80, 99–100, 106,
    232
  java, 5, 27
  mining, xv, 13–14, 23, 179, 190, 194,
    200, 201–204
  searching, 140–146
  servlet, 23 *see also* servlets (main entry)
  small (applets), 14
  spreadsheet, 216, 228

SQL, 217
  vertical, xii
  web, 13–15, 23, 29–30, 120, 189
ASP *see* Active Server Pages
association, 3, 216, 219–224, 228
attributes, association and, 220
  classification based on, 217–218, 226
  HTML, 40, 62
  mail, 175
  table, 46
  tag, 40, 45–47
  XML, 65
authentication, 28–29, 32, 36–37, 256,
    258

browsers (web), xi, 23, 30, 74, 77, 138
  Internet Explorer, 17–18, 127
  Java Plug-in and, 14–15, 17–19, 27, 119,
    127
  Netscape Navigator, 18, 127
  queries through, 149
  Refresh, 111, 114
  ViewSource option, 233
browsing (web), 11, 73

caching mechanism, 189–190
callback, 34, 41–44, 46–49, 54–55, 57,
    59–60, 64–65, 83, 132–133, 141–142,
    147–148
centers-of-gravity, 224, 226–228
centroids, 227–228
CGI *see* Common Gateway Interface
class dependency, 7, 33–34, 68, 110, 133,
    154, 179, 208
class diagrams, 6–7, 12, 33–34, 67–68,
    109–110, 133, 154, 179, 208
class hierarchy, 251–253

classes and interfaces, implemented in this book, 251–270
Java API, 9, 31–32, 64–65, 106–108, 175, 205, 244
classification, in data mining, 3, 120, 216–219, 223–226, 228
parts of speech, 177–178
CLASSPATH, 244–246
clustering, 3, 120, 216, 224–228, 287–289
code presentation, 1, 8–9, 12
collaboration diagram, 7
Common Gateway Interface (CGI), 13, 19, 22, 26, 291
compiling and running,
CensusDataFetcher, 212–213
FeatureExtractor, 198–201
FilterViewer, 84–85
Function class, 215–216
HTTPApplet, 26–27
MailParserWrapper, 163–164
parsers, 60–61
PortalApplet, 127–129
QueryEngine, 97–99
SimpleApplet, 18
SimpleSearcher, 144–145
SimpleServlet, 23
SMSRelay, 170
SqlGui, 104
TextParserWrapper, 185–187
WileySearcher, 149–151
confidence, 220
connections, dial-up, 30
HTTP, xii, 13, 37, 240
Internet, 30, 110, 125
network, 32, 164
content, and filters, 78, 82–83
dynamic, 4–5, 19, 22–23, 27, 30, 120
email, 153–154, 157–162, 167, 170, 172, 174–175, 189
HTML, xiii, 30–31, 33, 35–39, 44–45, 67, 72–73, 100, 141, 153–155, 158–162, 170, 174–175
plain text, 31, 154–155, 160, 162, 170, 175
RDF and, 236
resource, 231
static, 4–5, 27
web, 3–5, 12, 133, 135–136, 145, 158,

172, 180, 209, 236, 238
XML, xiii, 31, 33, 53, 57–58, 64, 67, 72–73, 100, 141, 153, 158, 160, 170, 172, 175, 200, 238, 240
context, 93–97, 106
copyright, 11–12, 180, 209, 275–278
coverage, 220–222

data cleansing, 222
data retrieval, 2, 12, 22, 209–216
data sets, xiii, 219, 226, 228
data sources, 2, 3–5, 4–5, 12, 13, 109–111, 118, 124, 128, 130, 133, 165, 180, 209
data warehouses, 3
database schema, 189, 132
database tables, 85–86
databases – see also JDBC, 14
structure of, 207
corporate, 3
relational, xi, 5, 67, 86, 99–100, 232–233, 240
WordNet, 180, 189–190, 276
delivery channels, 4–5, 12–13, 30, 120, 238
applets as, 14–19
servlets as, 19–23
deployment, 19, 23–24, 246–249
design notation, 1
dictionary, 178
Document Object Model (DOM), 33–34, 57–60, 63–65, 213, 256, 271, 273, 291
Document Type Definition (DTD), 61–62, 171, 212, 279
DOM see Document Object Model
drivers, 105, 154, 240
DTD see Document Type Definition

EJB see Enterprise Java Beans
element content, 72, 83, 135
element keys, 72, 83, 160, 162
elements, filtered, 82
HTML, xv, 9, 33, 36–37, 44, 68, 72–75, 106, 141, 156, 161, 233, 236, 257–260, 267
in mail, 158, 163, 168
input, 76

list, 120–121, 125
marked-up, 63
meta-, 233–234, 236
parsed, 182
root, 191
table data, 40
textual, 44, 50, 82–84, 90–96, 98, 156, 267
XML, xv, 9, 33, 34, 36–37, 52–53, 58, 68, 72–73, 100, 106, 141, 161, 237, 257–260
Xpath and, 237
elements variable, 43–45
email, 2, 4–5, 151, 153–175, 179, 189, 194, 201, 236
Enterprise Java Beans (EJB), 19, 146–147, 149
Extensible Hypertext Markup Language (XHTML), 34, 61–63, 234, 236, 293
Extensible Markup Language (XML) – *see also* JAXP & SAX, content, xiii, 31, 33, 53, 57–58, 64, 67, 72–73, 100, 141, 153, 158, 160, 170, 172, 175, 200, 238, 240
    data, xi, 23–24, 31, 94, 207, 231, 234, 236, 279–286
    definition, 293
    document, 213
    elements, xv, 9, 33, 34, 36–37, 52–53, 58, 68, 72–73, 100, 106, 141, 161, 237, 257–260
    files, 133, 151, 165, 180, 209, 213, 215, 237, 256
    in email, 170–172
    open standard, 3
    output, 198–200
    parsing, xii–xiii, 8, 13, 35, 52–62, 141, 256, 271
    tags, xvii, 52, 54, 62, 177, 209, 213
Extensible Style Language Transformation (XSLT), 236, 238, 239, 241

feature extraction, xvii, 194–201, 268
filter, WordNet, 183
filtering and querying, of email messages, 153, 158, 165–166, 168, 170, 172–173, 175

of web data, xii, xv–xvi, 2, 5, 7, 30, 40, 67–108, 111, 124–125, 129, 183–184, 186, 234, 237
firewall, 27–28, 30, 256
FROM clause, 105
get (HTTP method), 21–27, 30, 35–37, 74, 80, 82, 115–118, 137, 259

GIF *see* Graphical Interchange Format
grammar, 177, 191–192, 204, 207
Graphical Interchange Format (GIF), 160
Graphical User Interface (GUI), 16, 21, 40, 67, 73–74, 79–81, 99–105, 122–124, 138, 208, 254–255, 260–261, 291
GUI *see* Graphical User Interface

heuristics, 192–194, 201
hosting, 19, 189
HTML *see* Hypertext Markup Language
HTTP *see* Hypertext Transfer Protocol
hubs, 132
hyperlinks, 22, 23, 40, 131–132, 134–135, 138, 142–143, 151, 236–237
Hypertext Markup Language (HTML) – *see also* XHTML, content, xiii, 30–31, 33, 35–39, 44–45, 67, 72–73, 100, 141, 153–155, 158–162, 170, 174–175
    data, 3, 40, 43, 62, 64, 158, 208
    definition, 291
    documents, 64, 236
    elements, xv, 9, 33, 36–37, 44, 68, 72–75, 106, 141, 156, 161, 233, 236, 257–260, 267
    files, 17, 22–23, 26–27, 41, 47, 62, 127–128, 133, 151, 165, 180, 209, 237
    forms, 19–20, 22, 74, 106, 113–118, 165, 202
    headers, 21, 116
    links, 137
    mark-up, xi, 207
    open standard, 3, 19
    pages, 15, 19, 39, 62, 85, 153, 231, 233–234, 236, 238
    parsing, xii–xiii, 13, 33, 35–52, 60–63, 141, 159–161, 256
    tables, xi, 67, 86

Hypertext Markup Language (*cont.*)
  tags, xvii, 17, 39, 43–44, 54, 62, 64,
    115, 177, 233
  tokens, 42
Hypertext Transfer Protocol (HTTP), xiii,
    3, 5, 13, 17, 21, 22, 23, 24–27, 29, 30,
    32, 115–116, 153, 213, 240, 254, 291
  communication, xii, 13, 17, 24–29
  connections, xii, 13, 37, 240
  definition, 291
  get and post, 21–27, 30, 35–37, 74, 82,
    115–118, 137, 259
  obtaining data via, xiii, 29, 213
  open standard, 3, 5
  requests, 23, 30, 32, 35, 38, 189–190,
    254
  responses, 21, 115–116
hyponyms, 189, 202–204

IDE *see* Integrated Development
    Environment
IMAP *see* Integrated Message Access
    Porotocol
indexes and indexing, 40, 45, 88–89,
    94–97, 145, 201–202
information services, xii, xiii, 172–173
Integrated Development Environment
    (IDE), 34
Integrated Message Access Protocol
    (IMAP), 155, 291
Integrated Services Digital Network
    (ISDN), 30
interfaces, applet, 31, 120
  java, 8
  on-line, 2, 13, 19, 22, 26, 145, 150, 165,
    180, 184, 189, 202
  parser, 33, 37–38, 43–44, 52
  search engine, 2, 139
  servlet, 120
  user, 14, 15, 22, 23, 24
  WAP, 120
  web, 2, 13, 14, 26, 27, 145, 150, 165,
    172, 180
interface hierarchy, 253
interface implementation, 7–8
interfaces and classes, implemented in this
    book, 251–270
  Java API, 31–32, 64–65, 106–108, 175,
    205
Internet – *see also* World Wide Web, 2–4,
    13, 19, 23–24, 27, 29–30, 110–111,
    125, 153, 293
Internet Service Provider (ISP), 30, 120,
    163, 164, 174, 291
intranet, 3, 19, 153
ISDN *see* Integrated Services Digital
    Network
ISP *see* Internet Service Provider
J2EE *see* Java 2 Enterprise Edition
J2SE *see* Java 2 Standard Edition
JAF *see* JavaBeans Activation Framework
JAR *see* Java Archive
Java 2 Enterprise Edition (J2EE), 19, 34,
    38, 154, 243, 271, 274, 292
Java 2 Standard Edition (J2SE), 38, 154,
    243–244, 292
Java API for XML processing (JAXP), xiii,
    13, 34, 38, 52, 243–244, 271–274,
    292
Java Archive (JAR), 15, 244–246, 292
Java Data Mining API (JDMAPI),
    239–240, 241
Java Database Connectivity (JDBC), 105,
    154, 239–240, 292
Java Exception, 71
Java Server Pages (JSP), 23, 236, 238–239,
    241, 292
Java Virtual Machine (JVM), 14, 27–28,
    140
JavaBeans Activation Framework (JAF),
    243–244, 292
JavaDoc, 9–10, 12, 246, 251
JavaMail, xii–xiii, 6, 154–156, 160, 164,
    174, 175, 243–244
JAXP *see* Java API for XML processing
JDBC *see* Java Database Connectivity
JDMAPI *see* Java Data Mining API
JSP *see* Java Server Pages
JVM *see* Java Virtual Machine

latency, 125
lexicons, 178, 180, 205
libraries, 13

mail stores, 156
mean, 227–228

messages, email, xii, xv–xvi, 2, 5, 115, 151, 154–164, 166–172, 174, 175, 179, 194–195, 201, 267
  error, 62
metadata, 231–236, 239, 241
MIME *see* Multipurpose Internet Mail Extensions
mining, data, xi–xiii, 1, 3–5, 12, 120, 177, 207–229, 239–240, 241, 245, 269
  mail, xiii, xv–xvi, 154–175, 245
  text, xi–xiii, 1, 3–5, 12, 177–205, 207, 245
  web, xi, xiii, 1, 3–4, 12, 13–14, 23, 191, 202, 236, 241
Multipurpose Internet Mail Extensions (MIME), 24, 31, 244, 292

natural language analysis and processing, 3, 191
news groups, 2, 150
normalization, 224, 228, 287

open standards, 2–3
operations, comparison, 68–72, 74
  data mining, 208–209, 228
  text mining, 179
operators, comparison, 67–71, 90, 102–103, 191, 261
Outlook (Microsoft), 162–163

packages, xiii, 5–7, 12–13, 34, 41, 62, 68, 110, 133, 154, 179, 208, 251–270
page refresh, 15, 20
pages, home, 138
  HTML, 15, 19, 39, 62, 85, 153, 231, 233–234, 236, 238
  portal, 113
  root, 132, 134–135, 137, 138
  source, 109, 118
  web, xv–xvi, 2–4, 11, 30–31, 38–39, 67, 74–75, 77, 109, 111–112, 130, 131–132, 134–138, 158, 174–175, 179, 181–182, 201–202, 233, 236, 238
  XHTML, 62
  XML, 236
parameters, 20, 26, 59, 73, 76–78, 106, 115, 128, 154, 166–167, 210–211, 214
parsers, HTML, 13, 38, 41, 47, 57, 60–63, 141
  web, 102–103
  XML, 57, 60, 62–63, 141
parsing, bottom up, 191–193
  email messages, 155–164
  generic, 6, 35–38
  HTML, xii–xiii, 5, 13, 26, 33, 35, 38–52, 61, 141
  text, 180–190, 205
  top down, 191–193
  XHTML, 61–63
  XML, xii–xiii, 5, 13, 33–34, 35, 52–60, 61, 64, 141, 170
performance, 29–30, 131, 189–190, 236
phrase structure, 178–180, 190–194, 204
plain text, xi, 24, 31, 49, 153–154, 155–156, 158, 160, 162–163, 170, 175, 181, 267
Plug-in, 15, 17, 19, 27–28, 119, 127–129, 151
POP *see* Post Office Protocol
portals, applets and, xv, 4, 109, 119–129, 151, 172, 263
  building, xii, xviii, 13, 109–130
  example share price information, xv, 109–129, 224
  on-line, 151
  servlets and, xv, 4, 109, 111–119, 129
  SMS, 172
post (HTTP method), 21–27, 30, 35–37, 74–78, 80, 82, 115, 137, 254, 259
Post Office Protocol (POP), 3, 5, 154–155, 156, 163, 168, 267, 292
prediction, 3, 223
presentation techniques, 236, 237–238
production rules, 191–192
protocols – *see also* HTTP, IMAP, POP, SMTP, TCP/IP & WAP, access, 12, 175
  communication, xi, 2, 5
  internet, 13
proxy, 27–29, 30, 256, 258

query, simple SQL, 217–218
  example, 116
  submitting a, 149, 189

query engine, xviii, 67, 87–99, 102, 105, 109, 118, 124, 171, 179, 184–186, 208, 210, 214–215, 219, 228, 261
query term, xv
querying and filtering *see* filtering and querying

RDF *see* Resource Description Framework
recursion, 60, 139
Resource Description Framework (RDF), 231, 236–237, 239, 241

sandbox, 15
SAX *see* Simple API for XML
SDK *see* Software Development Kit
search, breadth first, 132, 151
    depth first, 135
    on-line, 210
    similar documents, 202–203
    single site, 145–146
    submitting a, 131
    web site, 75, 175, 202–203
search engine, Alta Vista, 146
    Google, 146, 150–151
    Lycos, 146
    Yahoo, 109–110
search engines, xii, xv, 2, 130, 131–151, 174, 202–203, 233, 237, 264–265
    meta-, 2, 145–151
search scope, 202
search sequence, 135
search text, 15–16, 20–22
search thread, 138–139
searching, xii, 11, 15, 131–151, 173, 202, 236
security model, 14, 15
SELECT clause, 99, 103
semantic networks, 179, 237
semantics, 178–179, 192
servers, 15, 17, 19–20, 22, 27, 128, 156, 163, 168, 172, 175, 189, 273
servlets, a brief history, 19
    and HTTP communication, 22, 25–26, 32
    and performance implications, 29–30
    as a delivery channel, 13–14, 19–23
    building a portal using, xv, 4, 109, 111–119, 129, 151

coverage, 23
    for application delivery, 23
    simple example, 20–23
    vs.applets, 15, 17, 24
SGML *see* Standard Generalized Markup Language
Short Message Service (SMS), xv–xvi, 4–5, 154, 164–170, 172–175, 238, 267, 292
Simple API for XML (SAX), 33–34, 52–53, 57–59, 62, 63–65, 240, 256, 259, 272, 292
Simple Mail Transfer Protocol (SMTP), 155, 292
SMS *see* Short Message Service
SMSRelay, xv–xvii, 167–170
SMTP *see* Simple Mail Transfer Protocol
Software Development Kit (SDK), 10, 19, 33–34, 38, 41, 47, 62–63, 154, 164, 243–244, 251, 292
spider, 131
spreadsheets, 216, 228
SQL engine, 208, 216, 228
SQL *see* Structured Query Language
SqlGui class, 67–68, 99–106, 208, 218, 261
Standard Generalized Markup Language (SGML), 47, 292–293
Standardization, 231, 236, 239
Structured Query Language (SQL), xv, 67–68, 99–106, 191, 208, 214, 216–223, 228–229, 232–233, 237, 240, 260–261, 292
submission, 17, 20–21, 25, 36–37, 74–79, 82, 115, 118, 137, 165–168, 180, 183, 202, 212
summarization, 233
Sun Microsystems, 243
support, 220–222
syntax, 105, 178, 192, 219, 237

tags, applet, 127, 129
    embedded, 196–197
    empty, 48–49
    end, 44–45, 47–48, 53
    formatting, 44, 49
    HTML, xvii, 17, 39, 43–44, 54, 62, 64, 115, 177, 233

JSP, 238
meta-, 233
parent, 40
simple, 48
start, 44–46, 53
structural, 39, 44, 49, 55, 62
text, 50
XML, xvii, 52, 54, 62, 177, 209, 213
TCP/IP *see* Transmission Control Protocol
/ Internet Protocol
test data, 208, 210, 212, 222, 269
threads, 120, 123–125, 131, 133, 138–140
Tomcat, 18, 23, 26, 243, 245, 247, 249
transformation rule, 178–179
transformation techniques, 204
Transmission Control Protocol / Internet
Protocol (TCP/IP), 3, 13, 292

UML *see* Unified Modeling Language
Unified Modeling Language (UML), 5–8,
12, 34, 68, 110, 133, 154, 179, 208,
293
Uniform Resource Locator (URL), 13, 18,
20, 22–23, 26–27, 32, 47, 73, 76–77,
98–99, 105–106, 110–111, 119, 128,
134, 136, 138, 140–143, 146,
148–149, 153–154, 156, 161,
172–174, 186, 204, 211, 215, 249,
265, 293
URL *see* Uniform Resource Locator

WAP *see* Wireless Application Protocol
web, language of the, 13–32
web crawler, 131–132, 133–140, 151, 142,
145, 148, 202, 264–265
web host, 19, 120
web services, 1–2, 12, 26, 237
web sites, impact of changes to, 110–111,
133, 165, 170, 180, 209
web sources, 3, 112–113, 237–238
web technology, 1–2, 12
WebData(Tool)Kit, 208, 219, 229
Web–Start, 15
WHERE clause, 99, 102–103, 105
wildcards, 69–71, 74, 82, 85, 88–90,
94–95, 195
Wireless Application Protocol (WAP), 120,
173, 293
WordNet, 180–184, 189–190, 201–204,
205, 276–277
World Wide Web – *see also* Internet, xi,
xiii, 3–4, 12, 32, 34, 52, 131, 145,
165, 180, 202, 236, 239, 293

XHTML *see* Extensible Hypertext Markup
Language
XML *see* Extensible Markup Language
Xpath, xv, 237, 239
Xpointer, 151, 237, 239
XSLT *see* Extensible Style Language
Transformation